Free and Enslaved African Americans

in

St. Francois County Missouri

1822–1920

Dawn C. Stricklin

HERITAGE BOOKS
2020

HERITAGE BOOKS

AN IMPRINT OF HERITAGE BOOKS, INC.

Books, CDs, and more—Worldwide

For our listing of thousands of titles see our website
at
www.HeritageBooks.com

Published 2020 by
HERITAGE BOOKS, INC.
Publishing Division
5810 Ruatan Street
Berwyn Heights, Md. 20740

Heritage Books by the author:
Cherokee Claims for Transportation and Subsistence, Special File 154: Volume 1
Free and Enslaved African Americans in St. Francois County, Missouri, 1822–1920

International Standard Book Number
Paperbound: 978-0-7884-5896-5

Civil Circuit Court Records Indexes

Vol. 3-4: 66, 03 Nov 1845. State of Mo. vs. Gabriel (a slave). Indictment for Assault with Intent to Commit Rape.

Vol. 3-4: 103-104, 09 May 1846. Petition for Partition of Real Estate & slaves, Belonging to the Estate of Dubart Murphy, deceased. Slaves: Peter, man about 32; Nelly, woman about 30; Ann, girl about 15; and 3 children: Nat, Moses, and Ginette.

Vol. 3-4: 107, 03 Nov 1846. Petition for Partition of Real Estate and Slaves, belonging to the estate of Dubart Murphy, deceased. The county sheriff is directed to sell these slaves.

Vol. 3-4: 128, 03 May 1847. Robert J. Hill et al., vs. Thomas Haile. Detinue for Slaves.

Vol. 3-4: 204-205, 09 May 1849 . Mary Estes vs. The other heirs of Gainim Estes, deceased. Petition for Partition of Land and Slaves. Slaves: Sam, about 25; Jane, about 25 and her infant about 8 months old; Harriet, about 9; and Artemiss, about 8.

Vol. 3-4: 209-210, 09 May 1849. Gabriel Thomason and others vs. Felix G. Poston and Jeremiah Poston. Slaves: Dorcus, woman about 55; Peter, man about 36; Mary Ann, woman about 24; Green, boy about 8; Minerva, girl 6; Fillis, girl 4; Amanda, girl 3; James Henry, boy 7 months.

Vol. 3-4: 211, 09 May 1849. Andrew J. Murphy vs. Elezer G. Clay. Petition to Foreclose a Mortgage. Slave: Priscilla, "...of dark complexion aged about 15..."

Vol. 3-4: 223, 06 Nov 1849. Gabriel Thomason et al., vs. Andrew Thomason et al. Petition for Partition of Lands and Negroes.

Vol. 3-4: 224-225, 08 Nov 1849. Mary Estes vs. Henry Frey et al., Heirs of Ganim Estes, deceased. Petition for Partition. Bill of slave to Erasmus S. Clardy and John E. Clardy, woman Jane, about 25 and her infant child, about 9 months. Bill of sale to B.S. Fatum and B.F. Morrison for two salves, girls Harriet, about 9 and Artemisia, about 8. Bill of sale to James Howerton, Sam, about 25. Bill of sale to George Taylor, woman Letty, about 20, on 07 Nov 1849.

Vol. 3-4: 226-228, 09 Nov 1849. Henry Estes, et al., vs. Irvin Estes, et al. Negro slave woman Alesy to be sold on 31 Dec 1849.

Vol. 3-4: 228, 09 Nov 1849. Gabriel Thomason, et al., vs. Andrew Thomason, et al. Petition for Partition of Real Estate and Slaves.

Vol. 3-4: 229-230, 09 Nov 1849. Philip Pipkin, Public Administrator of Jefferson County and Administrator of John Keeton, deceased vs. William Spradling, Administrator of William Keeton, deceased. Slaves: Nat, $300; Bob, $300; Wayne, $700; Caroline, $600; Sophronia, $600; Maria and child, $700; Ellen, $600; Baptiste, $600; Green, $600; Paul, $600; Margaret, $500; Susan, $300; Missouri, $300; Nancy, $350; Kitty, $250; Caroline's boy aged two or three years old, $250; Caroline's girls, aged one year and upwards, $150.

Vol. 3-4: 231-232, 10 Nov 1849. George W. Sebastian vs. James M. Cook, Erasmus P. Cook, and Nicholas Counts, Garnishee. Petition for Partition. Slaves: George, man 42; Andrew, man 19; Harriet, woman 23; Margurett, girl 12; George, boy 10, Jesse, boy 8; Henry, boy 7; Frank, boy 4.

Vol. 3-4: 233, 10 Nov 1849. Mary Estes vs. The Heirs of Gainem Estes, deceased. Petition for Partition of Slaves.

Vol. 3-4: 241, 07 May 1850. Alexander Moore and Jane Moore, his wife, vs. Sarah Boyce and Others, Heirs of John Boyce, deceased. Petition for Partition of Slaves.

Vol. 3-4: 244-246, 08 May 1850. Alexander Moore and Jane Moore, his wife vs. The Heirs of John Boyce, deceased. Petition for Partition of Slaves. Slaves: Charlotte, woman 45; Janette, woman 36; Anderson, man 28; Gabriel, man 25; Adeline, girl 19; Margarett, girl 12; James, boy 10; Henry, boy 10; Lewis, boy 9; Mary Jane, girl 6; Samuel, boy 4; Abraham, boy 8 months.

Vol. 3-4: 246, 08 May 1850. Nancy Mitchell et al., vs. John D. Mitchell. Petition for Partition of Slaves.

Vol. 3-4: 248, 21 Jun 1850. Ambrose L. Barnes, Reuben A. Barnes in his own right and as guardian of John M. Barnes, George H.C. Barnes, Mary S. Barnes, David Lassater and Isabella his wife (formerly Barnes), George C. Laws and wife Frances (formerly Barnes), and Martha C. Barnes vs. Milton P. Cayce. Civil Action. Slave: Hunter.

Vol. 3-4: 262, 07 Nov 1850. Alexander Moore and wife vs. Heirs of John Boyce, deceased. Petition for Partition of Slaves.

Vol. 3-4: 264, 07 Nov 1850. Alexander Moore and wife vs. Heirs of John Boyce, deceased. Partition of Slaves.

Vol. 3-4: 266, 07 Nov 1850. Philip Pipkin, Public Administrator of Jefferson County and Administrator of John Keeton, deceased vs. William Spradling, Administrator of William Keeton, deceased. Action of Detinue. Injunction against selling and dispossession of slaves.

Vol. 3-4: 269, 05 May 1851. Reuben Barnes and Others vs. Milton P. Cayce. Action of Petition for Partition of a Slave.

Vol. 3-4: 269, 05 May 1851. Britton Bridges vs. Daniel Williams, a free mulatto man. Recognizance to Keep the Peace.

Vol. 3-4: 283, 08 May 1851. Alexander Moore and Jane Moore, his wife, vs. William S. Boyce, et al. Petition for Partition of Slaves.

Vol. 3-4: 327, 05 May 1852. Reuben A. Barnes vs. Milton P. Cayce. Petition for Partitions. Cayce entitled to recover slave, Hunter.

Vol. 3-4: 339, 08 May 1852. Mary Estes, widow of Gainem Estes vs. Heirs of Gainem Estes, deceased. Petition for Partition of Land and Slaves.

Vol. 3-4: 339, 08 May 1852. Alexander Moore and Jane Moore, his wife, vs. William S. Boyce and Others. Petition for Partition of Slaves.

Vol. 3-4: 473-474, 06 May 1854. George W. Hilderbrand, James Adams and Elmira his wife (formerly Hilderbrand) vs, Rebecca Hilderbrand, widow of George, and Samuel, William, Franklin, Mary, Henry, and Margaret Hilderbrand. Petition for Partition of Land and Slaves. Slaves: Mariah, woman 45; Polly, 6; Anderson, 7 months.

Vol. 3-4: 507-508, 10 Nov 1854. George W. Hilderbrand, James Adams and Elmira his wife (formerly Hilderbrand) vs, Rebecca Hilderbrand, widow of George, and Samuel, William, Franklin, Mary, Henry, and Margaret Hilderbrand. Petition for Partition of Land and Slaves. Slaves: Mariah, woman 45; Polly, about 6; Anderson, about 7 months. All to be sold.

Vol. 3-4: 534-535, 08 Feb 1855. William C. Haile, James M. Haile, Lovick B. Haile, Samuel B. Herrod and Nancy his wife, and Elizabeth Haile vs. Thomas J. Haile, Mary D. Haile, Catherine Haile, Ann Carrow, Sarah Carrow, Catherine Carrow, and Mary Carrow. Petition for Partition of Land and Slaves.

Vol. 3-4: 558-559, 08 May 1855. State of Mo., vs. John A. Weber. Indictment for Dealing with Slaves.

Vol. 3-4: 563, 09 May 1855. State of Mo., vs. John A. Weber. Indictment for Selling to a Slave.

Vol. 3-4: 571-572, 10 May 1855. Walter E. Evans and Frances A. Evans his wife vs. Wade H. Clay and Mary his wife; Aaron J. Van Mormor and Matilda D. his wife; Mary J. Sutherland, widow of Richard L. Sutherland, deceased; Richard L. Sutherland, a minor under 21; Eliza L. Sutherland, minor; Maria V. Sutherland, minor; and Martha A. Sutherland. Petition for Partition of Slaves. Slaves: Nelson, man; Hiram, man; Overton, man.

Vol. 3-4: 576-578, 19 May 1855. William C. Haile, James M. Hale, Lovick B. Haile, Samuel B. Herrod and Nancy his wife, and Elizabeth Haile vs. Thomas J. Haile, Mary D. Haile, Catherine Haile, Ann Carrow, Sarah Carrow, Catherine Carrow, and Mary Carrow. Petition for Partition of Land and Slaves. Slave: Charles, a negro man, aged about 20, to be sold.

Vol. 3-4: 583, 10 May 1855. George Hilderbrand and Others vs. Rebecca Hilderbrand and Others. Petition for Partition and Sale of Slaves.

Vol. 3-4: 597, 05 Nov 1855. State of Mo. vs. Charles Hamilton. Indictment for Dealing with a Slave.

Vol. 3-4: 617-618, 09 Nov 1855, James B. Mitchell and Elizabeth his wife, formerly McKee; Finis E. Walker and Louisa his wife, formerly McKee vs. William Mitchell and his wife Mary, formerly McKee; Isaac Baker and wife Rachel, formerly McKee, Erastus M. Walker and wife Louvina, formerly McKee; and Thomas McKee. Petition for Partition of Land and Slaves. Slaves: George, boy about 18; Harve, man about 65. To be sold for cash.

Vol. 3-4: 654, 08 May 1856. James B. Mitchell and Others vs. Isaac Baker and Others. Petition for Partition of Land and Slaves.

6

Vol. 3-4: 654, 08 May 1856. William C. Hale et al., vs. Thomas J. Hale et al. Petition for Partition of a Slave and Real Estate.

Vol. 3-4: 661-662, 09 May 1856. Aaron Isenberg vs. Mary Jane Sutherland. Civil Action and Petition to Foreclose a Mortgage. Slaves: negro child named George, about 6; Jim, about 4.

Vol. 5: 1, 08 Nov 1856. Richard L. and Martha A. Sutherland vs. Aaron Isenberg. Court finds that Richard who is deceased and former owner of slaves George and Jim, bequeathed them to his widow Mary Jane Sutherland; they are to be returned to her after previously being sold at a sheriff's sale.

Vol. 5: 2, 08 Nov 1856. James F. Henry and Martha Henry, his wife, next of friends of William Wilson and Giles Wilson, minors under age of 21 vs. Daniel Williams, curator of the above. Petition for sale of slaves belonging to William and Giles: Fount; Isaac, about 50; Louisa, about 17; Martha, 15. All to be sold at the courthouse.

Vol. 5: 8, 08 Nov 1856. State of Mo., vs. John M. Griffin. Indictment Dealing with a Slave.

Vol. 5: 19, 04 Apr 1857. Nicholas L. Fleming vs. Stephen E. Douthit. Fleming claims to own: Ann, about 22; and her children: Frances, John, William, and James. Sheriff commanded to take possession of slaves and return to Fleming.

Vol. 5: 24, 04 May 1857. State of Mo., vs. John W. Griffin. Indictment for Selling to a Slave.

Vol. 5: 24, 04 May 1857. Nicholas L. Fleming vs. Stephen E. Douthit. Civil Action. Douthit filed motion to strike out Fleming's affidavit. Overruled.

Vol. 5: 26, 05 May 1857. John Patterson and Wm. D. McCracken vs. Wm. T. McFarland and wife and others. Petition for Partition of Slaves.

Vol. 5: 34, 08 May 1857. John Fulton presents instrument of writing from Charles Sandy, negro. Sandy paid $700 and Fulton emancipated the following: Amanda, about 25 with a dark complexion and her children: Burrel, boy aged about 4; John, boy aged about 2; infant, about 3 days old, sex and name unknown.

Vol. 5: 35-36, 08 May 1857. John Patterson and Wm. D. McCracken vs. William T. McFarland and Irena his wife, nee Crawford, Ludora Crawford and Edgar W. Prewitt, their guardian. Petition for Partition of Slaves: Nancy, woman, 45; Maria, 22; Francis, girl, 5; Mary Ann, child, 7 months; William, boy, 7 months; Catherine, woman, 20; Mary Jane, girl, 3; Simon, boy, 18 [months?]; Penny, woman, 18; Andy, boy, 14; Lucy, girl, 16.

Vol. 5: 36, 08 May 1857. Nicholas L. Fleming vs. Stephen E. Douthit. Civil Action. Douthit by attorney files.

Vol. 5: 37, 09 May 1857. Nicholas L. Fleming vs. Stephen E. Douthit. Civil Action. Plaintiff files motion to strike out part of Douthit's answer.

Vol. 5: 38, 09 May 1857. John Patterson and Wm. D. McCracken vs. Wm. T. McFarland and others. Petition for Partition of Slaves.

Vol. 5: 38, 09 May 1857. John Patterson and Wm. D. McCracken vs. Wm. T. McFarland and others. Petition for Partition of Slaves. Ordered by court that slaves be sold: Nancy, Maria, Francis, Mary Ellen, William, Catherine, Mary Jane, Simon, Penny, Andy, Lucy, and Alexander.

Vol. 5: 52, 02 Nov 1857. State of Mo. vs. Henry Potete. Indictment for Selling to a Slave.

Vol. 5: 54, 03 Nov 1857. John Patterson vs. William T. McFarland and wife, Ludon Crawford, and Edgar W. Prewitt, guardian. Petition for Partition of Slaves.

Vol. 5: 56, 05 Nov 1857. Nicholas Fleming vs. Stephen E. Douthit. Civil Action.

Vol. 5: 57, 06 Nov 1857. Nicholas Fleming vs. Stephen E. Douthit. Civil Action.

Vol. 5: 61, 07 Nov 1857. John Patterson vs. W.T. McFarland and Others. Petition for Partition of Slaves.

Vol. 5: 75, 21 May 1858. State of Mo. vs. Alexander Boyer. Indictment for Dealing with a Slave.

Vol. 5: 76, 24 May 1858. State of Mo. vs. James R. Turley. Indictment for Dealing with a Slave.

Vol. 5: 76, 24 May 1858. State of Mo. vs. William Goff. Indictment for Dealing with a Slave.

Vol. 5: 78, 25 May 1858. State of Mo. vs. John A. Weber. Indictment for Selling to Slaves.

Vol. 5: 83, 26 May 1858. State of Mo. vs. Milton P. Cayce. Indictment for Selling to Slaves.

Vol. 5: 83, 26 May 1858. State of Mo. vs. Luther K. Peers. Indictment for Dealing with Slaves.

Vol. 5: 84, 26 May 1858, State of Mo. vs. Stephen E. Douthit. Indictment for Dealing with Slaves.

Vol. 5: 86, 26 May 1858, Edwin C. Sebastian emancipates slave, Green, aged about 40, "...yellow or Copper Color and about five feet seven inches high..."

Vol. 5: 113, 22 Nov 1858. State of Mo. vs. Daniel O'Donnell. Indictment for Dealing or Selling to Slaves.

Vol. 5: 117, 24 Nov 1858. Nicholas Fleming vs. Stephen E. Douthit. Civil Action. Plaintiff to recover costs from defendant.

Vol. 5: 141-142, 27 Nov 1858. Hardy Koen and Nancy Koen his wife vs. William G. Poston, Luke D. Poston, and Richard I. Poston, minor children of Julia Poston, deceased, nee Davis by their guardian William Poston. Petition for Partition of Lands and a Slave. Slave named Harve, about 60 years old.

Vol. 5: 151, 11 May 1859. State of Mo. vs. Joseph Degierre. Indictment for Buying of Slaves.

Vol. 5: 152, 11 May 1858. Nicholas Fleming vs. Stephen E. Douthit. Civil Action to Recover Slaves.

Vol. 5: 156, 11 May 1858. Nicholas Fleming vs. Stephen E. Douthit. Civil

Action to Recover Slaves.

Vol. 5: 172, 14 May 1859. Nicholas Fleming vs. Stephen E. Douthit. Civil Action Appeal from County Court.

Vol. 5: 189, 15 May 1860. James W. Smith appears, "...whereby he emancipated his Negro Slave named Rufus, aged about thirty five years of a dark copper color about five feet ten inches..."

Vol. 5: 194, 15 May 1860. Nicholas Fleming vs. Stephen E. Douthit, Executor of Britton Bridges, deceased. Plaintiff claims court is prejudiced and asks for a change of venue. Case ordered to Reynolds Co., Mo.

Vol. 5: 243-244, 12 Nov 1860. Indictment for Selling to Slaves.

Vol. 5: 254, 15 Nov 1860. Nicholas Fleming vs. SE Douthit, Executor of Britton Bridges Estate. Appeal from County Court. Fleming by attorney files motion to dismiss.

Vol. 5: 263-264, 17 Nov 1860. State of Mo. vs. Jim (a slave). Indictment for Maliciously Killing Cattle.

Vol. 5: 264, 17 Nov 1860. State of Mo. vs. Jim (a slave). Indictment for Maliciously Maiming Cattle.

Vol. 5: 280, 12 May 1862. State of Mo. vs. Jim (a slave). Indictment for Maliciously Killing Cattle.

Vol. 5: 280, 12 May 1862. State of Mo. vs. Jim (a slave). Indictment for Maliciously Maiming Cattle.

Vol. 5: 286, 13 May 1862. State of Mo. vs. Jim (a slave). Indictment for Maiming Cattle.

Vol. 5: 287, 13 May 1862. State of Mo. vs. Jim (a slave). Indictment for Killing Cattle.

Vol. 5: 314-315, 12 May 1863. State of Mo. vs. Jim (a slave). Indictment for Maliciously Killing Cattle.

Vol. 5: 315, 12 May 1863, State of Mo. vs. Jim (a slave). Indictment for Maliciously Maiming Cattle.

Vol. 5: 323, 13 May 1863. State of Mo. vs. Jesse, a slave. Indictment for Murder.

Vol. 5: 325, 14 May 1863. State of Mo. vs. Paul (a slave). Indictment for Grand Larceny.

Vol. 5: 333, 15 May 1863. State of Mo. vs. Jesse, a slave. Indictment for Murder.

Vol. 5: 336, 16 May 1863. State of Mo. vs. Jesse, a slave. Jesse found guilty of 2nd degree manslaughter. To receive, "…thirty nine lashes on his bare back well laid on…"

Emancipation Records—Slave Records Box 5 File 175

[frame 1]

"Know all men by theses [sic] presents that I Edwin C Sebastian of St Francois County in the State of Missouri for and in Consideration of divers good Causes to me moving and also the sum of one dollar [sic] to me in hand paid by a certain slave named Green now belonging to me, the receipt of which is hereby acknowledged, have and do hereby emancipate and forever set free the said negro Green from servitude or involuntary labor. The said Green being aged about forty years, of Yellow or Copper Color and about five feet seven inches high.

In witness whereof I have hereunto set my hand & Seal this 24th day of May AD1858

Test
I.G. Beal [his signature]   E.C. Sebastian [his signature] Seal
Geo. W. Williams [his signature]

State of Missouri   }
County of St Francois   } In the Circuit Court said County May term AD1858

Be it remembered that on the 27th day of May AD 1858 in open Court, Came Edwin C Sebastian, who is personally known to the Court to be the same person whose name is subscribed to the foregoing instrument of writing, as having executed the same, and acknowledged the Execution of the foregoing deed of Emancipation to Green his Negro Slave which said acknowledgment is entered on the record of the Court of that day. In testimony whereof I the undersigned Clerk of the said Circuit Court hereto [sic] subscribe my name and affix the seal of said Court at office at Farmington the 4th day of June AD 1858.

John Cobb Clerk [his signature]"

[frame 2]

"Edwin C Sebastian to Green a Slave
deed of Emancipation

e[illegible]

13

Fees Paid
$1. [illegible]"

[frame 3]

"Walnut Grove Dec 30th 1858

Col John Cobb or   }
Wm R Taylor Esqr   }

    Will you please to send me by the Bearer, a Copy of the instrument
of writing, by which I emancipated a Negro man named Green at the last
May Term of the Circuit Court of St Francois County and much oblige.
    E.C. Sebastian [his signature]"

[frame 4]

"Copy delivered

Col John Cobb or William R. Taylor
Farmington Mo"

[frame 5]

"Know all men by these presents that I William M Cruncleton of St Francois
County in the state of Missouri, do hereby set free and forever emancipate
my negro boy, named Bob from all further service, duty or obligation as my
Slave or in any other manner, as such; said negro Man is about thirty eight
years old, five feet nine inches high, and of dark complexion.
    I[n] witness whereof I the said William M Cruncleton have hereunto
set my hand and affixed my hand and Seal this 8th day of November in the
year one thousand eight hundred and forty eight.

Witnesses   W.M. Cruncleton [his signature]
Seal
Jas Ransom [his signature]   }
Ignatius G. Beal [his signature] }

State of Missouri   }
County of St Francois   } In the Circuit Court said leo [sic] November Term

14

1848

Be it remembered that on this 8th day November 1848 personally appeared in the court here W.M. Cruncleton, whose name is subscribed to the foregoing Instrument of writing, and whilst said court was in session acknowledged that he executed and delivered the same as his voluntary act and deed for the purposes therein mentioned
In Testimony whereof I hereunto sign my name and affix the seal of said Court at office in and for Said County this the 10th day of November 1848
John Cobb clerk [his signature]
Wm R. Taylor [illegible] [his signature]"

[frame 6]

"State of Missouri   }
County of St Francois   } SS

I John Cobb Clerk of the Circuit Court and exofficio [sic] Recorder within and for said County do hereby Certify that the foregoing deed was filed in my office for Record on June 21st 1849 and the same is truly Recorded therein Book D Page 522-3
In testimony whereof I hereunto set my hand and affix the seal of said Court at Farmington this 22 day of June 1849

[seal]   John Cobb Recorder [his signature]"

[frame 7]

William M Cruncleton To Negro-man Bob.
Deed of emancipation
Filed for record June 21st 1849
Attest. John Cobb, Recorder"

[frame 8]

"In the name of God Amen. I Henry Potts of the County of Saint Francois and State of Missouri, being in good health of body and of Sound and disposing mind and memory (praised be god for the same) and being desirous to Settle my worldly affairs, whilst I have Strength and Capacity so to do, do make and ordain this my last will and testament. And first and principally I

15

command my soul into the hands of my Creator who gave it. And my body to the earth to be buried in a decent and Christian like manner at the discretion of my executors herein after named, And as to such worldly estate as it hath pleased God to intrust [sic] me with, I dispose of the same as follows viz – I will that my Negro Man Commonly Called and known by the name of Jack, and my Negro Man named Fountain Shall both be free from involuntary Servitude from and after my decease, during their Natural lives and further that they the said two Negroes shall be and remain in full possession of all the land and plantation on which I now live and reside, together with all the buildings, improvements, rights privileges and appurtenances thereunto belonging, and be entitled to all the benefits and profits arising from the same during their Natural lives or so long as either of the Said Negroes Shall live, (saveing [sic] to those who may have a lease hold their respective rights) and after their decease that the said premises shall decend [sic] and be equally divided among My Brothers and Sisters or their decendants [sic] according to their respective rights. And as to my personal estate, I will that my Said two Negroes Jack and Fountain Shall have each one Horse Beast to be chosen by them at their discretion and that the balance of My personal estate be impartially appraised and that they the said Jack and Fountain Shall be entitled to select out of my other personal estate so appraised any articles they may see proper to the amount of fifty dollars each at the appraised value to their own use and benefit for which their receipt shall be a [inserted] Sufficient voucher for My executors hereinafter named, and the balance of my personal estate to be Sold and the proceeds after defraying all my debts, and the expense of Administering on the same to be equally divided among those of my relations as before directed, and I make and appoint My two friends John McFarland and George Marks Executors of this My last will and testament.

In witness whereof I have hereunto"

[frame 9]

"Set my hand and seal this twenty eighth day of December one thousand eight hundred and thirty nine

Henry Potts [his signature] (seal)

Signed and acknowledged by the testator in the presence of the Subscribers as his last will and testament
Reuben McFarland [his signature]
Mainyard S Harris [his signature]

16

State of Missouri   } SS
County of St Francois   } County Court of St Francois County in Vacation
July 15th 1851

Be it remembered that Reuben McFarland one of the Subscribing witnesses to the written foregoing Will, personally appeared before me John Cobb Clerk of said Court, and being by me duly sworn, deposes and says, that he saw the above named testator, Henry Potts, sign the foregoing instrument of writing which he published as his last will; that he the said Testator, was at the time of sound mind and over the age of twenty one years, and that this deponant [sic] attested said Will as one of the Witnesses thereto by Subscribing his name to the same in the presence of said Testator—Deponant [sic] further States and deposes that, he sew [sic] Mainyard S. Harris Sign his name as a witness to the foregoing Will in the presence and at the request of the said Henry Potts, and that the said Signature of the said Mainyard S. Harris which now appears to said Wills as a witness thereof is genuine.

In testimony where I John Cobb Clerk of the County Court for said County hereunto Subscribe my name and affix the Seal of said Court at office at Farmington the 15th day of July AD 1851

LA[?] [seal]   John Cobb, Clerk [his signature]"

[frame 10]

"State of Missouri   } SS
County of St Francois   } County Court of St Francois County July 15th
1851

Be it remembered that on the fifteenth day of July AD 1851 Davis Marks, a credible witness of lawful age, appeared before me the undersigned Clerk of the County Court within and for the County aforesaid, and being duly sworn by me, deposes and says, that he personally knew Mainyard S Harris whose name is subscribed to the within Will as a witness thereto, that he well knew his signature and often seen him write his name, and that he has good reason to believe, and does believe that the said signature of the said Mainyard S Harris subscribed to this Will as a Witness is genuine.

(The proof aduced [sic] by the two before named Witnesses is deemd [sic] sufficient to establish this Will)

In testimony whereof I John Cobb Clerk of the said County Court have hereunto subscribed my name and affixed the seal of said Court at office at Farmington the day month and year aforesaid

LS [seal]   John Cobb, Clerk [his signature]

State of Missouri   } In the County Court said County August term
1851
County of St Francois   } Tuesday August 19th 1851, was the following
proceeding to w[it]

    Now at this day the Clerk of this Court presents the proof of the Will of Henry Potts deceased taken by said Clerk in Vacation, and the Certificates thereof endorsed on said Will, which is seen and examined and ordered by the Court that the same be, and it is hereby approved and confirmed.
    In testimony that the foregoing is truly Copied from the record of the proceeding of the said County Court in approving and Confirming the proof of the written Last Will and testament of Henry Potts deceased. I John Cobb Clerk of said Court hereunto Subscribe my name and affix the seal of said Court the 19th day of August 1851

LS [seal]   John Cobb Clerk [his signature]"

[frame 11]

"State of Missouri   } SS
County of Saint Francois}

I john Cobb Clerk of the County Court within and for said County, do hereby Certify, that the written and foregoing Will together with the Certificates of Proof and Confirmation thereon endorsed are truely [sic] recorded in my office in a Book therein left for that purpose on pages 213. 214. & 215
    In testimony whereof I hereunto subscribe my name and affix the seal of said Court the 29th of August AD 1851

LS [seal]   John Cobb Clerk

[the text below was written upside down on the page:]

State of Missouri   } SS
County of Saint Francois}

I John Cobb Clerk of the County Court within and for the County of Saint Francois aforesaid, Certify, that the foregoing two pages of writing Contain a true Copy of the last and testament Will and Testament of Henry Potts deceased, together with the certificates of Probate and the approval thereof by the County Court, and of record, as fully as the said original Will remains on file in My office.

In testimony whereof I hereunto Subscribe My name and affix the Seal of said Court at office at Farmington the 29th day of December AD 1852

John Cobb Clerk [his signature]"

[frame 12]

"Free Papers of Jack Potts a free man of Color in Saint Francois County"

[frame 13]

"In the name of God Amen. I Henry Potts of the County of Saint Francois and State of Missouri, being in good health of body and of sound and disposing mind and memory, praised be god for the same, and being desirous to settle my worldly affairs whilst I have Strength and Capacity so to do, do make and ordain this my last Will and testament. And first and principally I command my soul into the hands of my Creator who gave it. and my body to the earth to be buried in a decent and Christian like manner at the discretion of my executors herein after named, and as to such worldly estate as it hath pleased god to intrust [sic] me with, I dispose of the same as follows viz, I Will that my negro man commonly called and known by the name of Jack, and my negro man named Fountain shall both be free from involuntary Servitude from and after my decease, during their natural lives and further that they the said two negroes shall be and remain in full possession of all the land and plantation on which I now live and reside, together with all the buildings, improvements, rights privileges and appurtenances thereunto belonging, and be entitled to all the benefits and profits arising from the same during their natural lives, or so long as either of the said Negroes Shall live, (saveing [sic] to those who may have a lease hold their respective rights) and after their decease that the said premises shall descent and be equally divided among my Brothers and Sisters or their descendants according to their respective rights, And as to my personal estate, I will that my said two Negroes Jack, and Fountain shall have each one Horse beast to be chosen by them at their discretion and that the balance of My personal estate be impartially appraised and that they the said Jack and Fountain shall be entitled to select out of My other personal estate so appraised any articles they may see proper, to the amount

19

of fifty dollars each, at the appraised value to their own use and benefit for which their receipt shall be a sufficient voucher for My Executors, hereinafter named, and the balance of my personal estate to be sold and the proceeds after defraying all my debts and the expense of Administering on the same to be equally divided among those of my relations as before directed, and I make and appoint my two friends John McFarland and George Marks Executors of this My last will and testament

In witness whereof I have hereunto set my hand and seal this twenty eighth day of December one thousand eight hundred and thirty nine

Henry Potts [his signature] (seal)

Signed and acknowledged by the."

[frame 14]

"Testator in the presence of the Subscribers, as his last Will and testament.

Reuben McFarland [his signature]
Mainyard S. Harris [his signature]

State of Missouri } SS County Court of St Francois County in vacation July 15th 1851
County of Saint Francois}

Be it remembered that Reuben McFarland one of the subscribing Witnesses to the foregoing Will, personally appeared before me John Cobb Clerk of said Court, and being duly sworn by me, deposes and says, that he saw the above named Testator, Henry Potts, sign the foregoing instrument of writing which he published as his last Will. That he the said Testator was at the time of sound mind, and over the age of twenty one years, and that this deponant [sic] attested said Will as one of the witnesses thereto, by Subscribing his name to the same in the presence of said Testator, Deponent further states and deposes, that he saw Mainyard S. Harris sign his name as a witness to the foregoing Will in the presence and at the request of th said Henry Potts, and that the said Signature of the said Mainyard S Harris which now appears to said Wills as a Witness thereof is genuine

In testimony whereof I John Cobb Clerk of the County Court for said County hereunto Subscribe my name and affix the seal of said Court at office at Farmington the 15th day of July AD 1851

LS [seal]   John Cobb Clerk [his signature]

State of Missouri   } SS County Court of St Francois County
County of Saint Francois} July 15th 1851

Be it remembered that on the fifteenth day of July AD 1851 Davis Marks, a credible witness of lawful age, appeared before me the undersigned Clerk of the County Court within and for the County aforesaid, and being duly sworn by me, deposes and says, that he personally knew Mainyard S Harris whose name is subscribed to the written will as a witness thereto, that he well knew his signature and often seen him write his name, and that he has good reason to believe, does believe that the said signature of the said Mainyard S Harris subscribed to this Will as a Witness, is genuine. The proof aduced [sic] by the two before named witnesses is deemd [sic] sufficient to establish this Will. In Testimony"

[frame 15]

"whereof I John Cobb Clerk of said County Court have hereunto Subscribed my name and affixed the seal of said Court at office at Farmington the day month and year aforesaid

LS [seal]   John Cobb Clerk [his signature]

State of Missouri   } In the County Court said County August term
1851
County of St Francois } Tuesday August 19th 1851, was the following
proceeding to wit

Now at this day the Clerk of this Court presents the proof of the Will of Henry Potts deceased taken by said Clerk in vacation, and the Certificates thereof endorsed on said Will, which is seen and examined and ordered by the Court that the same be, and it is hereby approved and Confirmed.

In testimony that the foregoing is truly Copied from the record of the proceeding of the said County Court in approving and Confirming the proof of the Within last Will and testament of Henry Potts deceased. I John Cobb Clerk of said Court hereunto subscribe my name and affix the seal of said Court the 19th day of August 1851

LS [seal]   John Cobb Clerk [his signature]"

21

"State of Missouri   } SS
County of Saint Francois}

I john Cobb Clerk of the County Court within and for said County, do hereby Certify, that the within and foregoing Will together with the Certificates of proof and Confirmation thereon endorsed are truely [sic] recorded in My office in a Book therein left for that purpose on pages 213, 214 & 215.

In testimony whereof I hereunto subscribe my name and affix the seal of said Court the 29th day of August AD 1851

LS [seal]   John Cobb Clerk [his signature]

State of Missouri   } SS
County of Saint Francois}

I John Cobb Clerk of the County Court within and for the County of saint Francois aforesaid, Certify, that the foregoing 2 pages of writing Contain a true Copy of the last Will and testament of Henry Potts deceased together with the Certificates of Probate & the approval thereof by the County Court, and of record as fully as the said original Will remains on file in my office.

In testimony whereof I hereunto subscribe my name and affix the seal of said Court, the 29th day of December AD 1852

John Cobb, Clerk [his signature]"

[frame 16]

"Free paper of Fountain Potts. (a Man of Color)"

[frame 17]

"Know all Men by these Presents, That I Jesse P Davis of St. Francois County State of Missouri for and in consideration "that All Men are born free and equal" as well from Motives of benevolence and humanity, and for the further considerations of the sum of one dollar to Me in hand paid the receipt whereof I do hereby acknowledge, have Manumitted and hereby do Manumit and set free from Slavery, My Negro Boy Bob Aged About Twenty Five Years being of large Size and of black color, which said Negro is the same as was owned and belonged to Nancy Robinson of Washington County, and State aforesaid, and formed a part of said Estate, Subject however to the following Terms of Service, That whereas I have on the sixth day of October in the Year 1853 hired the said Slave Bob to John G. Scott of the County of St Francois State aforesaid from that date until the First day of January in the Year 1859. Here the said boy Bob is to remain with the said John G. Scott and faithfully discharge said Terms or time of service, And I do hereby Give, Grant, and release unto the said Bob all my right, title, and claim, of in and to his person, labour [sic] and service, and of in, and to the estate and property which he may hereafter acquire, or obtain, excepting only his service in Manner and during the Terms above Mentioned.

In Witness whereof I have this Eleventh day of October in the Year 1853 set My hand and seal in presence of Witnesses.

Witness[es]   Jesse P. Davis [his signature] seal [his seal]
John Cobb [his signature]
Walter K. Brady [his signature]"

[frame 18]

"State of Missouri   }
County of St Francois   } SS – In the Circuit Court said County November term AD 1853 first day of said Term and Seventh day of said Month was the following proceeding, to wit,----

Now at this day Jesse P Davis came into Court, whilst the same was in session, and produced a deed of Emancipation dated the Eleventh day of October 1853 whereby he emancipates and sets from Involuntary Servitude a negro boy named Bob of Black Color aged about twenty five years of large size described in said deed, executed by said Jesse P Davis and attested by John Cobb and Walter K Brady as witnesses thereto. And the said Jesse P Davis who is personally known to the Judge of said Court to be the same person whose name is subscribed to said deed of emancipation as the person executing the same acknowledges that he executed and delivered said deed for the purposes therein expressed on the day of the date thereof and it was ordered that the Same be Certified accordingly

I John Cobb Clerk of the Circuit Court within and for the County of St Francois in the State of Missouri, Certify, that the above is truely [sic] Copied from the record of the proceeding of the said Circuit Court in relation to the acknowledgment of the within deed of Emancipation by Jesse P Davis, as fully as the same remains in my office.

In testimony whereof I hereunto subscribe my name and affix the seal of said Court at office Farmington the Seventh day of November AD

1853

John Cobb, Clerk

State of Missouri   } SS
County of St Francois }

I John Cobb Clerk of the Circuit Court and Ex Officio Recorder in and for said County, do hereby Certify, that the foregoing deed was filed in my office for record on the 4th day of February 1854 and that the same is truely [sic] recorded therein in Book of pages 64 & 65 Witness my hand and official seal at Farmington the 22nd day of March AD 1854

John Cobb, Recorder [his signature]"

[frame 19]

"Jesse P Davis
To   } Deed of
Bob   } Emancipation

Filed for Record Feby 4th 1854
John Cobb, Recorder

Recorded in Book F Pages 64&65

$1.70 cts
1[.]00} 1.70"

[frame 20]

"State of Kentucky   }
Logan county [illegible] }

I Marmaduke B Morton as clerk of the said Logan county court do certify that at a county court held for said county at the court house in Russellville on the 25th day of May 1846 the following order was made to wit:

Daniel one of the slaves emancipated by the will of Robert Williams Decd appeared in court he is about twenty seven years old, about five feet seven inches high, stout, and well made he is a mulatto and yellow man.

In testimony that the foregoing order is truly and correctly copied from the Order & Record book of the said Logan county court, I hereto act my name and affix the seal of said county court the 30th day of June 1846 and in the 55th year of the Commonwealth.

> Marmaduke B. Morton [his signature]
> Clerk of Logan county court

State of Kentucky Logan county [illegible]:
I Tilghman Offutt presiding justice of the peace in and for the county aforesaid and President of the said Logan county court being a court of record do hereby certify that Marmaduke B Morton whose name is signed to the above certificate now is and was at the time of signing the same the clerk of the said Logan county court duly appointed and qualified as such, and that said certificate is in due form of law.

> I seal this 7th day of July 1846
> Tiln Offutt [his signature] JPLC [seal]"

[frame 21]

"Daniel Williams Certificate of Emancipation"

[frame 22]

"Appraisement List of the Personal Estate of James W. Smith deceased.

Slaves

1	General	aged	63	years	appraised		at	100
2	Jack	"	56	"	"	"	250	
3	Louis	"	43	"	"	"	250	
4	Talbot	"	30	"	"	"	550	
5	Major	"	25	"	"	"	600	
6	Frank	"	20	"	"	"	700	
7	George	"	20	"	"	"	700	
8	Peter	"	17	"	"	"	650	
9	Joe	"	14	"	"	"	450	
10	Charles	"	10	"	"	"	300	
11	Reuben	"	7	"	"	"	300	
12	Alvey	"	5	"	"	"	250	
13	Abram	"	3	"	"	"	200	
14	James	"	2	"	"	"	150	

15	Thomas "	2	"	"	"		125	
16	Phebee "	69	"	"	"		50	
17	Louisa "	50	"	"	"		100	
18	Julia Ann	"	47	"	"	"		100
19	Melissa "	26	"	"	"		400	
20	Jane "	20	"	"	"		450	
21	Henrietta	"	18	"	"	"		500
22	Lucinda"	16	"	"	"		500	
23	Mary "	13	"	"	"		500	
24	Mildred"	13	"	"	"		500	
25	Letty "	10	"	"	"		450	
26	Maria "	10	"	"	"		350	
27	Huldy "	9	"	"	"		350	
28	Harriet "	6	"	" 10.075	"		250	
1	Hick Port Bead Stead	"	"	"	10"			

[frame 23]

"St Francois County Missouri
On or before the twenty fifth day of December next I promise to pay to Patsey Hunt on order the Sum of one hundred and fifty collars it being a part of the consideration for the residue of the [sic] which Mary a Negro Girl (about 18 or 19 years of age) has yet to Serve the Said Patsey Hunt and which time I have this day purchased of the Said Patsey for the Sum of three hun[d]red dollars.

Witness my hand and seal this 30 day of March in the year of our Lord one thousand eight hundred and forty

Witness		his		
John,, Cobb. [his signature]	}	Shadrach	X	Caldwell
seal [his seal]				
Lawson Alexander [his signature] }		mark		
		a free man of color		

St. Francois County Missouri
On or before the twenty fifth day of December in the year of our Lord one thousand eight hundred and forty one, I promise to pay to Patsey Hunt or order the Sum of one hundred and fifty dollars It being a part of the consideration for the residue of the time which Mary a Negro Girl (about 18 or 19 years of age) has yet to Serve the said Patsey Hunt and which time I have this day purchased of the said Patsey for the Sum of three hundred dollars. Wit-

ness my hand and seal the 30th day of March AS 1840

Witness   his
John Cobb [his signature]   }   Shadrach X Caldwell
Seal [his seal]
Lawson Alexander [his signature] }   mark

Recorded March 31st 1840
John Cobb clk [his signature]"

[frame 24]

"Of the Honorable county court of St Francois County The following is a
true Statement of the hiring of the Slaves belonging to the estate of John Estes
decd Said Slaves, George & Elsey by name hired on the first day of Jan. 1838
for the term of one year [illegible] to Rolla B. Turly for one hundred & fifty
dollars Said negroes to be well clothed & treated by Said Turly & a deduction
out of their wages for any time lost by Sickness if sick at any one time for
more than three days—
                     by me
This Feb 1st 1838 -   H. Poston A. [his signature]

A List of the hire of the negro Slaves of the estate of John Estes decd (To wit)
The Slaves George & Elsey hired to Aaron Lowbeth on the 28th day of February last for one hundred & two dollars for their Services from that time till
the 25th day of December next to be clothed and paid [illegible] for by Said
Lowbeth & a deduction for Sickness if at any time Sick for more than three
days at a time by me

Mar. 9th 1838   H. Posten. Admr"

William Alexander will, pg. 8-10, 18 November 1831, recorded 29 February 1832

"…My negro woman Farmar and her three children I leave to be sold or disposed of by my son Corbin Alexander in such manner as he may deem most advantageous and the money so arising to be by him applied to the discharge of the debts which I owe towards their purchase…"

William Murphy Will, Pg. 10-11, 25 October 1833, 21 May 1836

"…I will that my negro name [sic] Cato to be sold and the money eaquallt [sic] divided between my five daughters (towit) [sic] Mary Elizabeth Dilila Kittvera and Sarah[.] I will that my wife have all the proper use and benefit of the service of my negro man Jim during her life and after her death the said negro Jim to go free…"

James Caldwell Will, Pg. 10-11, 5 May 1835, recorded 20 September 1836

[page one of four]

"35.

I[,] James Caldwell of the County of St Francois and state of Missouri being of sound and Disposing mind do make ordain and declare this my last will and testament, hereby revoking and declaring null and void all others made by me[.] Item 1st I give and bequeath to my beloved wife Meekee Caldwell the tract of land on which I now live with all the priviliges [sic] and appurtanences [sic] there unto belonging for her use and benefit and at her disposal, except one hundred and twenty-five Arpens [sic] which I give and bequeath to the bodily heirs of Lucinda Smith Deceased, an equal moiety to each to be laid off on the east end of Said tract of land on which I now live. I also give and bequeath to the bodily heirs of Lucinda Smith one negro woman named Maria which I loaned to Lucinda Smith as a nurse also her four children which she now has, an equal moiety to each-). Item 2nd I give and bequeath to Samuel Kinkead all my right title and interest to a tract of land pertaining to Bailey and McFarlands preemption rights on the waters of back creek. Item 3rd I give and bequeath to my adopted son Edwin C Sebastian all my houses and lots in the Town of Farmington also all my lands adjoining said Town and eighty acres adjoining the land of John Kennedy on the east side. Item 4th I give and bequeath to my adopted son Edwin C. Sebastian- my Plantation lying on the road leading from Farmington to Jackson at the crossing of Castor: Item 5th I give and bequeath to Mary Justus two hundred dollars to be paid by instalments [sic] of twenty give dollars [illegible] year [illegible] horse and saddle to be worth seventy five dollars a good Feather bed and Furniture and two good Milk cows to be paid out of my estate by Edwin [illegible] Sebastian."

[page two of four]

"36

Item 6th I give and bequeath [begin insertion] to my [end insertion] slaves Robin. Alvey Shadrack, Maria and Arnetta their Freedom at my death.- Item 7th I give and bequeath to Catherine McMurtrey the service of my slave Clay from this time untill [sic] the year eighteen hundred and forty give if she has any issue within that [t]hay [sic] time are to be free with her. Item 8th (I give and bequeath to Katherine McMurtrey my beloved wife Meeke Caldwell and Edwin C. Sebastian the service of my Slaves Jerry. Bill. Kitt. Anderson. and Harriet: four years each after my death, and equal moiety to each. Item 9th (I give and bequeath to my beloved wife Meeke Caldwell, and Edwin C Sebastian the service of my slave Ciller untill [sic] the year eighteen hundred and forty seven, and Ester and Lucy untill [sic] eighteen hundred and forty nine, and Amy until the year eighteen hundred and fifty six an equal moiety to each. Item 10th I give and bequeath to my adopted son Edwin C Sebastian the service of my slave Green untill [sic] the year eighteen hundred and fifty six. all of the above named negroes are to be free when their term of service expires. Item 11th I give and bequeath to Edwin C Sebastian all my Blacksmith Tools[.] Item 12th I give and bequeath to Edwin C Sebastian all my fire arms. Item 13th I give and bequeath to my beloved wife Meeke Caldwell and Edwin C Sebastian one equal moiety to each of all the stocks flocks clash in hand notes bonds and accounts and Farming utensils if a decision be necessary[.] In testimony whereof I have"

[page three of four]

"37.

hereunto set my hand and affixed my seal in the year of our Lord one thousand eight hundred and thirty five May fifth

James Caldwell [his signature and seal]

in Presence of
R.S. Josney [his signature]
H Poston [his signature]
Charles R Dulaney [his signature]

State of Missouri   } SS
County of St Francois   }

Be it remembered that on this twentieth day of September one thousand eight hundred and thirty six personally appeared before me the undersigned clerk of the county court within and for the county aforesaid Henry Poston and Charles R. Dulaney subscribing witnesses to the within foregoing last will and testament of James Caldwell deceased, and they and each of them after being duly sworn according to law upon their corporial oaths do say and declare that they and each of them the said Henry Poston and Charles R Dulaney whose names are subscribed to the foregoing instrument were personally present and that they saw the said James Caldwell sign his name to the said instrument of writing, and then and there is presence of each of them declare the same to to [sic] his last will and testament, and requested them the said Witnesses and each of them [begin insertion] to sign the same as witnesses [end insertion] the said [begin insertion] and further that they and each of them the said [end insertion] deponents believes that the said James Caldwell at the time of signing the same or said will, was of sound and disposing mind and memory."

[page four of four]

"38

All of which I do hereby certify this the day and date first above written

Given under my
hand and seal of office
the day and date first above
Written

John Cobb clk [his signature]

State of Missouri   } SS
County of St Francois   }

31

As Clerk of the county court County aforesaid, I Certify that foregoing Will was filed in my office on the twentieth day of September one thousand eight hundred and thirty six and that I have well and truly recorded the same together with the certificates thereon indorsed

September 20th 1836
John Cobb clk [his signature]"

Patsy Hunt, pg. 30, 10 October 1829, recorded 17 August 1839
"...my Negro boy Jack who was born the 15th of May 1810 I lend unto my brother Henry Hunt until he arrives to the age of twenty five years then I leave him free not be in Slavery no longer to no person- Also my Negroe girl Mary I lend unto my brother Henry Hunts daughter Patsey until said Negroe girl whoe [sic] was born the 11th of May 1821 dos [sic] arrive to the age of 21 years then I leave her free and all her encrease [sic] if any she should have to be in slavery no longer to no person, and I request my executor whoe I shall appoint to this my will, to have both the said Negroe boy jack and said Negroe girl Mary Emancipated according to law if it should be deemed necessary..."

Ezekiel Estes, pg. 36, 26 March 1820, 1 April 1820 (in Washington Co.)
"...to my daughter Anne and her heirs I give a Negro girl named Nance, to my son William I give a Negro boy Henry. The one the Negro woman is pregnant with I give so [sic] my son Gainem...the Negroes Phillip and Edmund to remain with my widow for her sole use Edmund to be under the control of my son Gainum until her death after which he and her and offspring is to be sold and the money divided agreeable to the above bequeaths..."

Pleasant Cayce, p. 44-47, 16 October 1840, 3 December 1846
"...I give and bequeath to Eliza Abbot formerly Eliza Robinson, Pleasant Robinson, Thomas Robinson and William Robinson (heirs and legal decendants [sic] of my deceased daughter Francis Robinson) of the State of Virginia one Negro woman named Edy which I placed in the hands of Christopher Robinson my said daughters husband together with her increase...I give and bequeath to my daughter Mary Glende one negro woman named Eliza and her increase which woman I placed in her and her husbands hands some time since...I give and bequeath to my son Newton F Cayce one Negro Girl named Sarah which he has had in possession also a negro man named Edmond and Elisha his wife a negro boy named Edmond or Edwin and a negro boy named Marshall now in my possession to be delivered to him my said son Newton at my death...I give and bequeath to my daughter Janetta Cayce

a negro Girl named Clarissa a negro boy named Joseph another named William and a negro girl named Emily...I Give and bequeath to my son Milton P Cayce my negro man Billy and also Nelson to be taken possession of by my said son at my deceased [sic] also a negro woman named Effy, a girl named Grace a boy named Dick...I Give and bequeath to my daughter Eliza Spencer a negro woman named Delila & her increase Also a boy named Tazwell said boy and woman being in her and her husbands possession...I give and bequeath to mt [sic] daughter Ann V. Kennedy a negro woman named A my [sic] now [sic] in her and her husbands possession and a negro boy named Coleman at my death...I give and bequeath to my step daughter Saplate B Covington a negro boy Briton...

William M. Whittenburg, pg. 59-60, 21 November 1842
"...I give and bequeath to my beloved mother Rachel Murphy formerly Rachel Whittenburgh...my negro man Alick slave now in the possession of Mr. Davis Murphy, and all and all manner of Interest I may now or hereafter have to any other slave or slaves..."

Samuel Vance, p. 68-69, 4 July 1843, 30 October 1843
"...I give to my beloved wife Lucy Vance her choice out of my negro slaves to take..."

William Edmonds will, pg. 78-80, 1 March 1826, recorded 28 November 1845
"...I William Edmons [sic] of County of Nelson, and State of Virginia... give and bequeath unto my beloved wife, Sally Edmons...if it should be the desire of my beloved wife, Sally Edmonds to remove from this County, it is my will and desire that...she should have five of my slaves, viz: Dover, Cate, Lucy, Scipio and George during her lfie [sic] time, and at her death, the said slaves namely Dover, Cate, Scipio and George and their increase, if any to be euqually [sic] divided between all of my children viz: James Edmonds, Elizabeth Edmonds, Jane Thomas formerly Jane Edmonds Samuel Edmonds, Nancy Adnrew [sic], formerly Nancy Edmonds Lavender Edmonds, Willis Edmons, Moses Edmonds, Rebecca Edmonds and Charles Edmonds. In the third place, it is my will and desire that the remainder of my slaves viz: Peter Phebe, Delphas, Phill Lucinda, Eady, David, Patrick and Minerva, and their increase (if any) be equally divided between my ten children above named, to them and their heirs forever, when my youngest son Charles Edmonds becomes of age..."

Richard L. Sutherland will, pg. 83-86, 28 February 1846, recorded 13

April 1846

"...I give to my beloved wife Mary Jane Sutherland and to her children Mary Elizabeth, Mildred D. Frances Ann Eliza L. Richard L. Maria V. Martha A. & Catherine F. Sutherland my Negro man Bill and his wife Fanny and their daughter Louisa, to be used and enjoyed by my said wife to her sole Benifit [sic] so long as she many remain single after my decease and at her death to he [sic] sole benefit of her and my children forever above named. Third. I give to my said wife and children above named all my other slaves to be used and enjoyed by her during her widowhood for her benefit and the support and education of my said children and at the Termination of her widowhood to the sole use and benifit [sic] of my said children forver [sic] and should my said children or any of them become of age or marry during the widowhood of my said wife, it is my will that the one so becoming of age or marrying shall have his or her share of my said negroes assigned and given to them..."

John D. Peers will, pg. 88-90, 30 April 1845, recorded 10 August 1846

"...I give and bequeath to my much loved wife Katherine Peers all my lands, town lots houses, slaves and other personal property...for her special benefit and the special benefit of our children, Valentine C. Peers, Eleanor K. Peers Sarah J. Peers, Philip E. Peers, Susan G. Peers. Luther K. Peers, William Peers, George B. Peers and John D. Peers and post humous child if any subject to the following arrangement...I wish my blacks taught to read (by my white family) and a small bible given to each of them..."

Thomas E. Burnham will, pg. 116-118, 18 February 1850, recorded 14 March 1850

"...I also given and bequeath to my said wife Mary Burnham during her widowhood, all my negro slaves...in case of the intermarriage of my said wife, I then give and bequeath to her absolutely my negro girl slave, Named Violet aged about 9 years. And that at the death or intermarriage of my said wife, all the property both real and personal hereby devised or bequeathed to her, except as herein before excepted, I hereby give, devise and bequeath to my two sons Charles M and William P Burnham and to my two daughters Lucy Jane and Mary Ann Burnham equally and to their assigns forever..."

Henry Potts will, pg. 124-126, 128, 8 December 1839, recorded 29 August 1851

"...I will that my Nrgro [sic] man Commonly called and known by the anme [sic] of Jack, and my Negro man named Fountain shall be free from involuntary servitude from and after my decease during their natural lives and further that they the said two negroes shall be and remain in full possession of all the land and plantation on which now live and reside, together with all the buildings improvements rights privileges and appurtenances thereunto belonging and be entitled to all the benefits and profits ariseing [sic] from the same, during their natural lives or so long as either of the said negroes shall live, (saveing [sic] to those who many have a leasehold their respective rights) And after their decease that the said premises shall decend [sic] andbe [sic] equally divided among my Brothers and Sisters or their decednants [sic] according to their respective rights- And as to my personal estate, I will that my said two negroes Jack and Fountain shall have each one horse beast, to be chosen by them at their direction, and that the balance of my personal estate to be impartially appraised and that they the sd Jack and Foundation shall be entitled to select our [sic] of my other personal estate so appraised any articles they may see proper to the amount of fifty dollars each, at the appraised value, to their own use and benefit for which their receipt shall be sufficient voucher for my executors hereinafter named, and the balance of my personal estate to be sold..."

Mary Estes will, pg. 129-132, 128, 14 August 1851, recorded 10 November 1851
"...After paying my debts, whatever shall remain from the sale of my perishable property shall be applied to the payment of said sums. In case there should not be a sufficient sum to pay the one hundred dollars to each [grandchild]. It is my desire that my negro girl Artemisia be sold and the money ariseing [sic] therefrom be applied to the payment of the same, and the remainder of the price of said negro girl go to and belong to my said niece Nancy Davis...It is my desire and I so will it that my said niece Nancy Davis have my two other slaves Harriet and Jones to be hired out for her use and benefit till she arrive to the age of twenty one years and it is further my will that she have all my other estate both real and personal that may belong to me at the time of my decease to be disposed of as she may think proper..."

Jas Reyburn Heirs, pg. 138, February and May 1824
"...By 1 negro by named   325.00
[By] 1 " Girl   400.00..."

John McKee Will, p. 2-3, 26 June 1854, recorded 14 November 1854
"...My Negro Woman Maria I wish to be free at my death and to have fifty dollars out of my estate..."

George W. Day, p. 4, 19 July 1855, recorded 16 August 1855
"...I give and bequeath to my son George Thomas Day my negro boy known by the name of Frank of black color and aged about eight years..."

Andrew Patterson, p. 5-7. 24 July 1855, recorded 31 August 1855
(p. 7) "...I give and bequeath to my said Son John Patterson all my right, title interest and claim of every kind whatsoever which I purchased of Gilbert Nettleton by deed dated July twenty first Eighteen hundred and fifty five, it being the undivided one third part of the following described negroes Slaves for life to wit. Nancy a Negro woman aged about thirty nine years, Maria a Negro Woman aged about twenty four years, and her two children, Catherine a mulatto negro woman aged about twenty two years, and her three children; Penny a negro woman aged about twenty years and her child; and Lucy a negro girl aged about eighteen years; together with all my right, title, claim, interest and demand of, in and to the said negro Slaves..."

David Sherill, p. 8-9, 15 December 1854, recorded 15 October 1855
"...I give and bequeath to my Son Pinckney H. Sherill one Negro boy named Sam...I give and bequeath to my Son Aaron L. Sherrill my negro boy named Lacy...To my Son De Lafayette G. Sherrill, I give and bequeath my negro boy named Joe...I give and bequeath, to my daughter Elizabeth Cooley my negro boy named Mark...I give and bequeath to my daughter Sarah Ann Dent my negro boy named Stephen...I give and bequeath to my daughter Mary Caroline Dent my negro Girl named Angeline...I give and bequeath to my daughter Mahaly Jane Dent my negro boy named Allen...The residues of my negro Slaves, and all other property of every kind and description not herein before disposed of it is my wish and will Shall be Sold by my Executors..."

Mary Glendy, p. 11-13, 22 May 1856, recorded 22 July 1856
"...1st I Give and bequeath to my negro Slave Julia her freedom at my death. 2nd I Give and bequeath to my Slave Kitty a yellow girl aged about sixteen years her freedom when she shall have arrived at the age of twenty year[s] and all her children at that time are to be free also. 3rd I give and bequeath to my Slave a negro boy of a black Color known by the name of Dick aged about

twelve years his freedom when he shall have arrived at the age of twenty five years[.] 4th I give and bequeath to my two Nephews Ferdinand Kennedy and Nettleton Cayce Jointly, the tract of land which was my late residence situate in St Francois County and state of Missouri, being the South East Quarter of section No 29 in Township No 36 North of Range No 6 East Containing 159 50/100 acres. To have and to hold the Same to them and their heirs and assignees forever upon the following consideration or condition however, that they shall and will cause the Said negro woman named Julia to whom I have herein bequeathed her freedom to have and receive at their instance and expense, a comfortab[le] and competent support, food clothing & other necessary comforts during her natural life[.] 5th I give and bequeath to my Said Nephews Kennedy & Cayce Jointly the service of my negro Slave Kitty untill [sic] she Shall have arrived to the age of twenty years at which time she is to be free[.] I also give to my Said Nephews Jointly the services of my negro Slave Dick untill [sic] he shall have arrived at the age of twenty five years at which time he is to be free...8th It is my desire, and I so will it, that the sum of five hundred dollars be and it is hereby appropriated, if there shall be that much remaining of my estate after paying the legacies herein before bequeathed, and if not then, whatever Sum Shall remain, to the use, benefit and support of the yellow girl Kitty, and the boy Dick the slaves herein before mentioned when the terms of their servitude shall have expired, the money to go to interest for their benefit untill that time. Said money with the interest to be held in trust by my brothers Milton P Cayce & John Kennedy who are hereby appointed Trustees for the purpose, or either of them, and to be laid out for the purchase of a tract of land, to be held in the name of said trustees or trustee and their heirs, for the sole use and benefit of the Said Kitty and Dick and should they at some future time desire to go to Liberia the Said land so held in trust, may be sold, and the proceeds appreiated[?] to defray their outfit and expenses, to their country and the remainder, if any to be given to them when they depart from here to their future home..."

Britton Bridges, p. 14-15, 28 March 1857, recorded 2 April 1857
"...I give devise and dispose of my Estate (Save what shall be necessary for the payment of my Just debts and funeral charges) in the following manner. That all my Good chattels &c. at my death to be sold for the purpose of paying my debts and funeral charges and distribution except my Slaves for their kind treatment to me I set free to wit: Tobitha a woman about Forty six years old[,] Ann a woman about Twenty four years old. Jerry a Man about Forty three years old. Frances a Girl about six years old[,] John Westley a boy about five years of [age,] William Daniel a boy about one year old to be free and the four last named children to be and remain with their mother untill [sic] they be-

come of the age of twenty one years and if the mother neglects to provide or shall die then the executor shall have the power to provide suitable homes for the same and after paying all debts and funeral expenses I request that Jerry shall have fifteen dollars and the ballance [sic] be equally divided between my three servants to wit Tobitha[,] Ann and Jerry…"

William A. McFarland, pp. 24-25, 21 March 1860, recorded 23 April 1860.
"…It is my will that all my Just debts be paid and to provide means for that purpose I direct that my Negro boy Reuben be Sold and the proceeds of said sale so far as it may be necessary applied to that purpose said sale to be made by my Executrix herein named in any manner she may deem proper…I give and bequeath to my beloved wife Elizabeth H McFarland all my Estate both real and personal together with all my slaves…"

Thomas Glendy, pg. 30-32, 10 April 1849, filed 5 December 1860
"…I also give and bequeath to my said wife [Mary Glendy] all my Slaves…I also give and bequeath to my said Nephews Kennedy and Cayce Jointly My Negro Girl Kitty aged about ten years, and my Negro boy Dick aged about five years. The Girl Kitty is to serve until she is twenty years of age and the said boy Dick to serve until he arrives at the age of twenty five years and No longer…I give and bequeath to my Negro Slave Woman Julia her Freedom at my death, and in consideration of the bequests herein before made to my two Nephews Ferdinand Kennedy & Nettleton Cayce, I do enjoin upon them that they shall cause the said Negro woman to have and receive at their instance & casts a comfortable and competent support during her natural life. 5th. I give and bequeath unto my Negro Slave Kitty Now aged about ten years her freedom when she arrives at the age of twenty years and all her children (if any) to be free at that time with her. 6th I give and bequeath unto my Negro Slave Dick Now aged about five years his freedom when he shall have arrived at the age of twenty five years…"

Isaac Baker, p. 36-38, 10 February 1862, 4 March 1862
"…I also give to my wife Emily my negro man George and my negro Woman Angeline and all her children to hold during her natural life and if said Emily die leaving heirs of her boddy [sic] they shall inherit Said negroes otherwise Said negroes shall revert to my legal heirs provided Said Emily have the right to give a Negro Girl Phebe to my Grand Daughter Catharine Ann Evans… I also give to my daughter Catharine my negro named Tom and my negro Woman America and all her children…I Give to my daughter Narcissa Evans my negro man John…I also give to my Grand Son John F McIlvaine my ne-

gro Man Sam and and [sic] to my Grand Daughter Minerva Ann McIlvaine I give my negro man wash [sic]...I also wish my negro Woman Sophy to remain in posession [sic] of my wife Emily and my daughter Catharine..."

Samuel Kinkead, p. 39-41, 3 December 1857, 24 October 1862
"...I devise and bequeath the children of my deceased Son Andrew B. Kinkead...one Negro Boy a Slave for life known by the name of Green. Third- I give and bequeath to my Grand children who reside in the State of Tennesse, to wit, Harriet Ann Esselman[,] James C. Esselman and Margaret C. Esselman each an equal Share one negro Girl named Arnetta, and her child, also one negro Girl named Jane, all Slaves for life...Fourth- I give and bequeath to my Daughter Lydia R. Baker and the heirs of her body the tracks of land heretofore conveyed to her by dee[d] bearing date December 2nd 1857. I also give and bequeath to my Said Daughter one Negro Girl named Dilla, and one negro boy named John and a Negro Girl named Harriet all slaves for life. Fifth- I give and bequeath to my Daughter Martha Kinkead the property of a residence and home on the Farm and in the House of said Farm in and upon which I now reside during her natural life. I also give and bequeath to her one Negro woman named Emma and one Negro boy named George both Slaves for life...I also give and bequeath to my Said Daughter Meeke Frances one Negro woman known by the name of Mary and her daughter a negro child named Lucinda, also one Negro boy named Louis..."

Eleazor Clay, pg. 43-44, 28 July 1860, 2 March 1863
"...It is my will and I so direct that my executor Shall sell my Slaves at private Sale on a credit of twelve months each of my Woman [sic] who have children to be Sold with their children and in the sale not to seperate [sic] the children from the mother and further that my said Executor will endeavor to procure for my slaves good homes and humane Masters and not to be sold to Negro traders to be taken out of the State..."

Samuel P. Harris, pg. 45-47, 25 August 1858, 29 January 1864
"...I also give and bequeath to my said wife Elizabeth Harris as her absolute property to dispose of as she may desire my slave Charles a boy of mulatto colour aged about nineteen years. Also my slave Frances a girl about Twelve years of Mulatto colour with her offspring. Also my slave known by the name of Ritter a woman of black colour aged about Sixty years....I also give and bequeath to my said son John K Harris my slave named Annie a woman aged about 17 years, also her child a boy named Ellis and all said womans [sic] future offspring also to have and to hold the same to him his heirs and assigns forever. I give and bequeath to my slave a woman named Esther, aged

about sixty eight years her freedom at my death I and further give and bequeath to the said Esther the sum of forty dollars for each year she may live after my death to be paid annually by my wife Elizabeth Harris during life from the proceeds of the farm bequeathed herein to her and after her death to be paid by John K Harris. It being my object and intention that the said Esther shall have support & maintenance from said farm during her life[.] I give and bequeath to my slave Nancy Edna a girl twenty two years of yellow colour her freedom at my death. And I do hereby emancipate set free release and discharge the said girl Nancy Edna from slavery or involuntary servitude together with all her offspring for all future time[.] And I further give and bequeath to the said Nancy Edna a house and maintenance from and on the farm which I have herein devised to my wife and Son Elizabeth and John K Harris, said maintenance & support to be received from the proceeds of said farm in whose ever hands [inserted] possession or ownership the same may be during her natural life[.] I give and bequeath to my son Josephus L Harris my mulatto slave a boy known by the name of Paris aged about 9 years to have and to hold the said boy Paris to him his heirs and assigns forever[.] I give and bequeath to my son Thos M Harris…the following named slaves viz Giles a man of yellow colour aged about forty six years, Hulda a woman of yellow colour aged about 43 years, also her said Hulda's youngest child named Sally Jane aged two years to have and to hold the said tract of land and slaves to him the said Thos M Harris his heirs and assigns forever. I give and bequeath to my daughter Mary Jane Carruthers my yellow girl Cyntha Ann, now aged about sixteen years. To have and to hold the said girl together with her offspring to her the said Mary Jane Caruthers her heirs & assigns forever[.] I give and bequeath to my grand daughter [sic] Elizabeth Fleming my slave a girl of yellow color aged about three years and known by the name of Melissa to have and to hold said girl to her the said Elizabeth Fleming her heirs and assigns forever[.] I give and bequeath to my two slaves Edmund & Paris their freedom at my death, the first named being a man of bright mulatto colour 24 years of age 5 feet 9 inches high. The other, Paris a man of mulatto color about 5 feet 7 inches hight [sic] and aged about 39 years. And I do hereby emancipate set free release and discharge the said Edmund and Paris from slavery & involuntary servitude for all future time…"

William Haile estate, pg. 1, 15 February 1855
"...1 Slave Charles $800 [.]00..."

George W. Day inventory estate, pg. 7, filed 13 October 1855
"1 Slave a Boy James $529.75
Frank 8 years old 500[.]00..."

David Sherrill, pg. 19, filed 12 January 1856
"...Negro Man named Sam, also Man Named Mark, boy Named Joe[,] Girl named Angeline, boy Named Lacy, boy named Stephen, boy named Allen, which were bequeathed to certain persons by the Will, also negro Woman named Sal and child Named Harriet, and Negro boy Named Marshall which were desired to be Sold..."

David Sherill, pg. 20, 19 November 1855
"...Slave Bequeathed by Will   Dollar[s]   cents

1	Negro	Man	Named	Sam	appraised to		900	00
1	Negro	Man	Named	Mark	"	900		00
1	Negro	Boy	Named	Joe	"	850		00
1	Negro	Girl	Named	Angeline	"		600	00
1	Negro	Boy	Named	Lacy	"	450		00
1	Negro	Boy	Named	Stephen "		250		00
1	Negro	Boy	Named	Allen	"	200		00
				Total amount		$4150		00
1	Negro	Woman Named	Sal and }					
	child Named Harriet		}		800		00	
1	Negro	Boy	Named	Marshall			200	00
				amount-			1000	00

David Sherill, Bill of Sale, pg. 22-23, 13-14 December 1855
"...Articles Sold Purchasers name amt...
1 Negro Woman Sal & Child Harriet   William Dent   1040   00
1 Negro Boy Marshall   William Dent   402   00..."

Inventory of Estate of John W. Hill, pg. 29, appraised 8 January 1856, filed 16 January 1856

1	Negro	Man	Henry	1000	00
1	"	Boy	James	1000	00
1	"	"	John	800	00

1	"	"	Sanford 500	00	
1	"	Woman Katherine		500	00
1	"	Girl	Betsey 500	00	
1	"	"	Fanny 400	00	
1	"	"	Louivinia	250	00
1	"	Woman Rose and Child Sally		1000	00

Inventory of Estate of John W. Hill, pg. 38, filed 11 February 1856

"Slaves. One Negro Man Henry, one Negro Boy James, one Negro Boy John, one Negro Boy Sanford, one Negro Woman Katharine, one Negro Girl Betsey[,] one Negro Girl Fanny, one Negro Girl Louvina, one Negro Woman Rose & child Sally..."

Inventory of Estate of Susan M. Conway, pg. 39, 16 January 1856, filed 25 February 1856

"...1 Negro Slave Man Alexander aged 17 years, 1 Woman 40 Named Nancy[,] 1 Girl 8 Fillis[,] 1 Girl 3 Fanny[,] 1 Boy 6 months old, George..."

Appraisement Bill of Estate of Susan M. Conway, pg. 40, 16 January 1856, filed 25 February 1856

1	Slave a Man	Alexander			about	17	year old	1100 00
1	Woman	Nancy	age	40	years	200	00	
1	Girl	Fanny	age	3	do	250	00	
1	do	Fillis	"	8	"	450	00	
1	Boy	George	age	6	Months	100	00	

Inventory of Estate of W.R. Vance, pg. 41, filed and recorded 1 March 1856

"1 Negro Man Named Jim, 1 Negro Woman Named Betty..."

Inventory of Estate of Mary Glendy, pg. 69, filed and recorded 25 August 1856

"...Slaves. Julia a Negro woman about 50 years old. Kitty a girl 17 years old. Dick a boy 11 years old. William boy 2 years old & child of Kitty..."

Inventory of Estate of William Patterson (heir is minor William Patterson), pg. 77, 16 September 1852

Jane a woman (valued by Coms appointed to make partition of) $500 .00

Hiram a boy " 400 .00

Eliza   a Girl   "   225   .00

Inventory of Estate of William Patterson (heir is minor William Patterson), pg. 81, 5 August 1856
"…Received of Columbus Price, Curator of William Patterson a minor and heir at law of William Patterson late of Perry county deceased, one Negro Woman named Jane and four children it being in full of all personal property and three hundred and seventy seven dollars and ninety nine cents in Money and Notes approved of by the County Court of Perry County Mo transacting Probate business this augs [sic] '5' 1856

Alexander Patterson [his signature]

Witness   Curator of Wm Patterson a minor
Henry T Burns…"

Inventory of Estate of John W. Hill, pg. 87, appraised 4 March 1857, filed 10 March 1857
"…Slaves—John a boy aged 13[,] Rose a woman aged 23[,] Betty a girl " 12[,] Sally " 2[,] Fanny " " 8[,] Louvina " " 6[,] Sanford a boy " 7[,] Jim " " 16[,] Catherine " woman 38 & child 5 mons old…"

Inventory of Estate of John W. Hill, pg. 91, appraised 4 March 1857, filed 10 March 1857
"…Slaves…

John a boy aged 13 years	800 00	
Betty " Girl " 12 years		500 00
Fanny " " 8 "		550 00
Sanford " Boy 7	600 00	
Catherine " woman 38 & child 5 mos		800 00
Rose a woman 23 years		800 00
Sally a girl 2 "		300 00
Louvina " 6 "		450 00
Jim a boy " 16		1000 00…"

Britton Bridges estate appraisal, pg. 117, 3 April 1857, filed 20 April 1857

1	Negro	Man	Named	Jerry	aged	43	years	a p -
praised at		$883	00					
1	"	Woman "		Tobitha "		47	"	
483	00							
1	"	"	"	Ann	"	24	"	
783	00							

1	"	Girl	"	Frances	"	6	"
433	00						
1	"	Boy	"	John	"	4	"
383	00						
1	"	"	"	James	"	½	"
200	00						
1	"	"	"	William	"	3	"
300	00						

William Bryan inventory, pg. 147, 16 September 1857

Slave	Isaac	$550	00
"	Sarah	500	00

Luke Davis inventory, pg. 162, 25 February 1858

"1 Negro Man Harvy about 60 years old   100 00..."

Nancy Poston inventory, pg. 116, filed 5 July 1858

Agness	a	Girl	aged	30	years		
Betty	"	"	"	14	"		
Phillis	"	"	"	10	"		
Sarah	"	"	"	6	"		
Emily	"	"	"	4	"		
Margaret		"	"	"	2	"	
Jim	"	boy	"	18	"		
Charle[s]		"	"	"	16	"	
Finley	a	Boy	"	12	"		
George	"	"	"	8	"		

Nancy Poston estate, pg. 178, 10 May 1858

Agness	Aged	30	years	500	00	
Betty	"	14	"	700	00	
Phillis	"	10	"	500	00	
Sarah	"	6	"	300	00	
Emily	"	4	"	275	00	
Margaret		"	4	"	300	00
				$2475	.00	
Jim	aged	18	"	900	00	
Charles	"	16	"	800	00	
Finley	"	12	"	700	00	
George	"	8	"	400	00	

William Spradling Inventory, pg. 208. Appraised 16 December 1858
"…1 Negro Man Slave named Albin aged 30 years 1 Eye out 700[.] 00
1 do do do do Jim do 28 do Diseased 300[.] 00…"

Andrew J. Murphy, pg. 213, 1 January 1859
"1 Negro Boy named Franklin aged 7 years appraised at   450 00
1 " " " William " 5 " " "   375 00
1 " " " Manuel " 3 " " "   225 00
1 " Woman " Henny " 65 " " "   50 00
1 " " " Charlotte " 25 " " "   800 00
1 " Infant of Charlotte " 5 days " "   50 00
1 " Girl named Susan " 15 years " "   800 00
1 " Boy " Lewis " 18 mons " "   125 00…"

William Keeton Inventory Appraisement, pg. 213, 4 January 1859
"…Slaves as Follows.

Nat aged 70 years	Green aged 24 years	Batist aged 24 years
Paul " 21 "	John " 8 "	Charles " 4 "
Cornelius " 1 "	Caroline " 5 "	Margaret " 24 "
Saphrona " 30 "	Mariah " 28 "	Hannah " 12 "
Josephine " 7 "	Thomas " 4 "	Kitty " 19 "
Missouri " 22 "	Allis " 2 "	Jefferson " 2 "
Nancy " 19 "…"		

William Keeton appraisement, pg. 214, 1 January 1859

Nat	age	70	appraised		to	300	00	Green
age	24	apprsd	to	1000	00			
Batiste "		24	"	"	1000	00	Paul "	
21 "		"	1000	00				
John "		8	"	"	600	00	Charles "	
4 "		"	350	00				
Thomas "		5	"	"	400	00	Jefferson	
"	2	"	"	200	00			
Cornelius		"	1	"	"	125	00	S o p h -
rona "		30	"	"	600	00		
Mariah "		28	"	"	800	00	Margaret	
"	24	"	"	700	00			
Missouri		"	22	" diseased	"	450	00	
Kitty "		17	"	"	900	00		

Hannah "	12	"	"	600	00	Nancy	"
14	"	"	900	00			
Josephine	"	7	"	"	500	00	Allis
"	2	"	"	200	00		
Caroline	"	5	"	"	500	00	
			$	11.120	00		

Marmaduke Berkley inventory estate, pg. 228, 31 January 1859

"...Slaves as Follows.
1 Negro Man Alfred aged 30 years
1 Negro Woman Martha and child Firman
1 Negro boy Harrison aged 12 years
1 Negro girle [sic] Amanda aged 6 years
1 Negro boy Gus aged 8 years
1 Negro Girl Angeline aged 4 years..."

Marmaduke Berkley estate, pg. 228, 31 January 1859

1 Negro Man Alfred	900	00
1 Negro Woman Martha & child Firman	950	00
1 Negro Boy Harrison	700	00
1 Negro Boy Gus	550	00
1 Negro Girl Amanda	400	00
1 Negro Girl Angeline	325	00

William Keyton [sic], pg. 238, 5 May 1859

"...Slaves, Nat Man aged 70 years   Green do do 24 do Babtiste [sic] do " 24 do Paul do 21 years John Boy " 8 do Charles do " 4 do Caroline Girl " 5 do Margaret Woman " 24 do Safrona do " 30 do Mariah do " 28 " Hannah Girl " 12 " Josephine do " 7 " Thomas Boy " 4 " Allis Girl " 2 " Kitty Woman " 19 " Nancy do 19 " Jefferson Boy " 2 "..."

Zeno Westover Inventory Appraisement, pg. 243, 18 April 1859

1	Negro	man	named	Henry	aged	46	years
1	"	Boy	"	Reuben	"	3	"
1	"	Woman	"	Sarah	"	44	"
1	"	"	"	Polly	"	25	"
"	"	Girl	"	Leese	"	6	"

Zeno Westover Inventory Appraisement, pg. 248, 6 June 1859

| 1 Negro Slave | named | Henry | aged | 46 | years | 850 | 00 |
| 1 negro Slave | " | Sarah | aged | 44 | years | 600 | 00 |

1 negro Slave	"	Polley	"	24	"	1000	00
1 negro Slave	"	Leese	"	6	"	400	00
1 negro Slave	"	Reuben	"	3	"	250	00

B.W. Yeargain inventory appraisement, pg. 263, 20 September 1859

1	Negro	Woman	Named	Henta[?]		Appraised	$800	00
1	"	Girl	"	Elizabeth	"	400	00
1	"	Boy	"	Thomas "	400	00
1	"	Girl	"	Dina "	200	00
1	"	Boy	"	Frank "	300	00

Wm. A. McFatton [sic] pg. 292, filed 30 June 1860

Clarissa & her child		aged	about	33	yrs	800	.00
Reuben "	"	16	"	900	.00
Mary "	"	9	"	650	.00
Lewis "	"	7	"	530	.00
Madison	"	"	5	"	400	.00
Drusy Ann	"	"	3	"	275	.00
Alan "	"	2	"	175	.00

George Carder Inventory Appraisement, p. 302, filed 17 December 1860

Susan	a Slave	15	years	appraised		to the sum of	$850	.00
Lewis "	15	yrs old "	"	300	.00
Sarah "	13	yrs old "	"	700	.00
Charles "	11	yrs old "	"	700	.00
Adaline "	7	do	"	"	300	.00
Jane "	4	Do	"	"	200	.00
George "	85	Do	valued at Nothing		

Rudolph Haverstick, pg. 310, 21 January 1861

"...1 negro man named John aged about 28 years
1 negro woman named Julie aged 28 yrs..."

Rudolph Haverstick, pg. 311, 8 January 1861

"...1 Negro Man named John   1000 00
1 Negro woman   "   Julia   700 00..."

John W. Smith, pg. 379, inventory appraisement, 4 April 1862

1	General	aged	63	years	appraised at	100	00

2	Jack	"	56	"	"	250	00		
3	Louis	"	43	"	"	250	00		
4	Talbot	"	30	"	"	550	00		
5	Major	"	25	"	"	600	00		
6	Frank	"	20	"	"	700	00		
7	George	"	20	"	"	700	00		
8	Peter	"	17	"	"	650	00		
9	Joe	"	14	"	"	450	00		
10	Charles	"	10	"	"	300	00		
11	Reuben	"	7	"	"	300	00		
12	Alvey	"	5	"	"	250	00		
13	Abram	"	3	"	"	200	00		
14	James	"	2	"	"	150	00		
15	Thomas	"	2	"	"	125	00		
16	Phoebe	"	69	"	"	50	00		
17	Louisa	"	50	"	"	100	00		
18	Julia Ann	"		47	"	"		100	00
19	Melissa	"	26	"	"	400	00		
20	Jane	"	20	"	"	450	00		
21	Henrietta	"		18	"	"		500	00
22	Lucinda	"	16	"	"	500	00		
23	Mary	"	13	"	"	500	00		
24	Mildred	"	13	"	"	500	00		
25	Letty	"	10	"	"	450	00		
26	Maria	"	10	"	"	350	00		
27	Huldy	"	9	"	"	350	00		
28	Harriet	"	6	"	"	250	00		

Isaac Baker Inventory Appraisal, Pg. 388, 2 May 1862

"…Slaves Negro man George aged 44 [,] Negro Woman Angeline 25 [,] Negro Girl Phebe age 8 [,] Negro Boy Lewis aged 6 [,] Negro Boy Billy 5 [,] Negro Boy Gussy 1 [,] Negro Woman America age 26 [,] Negro Boy Frank aged 7 [,] Negro Boy Charles aged 6 [,] Negro Boy Ellis aged 3 [,] Negro Man Tom 23 [,] Negro Woman Sophia aged 56 [,] Negro Man Sam aged 43 [,] Negro Man Wash aged 33[,] Negro Man John aged 32…"

Isaac Baker inventory, pg. 391, March 1862

1	Negro	Man	named	George	aged	44	500	00
1	"	Woman	"	Angeline	"	25	600	
00								

1	"	Girl	"	Phebe	"	8	325	00
1	"	Boy	"	Lewis	"	6	250	00
1	"	Boy	"	Billy	"	5	200	00
1	"	Boy	"	Gussy	"	1	150	00
1	"	Woman Named	Americaaged			26	600	00
1	"	Boy	"	Frank	"	7	400	00
1	"	Boy	"	Charles	"	6	300	00
1	"	Boy	"	Ellis	"	3	150	00
1	"	Man	"	Tom	"	23	500	00
1	"	Woman	"	Sophia	"	56	156	00
1	"	Man	"	Sam	"	43	500	00
1	"	Man	"	Wash	"	33	500	00
1	"	Man	"	John	"	32	700	00

Robert Sears estate and appraisement, pg. 397-401, filed 5 April 1862
"...Sale Bill of the Estate of Robert Sears (Colored Man) Decd..."

"...A bill of appraisement of the slaves and other personal Property belonging
to the estate of Robert Sears deceased
1 Negro woman Phillis..."

Richard C. Poston inventory appraisement, pg. 408, 24 April 1862
"...Negroes William 52 years old [,] Henry 52 " "[,] Dick 34 " "[,] George 34
[,] Henry 30[,] Sam 30[,] Jack 27 tears old[,] Blind George 40 " "[,] Jim 17
" "[,] William 16 " "[,] Alf 15 " "[,] John 15 " "[,] Josh 10 " "[,] Lee 8 " "[,]
Simon 7 " "[,] Furd 4 " "[,] Oliver 4 " "[,] Four 3 " "[,] Jake 3 " "[,] Charley
2 " "[,] green 24 " "[,] Louisa 33 " "[,] Hariet 31 " "[,] Loueas [sic] 33 " "[,]
Margret 17 " "[,] Ada 11 " " Fanny 10 " "[,] Gusta 6 " "[,] Diamond Child
9 months[,] child Mary two years old..."

Inventory of minor heirs of John W. Hill, pg. 425, 6 June 1862
"...Slaves of said minor Jim a boy aged 21 years "[,] John age 17 years "[,]
Sanford a boy aged 14 years "[,] Rose a Girl age 31 yrs "[,] Betty a girl age 17
yrs "[,] Fanny a girl 15 yrs age"[,] Vena a girl age 13 years"[,] Harriet a girl 5
years old"[,] Sally a girl age 8 years"[,] Lewis a boy age 6 years"[,] Peter a boy
age 3 years..."

Wm. D. Christopher, pg. 426, 6 June 1862

One	Negro	Woman	Named	Sarah	aged	35	years	
one	"	Girl	"	Angeline	"	7		"

One	"	"	"	Pricilla	"	4	"	
One	"	Boy	"	Charley	"	2	"	

Wm. D. Christopher, pg. 429, 6 June 1862

One	Negro	Woman	Named	Sarah	aged	35	years	200
00								
one	"	Girl	"	Angeline	"	7	"	
150	00							
One	"	"	"	Pricilla	"	4	"	125
00								
One	"	Boy	"	Charley	"	2	"	125
00								

William N. West inventory app., pg. 453, 2 February 1863

"...1 Negro Man George about 36 years old[,] 1 Woman Phebe & Two children Mary 3 years old Matilda Inft[,] 1 Girl Melvina 13 years old[,] 1 Girl Malissa age 6 years old[,] 1 Girl Hariet 9 do do..."

Wm. A. McFarland inventory app., pg. 477, 4 March 1863

1	Black	Slave	Girl	named	Mary	aged	11	years
1	"	"	Boy	"	Louis	"	9	"
1	"	"	Madison [sic]	"	Madison			"
8	"							
1	"	"	Woman	"	Clarissa	"	33	"
1	"	"	Girl	"	Dove	"	5	"
1	"	"	Boy	"	Alvin	"	4	"
1	"	"	"	"	Jerry	"	3	"

Samuel Long inventory app., pg. 492, 21 July 1863, filed 7 September 1863

"...Memorandum of the Slaves belonging to the Estate of Saml Long

one man Called Harry was		aged	Fifty five	years
Silas	aged	Forty five	years	
Green	age	Thirty two	"	
Zack	"	Twenty Seven	"	
Luther	"	Twenty five	"	
Allen	"	Twenty three	"	
Albert	"	Twelve	"	
George	"	Ten	"	
Robt	"	Two	"	
Henry	"	Two	"	

Maude	"	Twenty Nine	"
Harriett	"	Twenty	"
Maria	"	Seventeen	"
Mahaly	"	Seven	"
Alice	"	Two	years old

The above Negroes ran off and we got a warrant in Washington and the Sheriff arrested three and the [illegible] authorities released them before we got possession of them

> William Long [illegible]
> administrator [sic] of the Estate of Sam Long..."

Wm. Hunt appraisement list, pg. 523, 13 June 1864, filed 21 June 1864

1	Negro	man	named	Jim	50	00
1	"	woman	"	America	50	00
1	"	boy	"	Charles	50	00
1	"	"	"	Peter	50	00
1	"	Girl	"	Eliza	50	00
1	"	boy	"	Jim	50	00
1	"	boy	"	Moses	50	00

Thomas E. Burnham Inventory (Mary A. and Lucy I. Burnham his minor heirs), pg. 539, 8 March 1865, filed 8 March 1865.

"Four Slaves to wit Anderson a boy, about Eight years old. Charity a girl aged about six months, Manda a girl aged about Eighteen, Ann a girl aged about five years. Anderson and Charity belong to Mary A., and Manda and Ann to Lucy I. The girl Manda was appraised as appears in Inventory and appraisement of the said Corbin Alexander adm aforesaid to $20000..."

St. Louis Argus Newspaper Extracts, 1915-1920

Farmington, St. Francois County Extracts from the St. Louis Argus (St. Louis, Mo.), 1915-1920 with Commentary

Note: All extracts without a title are from "Farmington Notes/News" written by Dayse F. Baker and others; all others were extracted from various other parts of the newspaper. The ellipses found throughout the text do not indicate that textual matter has been removed. The sentences in the author's text—Dayse F. Baker—and the texts of other local St. Louis Argus columnists were printed with ellipses between them. On various occasions, these ellipses range from two to up to eight. For the transcriptions, the ellipses were reduced for ease in transcription to just three.

01 January 1915, pg. 3, col. 1-2.
"Mrs. Albert Simms is spending a short while in St. Louis as the guest of her husband...Messrs. Lindsey Clay and John Poston spent the week end [sic] with home folks...Mesdames Pugh and Franks have the sympathy of their many friends on account of the serious illness of their father, Mr. Richard Jones...Many children were the happy recipients of gifts from the municipal tree...Mrs. Lizzie Cole and granddaughter, little Miss Estacada Baker, attended the Christmas exercises of Miss Edith Cayce who teaches at Mineral Point...Mrs. Jane Hunt is spending the holidays in St. Louis as the guest of her sons, Oscar and Myrtle...Miss Ruth B. David, of Bonne Terre, is the house guest of Miss Dayse Baker...The children of the M.E. Sunday-school, under the direction of Miss Baker, tendered Grandma Evans a surprise sack party Christmas afternoon. She, though 86 years of age, was able to address the children. Many articles were given her and a pleasant time was spent... Mr. Otis Vaughn came to our city to accompany his wife to their home in Potosi...Little Nadine Baker is recovering from a recent illness...Mrs. Dora Carson and sister, Miss Edith Cayce, are visiting their parents, Mr. and Mrs. Thomas Cayce...Mr. and Mrs. P.M. Cayce entertained at four o'clock dinner on Christmas day, Messrs. and Mesdames Ed Harris, Otis Vaughn, Misses Rues [sic] B. Davis and Dayse F. Baker...Mr. Tom Cayce spent the week end [sic] with his family...Messrs. Pyrtle J. Evans, of Lincoln Institute and Harold Staten, of Sumner High, spent their Christmas vacation with home folks...Prof. J.C. Staten spent the holidays at home...Miss Sophia Mudd has been absent from school. She has been suffering from a painful injury to her thumb...Both churches appropriately and successfully celebrated the "Great Advent" Thursday evening...Mr. Talbert Burns has recovered...Mrs. Laura Kennedy spent last week at Charleston attending to business...Miss Ruth B.

Davis addressed the pupils of Douglass school Monday morning. At the same period, Rev. Brooks, on behalf of the pupils, presented to Miss Baker a gift which was gratefully received."

08 January 1915, pg. 3, col. 4-5.
"Mrs. Masohat [sic] Hill, of Herculaneum [Jefferson Co., Mo.], is here attending her father, Mr. Geo. Blackwell, who is quite ill...Mr. Lewis Murphy has accepted employment at Festus, [Jefferson Co.,] Mo...Mrs. Geo. Wright and her daughter Helen, of Bonne Terre, were guests of Mrs. Jas. Robinson, the latter part of the week...Mr. Jas. Robinson had a successful entertainment at Eagle Hall Thursday evening...Miss Lora Robinson, of Bonne Terre, attended to business here Saturday and was also the guest of Estacada Baker... Mrs. T.L. Watson is ill...Miss Dollean Poston, and little neice [sic], Costella Shaw, of St. Louis, had a pleasant sojourn with relatives last week[1]...Visitors from Coffman [Ste. Genevieve Co., Mo.] during the week were: Mesdames Maria Douthit and Cora Swink, Messrs. Roy Douthit and Wilson Chappelle, and Misses Alcesta Douthit and Imogene Staten...Mrs. Tulleck [sic], and grandson Herman, of Ironton [Iron Co., Mo.], spent a few days with Mr. and Mrs. Henry Amonette...Mrs. T.L. Watson managed an entertainment with the little folks Wednesday evening which was very interesting. Mr. Peter Swink and daughter Miss Alice, returned Wednesday from Champaign, [Champaign Co.,] Ill...Grandma Evans is ill at her home in South Farmington[2]...The Douglass School spelling contest was a feature of the New Year entertainment but a more interesting feature was the spelling bee of "grown ups." Miss Laura Amonette received the first prize. Mesdames S.O. Wilkins, E.J. Harris, and Mr. Fred Bridges contested equally and were given similar prizes. The judges were Messrs. J.C. Staten, John Douthit, V.E. Williams, J.L. Brooks and Miss Ruth B. Davis. Miss Baker was the conductress...Let every colored voter use his own judgment in voting next Tuesday. Let not it be said of you that you were bought for some small sum. Be a man. Exercise your ability to handle the ballot."

15 January 1915, pg. 3, col. 3.
"Miss Mae Baker is the guest of Mrs. P. Taylor, of St. Louis...Mr. and Mrs. F. Chappelle and daughters, of Coffman, returned home Monday...Mr. Joseph Galvin, of Peoria, [Peoria Co.,] Ill., was shaking hands with friends here the latter part of the week...Messrs. Gorda [sic] Taylor and Leonidas Baker, of Bonne Terre, were the guests of relatives here Sunday...Mr. Henry Hunt is quite ill at his home in West Farmington...Miss Cosetta and Dola Boddie entertained a few friends at their home Sunday afternoon. An enjoyable time was had...Miss Melview Kennedy delightfully entertained the Clever Bees

Thursday evening, at which time the ladies discussed "Woman Suffrage" with much spirit...Mr. Wm. Hill is able to be out on the streets...At the request of the campaign committee, Dr. B.F. Abbott came to Farmington last Friday and made an address that made the community wild with enthusiasm and praise. The court house was filled with people. The committee prevailed with him to return Monday. He spoke Monday night to a crowded house. The evils of liquor were so plainly shown that after the meeting men rushed to the stage expressing themselves, "I'll vote dry and thereby make the proper use of my ballot." Statesmen declared the speech of Dr. Abbott was the best that had been made during the campaign. Women, with their boys and girls, flocked there showing their interest in the movement."

22 January 1915, pg. 3, col. 3.
"Mrs. L.F. Smith accompanied Mrs. Eliza Overton to St. Louis Friday...Mrs. S.A. Smith is the guest of her sister, Mrs. W.A. Gunnell, of St. Louis...Mrs. Felix Poston spent the week end as the guest of Mrs. J.F. Ransom of Bonne Terre...Mrs. Jas. Robinson has been quite ill for more than a week...Miss Mattie Valle had a pleasant week with home folks at Coffman...Miss Dayse Baker attended a social at the residence of Mrs. Geo. Robinson at Bonne Terre, Saturday evening, at which time the number of fifteen "Poro Ladies" presented the hostess an operating chair[.] The evening was an interesting one on "Blue Street."...Miss Meyers and mother suffered an attack of ptomaine poisoning, caused from eating head cheese. They are both convalescent[3]... Mr. and Mrs. Wm. McCallister are rejoicing over the arrival of their son, Noam Willard, of a fortnight past...Mrs. Pugh and children left for Bethany, [Harrison Co.,] Mo., Sunday...Mrs. Randall Wilburn continues very weak... The teachers and pupils of Douglass School regret to learn of the serious illness of Master Aldrew Evans...Tuesday evening at 6:20 the bells proclaimed the town of Farmington dry. Rejoicings were galore...Mr. Thos. Cayce came in Tuesday and helped to make it more dry...Little Laurine Boddie is able to be out again...Several have paid up for their subscriptions to the Argus and many will pay soon."

29 January 1915, pg. 3, col. 1-2.
"Rev. J.D. Barksdale spent a day of last week with Rev. T.L. Watson...Mr. Percy Swink has returned from Sydney, Ill., where he has been engaged in agricultural pursuits...Mrs. J. Franks received the sad intelligence of the demise of her father, Mr. Richard Jones, which occurred at Fulton, Mo...Mr. and Mrs. Chas. Cayce are happy with their son, "Little Robert Talbert," who came a fortnight ago...Miss Vera Brooks and D.F. Baker represented the M.E. Sabbath school in presenting Aldrew Evans with a silver offering Sunday morn-

ing...Mesdames Jas. Robinson and Lewis Murphy are convalescent...The many friends of Mrs. W.A. Gunnell are glad to know she is improving... Mrs. Albert Simms returned from St. Louis, Friday, after a stay of more than a month...Miss Mabel Meyers was hostess for the Clever Bees Thursday evening. A delicious luncheon was served. "Crocheting and Honolulu" were discussed...Mrs. [sic] Chas. Baker had business in St. Louis Saturday. He reports the Pythian order growing rapidly, numerically and financially...Quarterly meeting will be held at the M.E. Church February 13-14...Mr. Wm. Cayce went to Cape Girardeau last Tuesday and accompanied his daughter, Mrs. W. Davis, home. She is growing better...Miss Gracie Anthony writes us from Western University that she is having a successful term and is well and happy."

05 February 1915, pg. 2, col. 4.
"The remains of Mr. Richard Jones, who died at Fulton [Callaway Co., Mo.], arrived here Tuesday. The funeral services were held at the A.M.E. Church, with Rev. T.L. Watson officiating. Goodwill Lodge had charge of the body... Messrs. Geo. Meyers and Louis Murphy spend a pleasant day with home folks Sunday...Mrs. F. Chappelle was called here from Coffman on the account of the illness of her mother, Mrs. Buford. She was accompanied by her nieces, Misses Ida and Mildred Chappelle...A letter from Mr. Lorillard Murphy, at Indianapolis, states that he is well and happy...Miss Edith Cayce spent the week's end with her mother, Mrs. T. Cayce...Mesdames P. Boddie [sic] and Eliza Overton are among the numbered ill...Mrs. Randall Wilburn grows weaker each week...Mrs. Lewis Murphy was hostess for the Clever Bees, Thursday evening. Although there was a splendid use given to the needle, much joking was in vogue. A delightful luncheon was served... News reached relatives of Mrs. Sara Amonette, Mrs. Annie Yeager and son, Kenneth—of their being taken to a hospital as a result of a bomb explosion, from which each received injuries. They reside in St. Louis[4]...Messrs. Chas. Douthit and Ben Chappelle, of Coffman, were here the first of the week... The Senior Class of Douglas [sic] School is preparing to present "Thompkins' Hired Man," a play which will be quite interesting...Mrs. Lewis Hill received a fall Saturday which caused him to be quite a cripple....Miss Amie Busch attended the funeral of her uncle, Mr. Peter Taylor, at St. Louis, Sunday[5]... Messrs. Wm. Baker and Jerry Bridges were up from the camp Saturday...The collector for the Argus will be around today; so open up the old sack and get ready to pay."

12 February 1915, pg. 2, col. 4.
"Mr. T. Bryant and daughter, of Fredericktown [Madison Co., Mo.] spent Sunday with relatives here...Mrs. Laura Kennedy attended to business at

Coffman last week...The friend of Miss Allie Cummingham [sic] are glad to hear that she found her affinity in Oklahoma City...Greeting are now going up to Mr. and Mrs. Alexander Anthony of St. Louis, who have recently launched out on the sea of matrimony...Rev. Bowles will be in this week preparatory to holding Quarterly Meeting Sunday...Mesdames J.F. Ransom and Daisy Martin, of Bonne Terre, were the guests of Mrs. F. Poston the latter part of the week...Mr. Peter Hunt was up from Knob Lick the first of the week... Miss Lorene Staten, of Coffman, was the house guest of Mrs. Lewis Murphy last week...The Allen Endeavour will render a programme Sunday evening in commemoration of the birthday of the late, and much beloved, Bishop Grant...Mrs. M. Harrison, of Festus, was the guest of Mrs. Jerusha Poston, Thursday...A donation given to Rev. T.L. Watson and wife by the members and friends of his church rendered them quite happy and grateful...Mr. and Mrs. Richard Occamore, of Spratt, spent Sunday with relatives here...Misses Luetta and Helen Matthias are absent from school this week. They are spending the week with home folks at Coffman...Mr. J.F. Sutherland is among the ill of the week...Some have renewed, many will renew, and you who have not ought to do so, for the Argus is a paper that stands for the uplift of the Negro race in all things."

19 February 1915, pg. 3, col. 2.
"Miss Annie Busch has returned from a trip to St. Louis...Miss Mary Barnes, of Washington, Mo., is the house guest of Mrs. T.L. Watson...Large audiences gathered at the M.E. Church Sunday to hear Rev. A.L. Woolfolk who conducted quarterly meeting. Rev. Woolfolk is an energetic young minister who needs our encouragement[6]..."Grandma Evans" is stricken with paralysis and is unable to speak, yet she is conscious and shows a desire to converse as her many friend[s] administer unto her wants...Prof. J.C. Staten is not able to be in the school room. He is at home for recuperation...Rev. Bowles, district superintendent, was here Monday night and held the last quarterly conference for this conference year. He also preached an interesting sermon at 8 o'clock...While at play Rossie Madison received a cut on his left hand, which has caused him great pain...Miss Melview Kennedy has returned to her home at Greenville [Wayne Co., Mo.]...Miss Dayse F. Baker was hostess for the Clever Bees Thursday evening, at which time Miss Hadassah Bridges sang a solo and Miss Lorene Staten addressed the ladies...Rev. Brooks and Rev. Woolfolk were visitors at school Monday. The latter addressed the student body...The friends of Mrs. Robt. Simpson are delighted to have her here again. She and her husband reside in Chicago. Mrs. Simpson will remain until her mother recuperates...Mrs. Laura Kennedy is visiting in De Soto [Jefferson Co., Mo.] and St. Louis this week...The angel of death visited

the home of Mr. Randall Wilburn and took away his wife at an early hour Sunday morning. Three small children survive her. She had been ill more than six months with tuberculosis. Rev. T.L. Watson conducted the funeral services Monday afternoon...Some of the gentlemen of our city are preparing to organize a club for social comfort. It is much needed...Mr. J.F. Sutherland is back on his job....Mrs. D. Buford is yet ill...The reason you did not know it had happened is because you do not read the Argus. It is a paper that will keep you posted as to the happenings and it will also while away those lonesome moments you have when you feel that you just have to visit Sister B to learn the news."

26 February 1915, pg. 2, col. 2.

"Mr. B.J. Wilkins spent Sunday with home folks...Mrs. H. Burks arrived Thursday to be at her mother's bedside...Mrs. Clay is convalescing...Prof. J.C. Staten continues to improve...Master Clayton Alexander is able to be out again. His wounds are healing nicely...Mrs. Hannah Allen, of Fredericktown, was the guest of Mrs. Eric Matthias the past week[7]...The "Boys' Day" program at Douglass School was largely attended Friday. The little lads were equal to the occasion. Prof. W.L. Johns, city superintendent, addressed the patrons and pupils...Principal Williams responded and remarks were made by Rev. Watson and Rev. Brooks...The messenger of death came at an early hour Saturday morning and bore the spirit of "Grandma Evans" away. The funeral services were conducted at the M.E. Church Sunday afternoon. The Sunday school turned out in a body. She was ninety years, two months and one week old at the time of her death...Revival services are now in progress at the A.M.E. Church...The Clever Bees enjoyed a hearty repast at the home of Mrs. Chas. Baker, Thursday night. Mrs. Robt. Simpson, of Chicago, addressed the Club on the subject of "Art." She brought with her quite a collection of her recent models...Mrs. A. Simms was not so well the past week... Messrs. Samuel Burke and Philip Thornton have shown us they can not [sic] do without the Argus[8]...A certain old gentleman said that another man told him that a woman told him that a young lady told her that a young man of our town said that he would wed soon. It certainly must be true...We told you that the "Argus Man" told us that if you did not pay you would be cut-off the list. Was it true?...Miss Alice Swink entertained Friday evening in honor of Miss Barnes of Washington...The school term consists of 180 days. Catch a brace of one of these days and visit the school. You have a welcome any day. Each patron owes it to himself or herself, also to their child or children, to visit at least one time."

05 March 1915, pg. 3, col. 1-2.

"Miss Melview Kennedy, accompanied Miss Edith Cayce to Potosi [Washington Co., Mo.] Sunday for a few days' stay...Messrs. Lewis Murphy and Geo. Meyers were at home Sunday...Rev. T.L. Watson is still engaged in revival services. Rev. Brooks is assisting in the meeting...Prof. J.C. Staten has resumed his work at Charleston [Mississippi Co., Mo.]...Mrs. Laura Valley, of Coffman, was the guest of her daughter, Miss Mattie, the first of the week... Messrs. Wayman and Ben Chappelle had business in Farmington last week... Miss Dayse Baker was present at a dinner party at the residence of Mrs. Geo. Maul, of Bonne Terre, Sunday. Those present were: Rev. Sanders and wife, Mrs. Benjamin Ransom and Miss Ruth B. Davis...Mrs. Fred Chappelle, of Coffman has been here for a week caring for her mother, Mrs. D. Buford, who is quite ill...Mr. A. Simms, of St. Louis, spent Thursday in our city on business...Rev. Brooks will soon be off to conference, which convenes at Louisiana, [Pike Co.,] Mo...Mr. Peter Swink has gone to Sidney, [Champaign Co.,] Ill., where he has employment...Mr. and Mrs. Geo. Villars, of Castor, were the guests of Mrs. Louisa Anthony the first of the week...Miss Hadassah Bridges delightfully entertained the C.B.C.'s Thursday night. Crocheting and tatting were the topics for the evening. The beautiful quilt made by the ladies has been sold and the proceeds will be given to a charitable purpose...Mr. Chas. Douthit and wife, of Avon [Ste. Genevieve Co., Mo.], did their usual shopping here last week...Mr. Benjamin Chappelle presented his daughters a beautiful piano...Miss Frankie Maul, of Bonne Terre, was the guest of Miss Ora Hunt, Thursday...Mr. Ben. Ransom, of Bonne Terre, Mr. Chas. Keeton, of De Soto, were shaking hand with Farmington friends Friday...Some girls do not get to go out at all at night, some get to go very little, and some are out every night—a few night too many. To which class do you belong? Mothers, schoolgirls cannot go out every night and then feel fresh for the next day's work. Their bodies are tired, their minds are crowded and you often wonder why they seem stupid."

12 March 1915, pg. 3, col. 2.

"Master Booker Baker has extended his agency into the territory of Mineral Point [Washington Co., Mo.] and Potosi...Miss Melview Kennedy returned Sunday from a visit with Mrs. J. Carson, of Potosi...Mrs. C. Baker has been quite ill for more than a week...Rev. T.L. Watson and wife were among the numbered ill of last week...The Pastime Club is thoroughly organized with Mr. Jas. Robinson as president. It is composed of twelve members...The cozy little cottage of Mrs. Louisa Anthony was consumed by fire at an early hour Tuesday night. The contents were tntirely [sic] burned. The origin of the fire is unknown. All of the family were away from home...Mr. Alexander Antho-

ny spent a day of last week at home looking after business for his mother...
Mrs. Laura Kennedy has returned from a visit to De Soto and other points...
Mr. Thomas Cayce was the guest of homefolks Sunday...We are glad to know
that Little Nadine Cherry will recover from her recent illnesss. aiyw [sic] illness [sic]....Miss Laura Amonette and Mrs. Minnie Clark accompanied Mrs.
David Buford to St. Louis Sunday morning. Mrs. Buford will be under the
care of a physician for a while...Mr. Fred Chappelle and wife returned home
Thursday, taking little Miss Laura Wilburn with them...The teachers and
pupils of Douglass School were quite generous to the members of Mrs. Anthony's family by way of silver offerings...Mrs. Charlotte Clay has recovered;
Mrs. Lucy Mooten has been quite ill for several days...There are only fifty-
five more days of school. Can you not give one hour for a visit there? Get your
name on the visiting list...Aldrew Evans, beloved son of Mr. and Mrs. Geo.
Evans, departed this life Sunday morning after an illness of many months.
His parents have the sympathy of a host of friends[9]...Mr. Lewis Murphy
was down from Festus the first of the week. Mr. P. Boddie is yet unable to be
out...There are more people ill in Farmington now than have been for years
i.e., at one time. Lend your presence and your means."

19 March 1915, pg. 3, col. 3.
"Master J.P. Boddie has been absent from school a week on account of illness...Mr. Lindsey Clay had a "scrumptious time" here Saturday and Sunday...Little Miss Hildrake Kennedy is improving very fast...The C.B.C.'s
had a very pleasant evening Thursday at the residence of Mrs. P.M. Cayce.
The hostess spared no means to make the affair enjoyable. Miscellaneous
quotations caused much mirth to be added to the evening...Mr. P. Hunt,
while working at Knob Lick, received injuries to his left hand which have
rendered him quite a cripple...Mr. Henry Hunt remains very much indisposed...Messrs. Chas. Baker and P.M. Cayce say, by their ways and actions,
that they, their wives and their children cannot do without the Argus. What
did they do? Just wrote the check...Those among the ill of the week are:
Miss Hortense Kennedy, Mrs. L. Murphy, Masters Kossuth Baker and Clifton Cooper, and Mr. J.F. Sutherland...Miss Mae Baker has returned from St.
Louis where she has been visiting for quite a number of weeks...The Illinois
breeze blew right for Mrs. Ella Cherry. She is now enjoying her honeymoon
at Champaign. Who will be next?...Queen of Honor Court will observe Palm
Sunday at highnoon [sic] with a candle-light service at the Masonic Hall...
The members of Burleigh Lodge will hold their anniversary services at the
A.M.E. Church March 28, at which time Rev. T.L. Watson will deliver a
sermon...Mrs. Chas. Baker is convalescent. News reached us from St. Louis
that Mrs. Buford is much better...Quarterly meeting services will be held at

the A.M.E. Church Sunday...When the sad intelligence was announced of the death of Miss Amy Busch Sunday night, a community grieved deeply. Her mother has the sympathy of a host of friends. Her daughter, Mrs. Lucas, of Belmont, was successful in reaching her sister's bedside ere death claimed her[10]...Mrs. Laura Kennedy received a fall which rendered her quite lame... Mrs. E.J. Harris is now able to dress you up for Easter in the very latest prints."

26 March 1915, pg. 3, col. 2.
"The friends of Master Ambus Drew are sorry to learn of his continued illness...Miss Estacada Baker is introducing Negro art into this city...Rev. A.J. Sanders, of Bonne Terre, assisted Rev. Watson in conducting quarterly meeting services Sunday...While en route home from Potosi, Mrs. Geo. Maul and Miss R.B. Davis spent Sunday in Farmington...Miss Helen Matthias improves very slowly...La grippe has formed acquaintance with Mesdames Geo. Meyers, J.L. Brooks, S.O. Wilkins, Misses Melview Kennedy, Mildred Taylor and Edna Harris and Mr. Lewis Kennedy. They don't like the introduction... Miss K.D. Townsend, of Bonne Terre, attended the play of the senior class of Douglass School Friday evening...Mr. Oscar Hunt, of St. Louis and Mr. Myrtle Hunt and family, of Fredericktown, were here the first of the week in answer to the death of their father, Mr. Henry Hunt, which occurred Saturday night. The funeral was held Monday afternoon...Mrs. Maria Staten, of Coffman, is visiting the Misses Matthias, her granddaughters...Misses Mabel Meyers and Hodassah [sic] Bridges and Mrs. P.M. Cayce were participants in the musicale [sic] given at the residence of Mrs. E.J. Harris Thursday evening the refreshments were more than refreshing...Rev. J.D. Barksdale attended to business here Tuesday...Mrs. Thos. Cayce spent last week with her daughters in Potosi..."Health Week" has been given attention and the results are seen. Many who crawled out of their winter shells crawled back this week as well as did the groundhog...The young folks of this city need a reading room where they could go and while away the hours of leisure. There they could read the best magazines and exchange ideas to a great advantage. Who'll be the first to give a dollar towards the movement?"

02 April 1915, pg. 3, col. 3.
"Queen of Honor Court assembled at the Masonic Hall Sunday noon and observed Palm Sunday with a special candle-light service...At three o'clock at the A.M.E. Church, Rev. T.L. Watson preached the annual sermon to the members of the Burleigh Lodge and Masoleot [sic] Court. At this time Mr. Chas. Baker discussed "The Negro and his faults." A response was given by Miss Dayse F. Baker, representing Masoleat [sic] Court in progress Mr. P.M

Cayce paid tribute to the deceased knights. Messrs. Ben, Arville and Weyman Chappelle. Mr. Joe Franks and Miss Imogene Staten were in attendance from Coffman. Mrs. Harriet Villais and daughter Miss Mary, of Castor, spent the week's end with relatives...Mr. Wm[.] Hunt, of Champaign, Ill., arrived here Tuesday and departed Wednesday[.] Among the ill of the week are Mesdames Geo. Blackwell, F. Poston, Antoine Murphy, Chas. Cayce, Mr. H[.] Overton and little Ruth Boddy [sic]...Rev. J.L. Brooks and family were terribly alarmed Saturday night by a score or more of intruders. Each intruder had been to the grocery or meat market. It was an agreeable alarm...Miss Stanley, of Columbia, [Boone Co.] Mo., made an interesting talk on "Home Economics" at Douglass School Friday afternoon, at which time a large number of ladies were in attendance...Mrs. Samuel Burke had business in Fredericktown last week...Since returning to her home at Coffman, Miss Helen Matthias has improved very rapidly...Miss Charlotte Valle, of Coffman, was the house guest of Miss Dayse Baker a few days of last week...Miss Melview Kennedy, of Greenville has recovered...Mr[.] J.F. Sutherland is again at his usual vocation."

09 April 1915, pg. 3, col. 2.
"Mrs. Lewis Burke remains ill...Miss Edith Cayce has just finished a successful term of school at Mineral Point...Mr. Geo. Blackwell is ill at his home in South Farmington...Sunday was a busy day at both churches as each observed Easter by way of appropriate exercises...Messrs. Lewis Murphy, Geo. Meyers and Thos. Cayce came home for Easter...Mrs. Chas. Baker is convalescing...A nice little cottage is being erected on the old home place of Mrs. Anthony...Master Clifton Cooper does not improve very fast...Mr. P.M. Cayce is building, repairing and planting on his home place...There are less than three dozen days of school. Will you select one day to visit us?...At the residence of Mrs. Geo. Meyers, with her daughter, Miss Mabel, as hostess, the C.B.C.'s enjoyed a spanking good time Thursday evening...Miss Charlotte Valle, of Coffman, was the guest of her sister, Miss Mattie, Sunday... The pugilist betters and the city voters had the day, Monday. Such blowing and swelling...Mrs. W. Davis returned to Cape Girardeau [Cape Girardeau Co., Mo.] Monday after a few months of visiting with her mother and other relatives...We are glad that the month has arrived that so many are to renew their subscription. We thank you in advance."

16 April 1915, pg. 3, col. 3.
"Miss Bertha Matthias has accepted a position in St. Louis...Mr. Tillman Cayce attended to business in St. Louis the first of the week...Mrs[.] Laura Kennedy has been quite ill for a week. Mrs. E. Overton is convalescent...

Mr. A.A. Simms, of St. Louis had a pleasant trip home, Saturday...Misses Corinne Wilkins, Hadassah Bridges, and Alice Swink, Mesdames Thos. Cayce, Robt. Simpson and Master Booker Baker attended the closing exercises of the school at Mineral Point...Mrs. David Buford has returned from St. Louis feeling much better...Prof. J.C. Staten returned to Charleston Monday accompanied by Master Oscar Smith who will spend an indefinite period of time at Cairo, Ill...Miss Dola Boddie is spending a fortnight with relatives in St. Louis...On Thursday evening at the residence of Mrs. Geo. Evans, Miss Melview Kennedy entertained the Clever Bees...Mr. Harry Cayce had a might shaking of hands with home folks the first of the week...Mr. Hildred Overton says, "Diptheria once, is once too many." He is clamoring to get out...Miss Ethel Swink, of Coffman, is here for an indefinite stay... Mr. and Mrs. Jno. Franks entertained Mr. E. Myree, of St. Louis Wednesday evening...Mr. Jno. Franks has employment at Poplar Bluff, Mo...The programme [sic] rendered at the M.E. Church Sunday evening under the management of Mrs. Robt. Simpson, was indeed interesting...Miss Dayse Baker attended to business in St. Louis Saturday in company with Miss Ruth B. Davis of Bonne Terre...Rev. Reynolds is the pastor of the M.E. Church. Rev. Brooks has been sent to Webster Groves...You bought your Easter gown and paid for it, you've read the Argus, now pay for it...A liberal reward is being offered by a certain young man for a cure for la grippe."

23 April 1915, pg. 3, col. 2.
"Rev. A.L. Reynolds preached two excellent sermons Sunday and returned to St. Charles Tuesday...Mr. Sterling Alexander underwent an operation in St. Louis last week. He has had an injured knee for some considerable time... News reached us here from Jefferson City that Mr. Tine Murphy had undergone an operation...Some one [sic] in Festus was delighted to greet Mr. J.F. Sutherland Sunday and he was delighted to be there. Mrs. Leora Simpson, Miss Hadassah Bridges and Miss Edith Cayce took a crowd of young people out Sunday afternoon, and they ate some goobers, too...The town boys played the " [sic] Douglass School boys a game of baseball Friday. The score was 9 to 8 in favor of the former, but the Douglass lads will be with them again today on the campus...Mrs. Jas. Cayce says she cannot do without the Argus any longer. Many are "newing" and renewing...Messrs. Ben.[,] Arville and Wilson Chappelle, of Coffman, were here last week...At the residence of Mrs. L. Murphy, Thursday evening, the Clever Bees enjoyed a pleasant evening. "Dining-room Etiquette" was discussed...We lament that Mr. John Bridges was taken to the hospital last week. We wish him a speedy recovery... Prof. V.E. Williams says turkeys grow larger in southeast Missouri and that is why he is buying eggs. They'll hatch in Chillicothe [Livingston Co., Mo.]...

Miss Barnes, of Washington, had a pleasant sojourn with Mrs. Watson and has returned home...Mr. Henry Amonette suffered an attack of illness last week. He is convalescent...Mrs. J.L. Watson is attending to business in St. Louis this week...Gardening and green hunting is the latest vocation here. The fields and valleys have guests galore...We have twenty-five days of school left. Get your name on the registered list. To visit the school is a patron's duty."

30 April 1915, pg. 3, col. 3.
"When the sad intelligence reached us of the painful accident of Miss Dola Boddie in being struck by a car in St. Louis Thursday, we were deeply grieved. Besides other injuries her nose was broken. Her mother, Mrs. P. Boddie, and Mrs. Laura Kennedy left Sunday to administer unto her needs...Mr. Chas. Baker had two very busy days in the city last week...The Junior League of the M.E. Church rendered a program Sunday evening much to the credit of their literary ability...Mr. and Mrs. Chas. Douthit, of Coffman, spent a day here last week shopping...Rev. Brooks spent last week here with his family and attending to business. His family will remain here until after commencement...Rev. Reynolds arrived Saturday from a business trip to St. Charles... Mr. Hildred Overton is well enough to be at his usual vocation. He has a horror for even the thought of quarantine...Rev. T.L. Watson is improving and is having a successful pastorate...Master Roy Kennedy had the misfortune of sticking a nail in his foot...The same faculty of Douglass School has been selected for the ensuing year...Mrs. Leora Simpson was hostess to the [two words illegible] Thursday evening at which time the ladies fared "sumptuously" and discussed "The Church of Today and Its Needs.".....Mrs. Chas. Baker is recovering rapidly...Mr. P.M. Cayce has added a merry-go-round to the collection of lawn amusements and it is proving quite a drawing card for the children...Mr. Jas. Robinson, Jr., has got the country beat at killing snakes. Hear his method if you have any fear of reptiles. It was a long distance stunt."

07 May 1915, pg. 3, col. 4-5.
"Mrs. G. Evans and Miss Melvieu [sic] Kennedy returned Sunday evening from a visit in St. Louis...The acquaintance entertainment given on the lawn of Mr. P.M. Cayce was largely attended. The decorations and illuminations were beautiful. It was a financial success...Rev. Reynolds and family have arrived and have received a hearty welcome to our community...The game of ball on the Douglass Campus, Friday evening, was a victory for the town boys. The D.S.B's still feel equal to the test...Fifteen more days of school and then comes vacation. Visitors are requested to come to the morning sessions, as the afternoons are given to examinations, etc...Messrs. Chas. Baker, Jas.

Robinson, and F. Poston have made improvements on their property, which adds much to the value thereof…Little Miss Ina Kennedy was hostess at a birthday party Saturday afternoon, when quite a number of tots had one of "Aunt Dolly's Times"…Some young man would do well to open a business where one might go and get refreshments in season and enjoy a social evening…The Evans croquet plot is open to the public from morning until night. Some are becoming professionals…Little Miss Odessa Cayse [sic], of St. Louis, is spending a few days with relatives[11]…The local paper announced the election of Miss Dayse Baker to the Bonne terre [sic] School. Miss Baker wishes to say she was not an applicant, but will teach at Farmington next term…The Bumble Bees of Farmington will meet the Fredericktown Boys on the ball ground Thursday."

14 May 1915, pg. 3, col. 4.
"The Bumble Bees of Farmington played the Honey Bees of Fredericktown, Friday. The game was a victory for the latter. The weather was very cool—too cool for those Bumble Bees to make many home trips. Messrs. Philip Thornton and Percy Swink have the right of way from Libertyville to Farmington… The teachers and pupils of Douglas [sic] School are glad to have Miss Dola Boddie back at her duties…Mrs. T. L. Watson received a message announcing the serious illness of her sister who lives in Kansas City…Some of the young people of the M.E. Church will present "Tattlewood Gossip" at the Masonic Hall Monday night…Miss Mamie Franks, of St. Louis, is a visitor to our city…Messrs. Lewis Murphy and Geo. Meyers have returned from Festus…Miss Dayse Baker entertained the Clever Bees Thursday evening. Miss Hadassah Bridges and Mrs. Lew Murphy introduced new ideas of crocheting. Mrs. Simpson rendered a vocal selection…Miss Edith Cayce spent the week's end at Potosi…Mr. and Mrs. Ben Chappelle, of Coffman, were the guests of Mr. and Mrs. Wesley Douthit last week…Prof. J.C. Staten attended to business here the first of the week…Queen of Honor Court had its installation of officers Friday night. Mrs. W.I. Roberts was installed as Most Ancient Matron…Mrs. Louisa Anthony is again enjoying the comforts of home…Mesdames E.A. Rozier and F.S. Weber addressed the school one day last week on Civic Improvements. Since Clean-up days have passed, the lawns and by-streets look very nice…We earnestly hope that each patron will proceed to assist their older children in finding employment for the summer days. Many have been employed throughout the school term and many are seeking employment. A change of work is play you know. The mind has been well employed. Let's employ the hands now.'"

21 May 1915, pg. 3, col. 1.

"An interesting feature of last week was the musical rendered by the young people of the A.M.E. Church Friday evening. It was a treat. After the rendition of the same, the evening was spent on the church lawn...Mrs. Jane Hunt attended to business at Fredericktown last week...Tomorrow the Douglass Boosters will play the Fredericktown school boys ball. Prof. Williams will accompany the boys on the trip...Mr. Geo. Blackwell continues very much disabled...Miss D.F. Baker has seen the granitoid man. He paid respects to her walkway...Mr. A. Simms has made improvements on his property which renders it quite valuable...Mr. Jno. Frank [sic] is convalescent...The Clever Bees enjoyed a treat at the residence of Mrs. Chas. Baker Thursday evening... Mr. Moses Hunt has the "croquet flag." Messrs. John Douthit, Lewis Hill, Geo. Evans and Chas. Cayce are on his trail...The Honey Bees, of Fredericktown, will find the Bumble Bees nest in Farmington, May 28...Mr. Chas. Baker enjoyed a fraternal good time at Festus Sunday...Mr. Lewis Murphy is the man that put the G. in granitoid...Everybody has his mitt out feeling for rain...Miss Mamie Franks has been quite ill...The exercises of Douglass School will be held May 28, 29. We're glad you're coming...The youths of the M.E. Church were organized into King's Heralds with Miss D.F. Baker, president, and Mrs. A.L. Reynolds, vice-president. These children are endeavoring to raise their annual assessment...Prof. V.E. Williams is quite athletic now-a-days. Something is doing when he makes a home run. Something is mashed."

28 May 1915, pg. 3, col. 3.

"Commencement exercises to night [sic]...The Douglass Boys defeated the Bumble Bees Friday afternoon and then went to Fredericktown and defeated the team there Saturday. Today the Fredericktown team will play the Bumble Bees on the Carleton Campus...On the evening of May 13 Mrs. Chas. Baker delightfully entertained the C.B.C's. They were likewise entertained by Miss Hadassah Bridges Thursday evening...Messrs. Chas. Sutherland and A. Simms have returned from St. Louis feeling "it was good to be here."... Mr. Peter Swink has returned from Champaign...Mr. and Mrs. Jas. Robinson entertained with evening luncheons Thursday and Friday with much joy to the guests...Miss Lottie Simms, of St. Louis, spent a pleasant time with home folks the first of the week...Miss Etta Jordan, of Charleston, is the house guest of Mrs. Laura Kennedy...Rev. Brooks has enjoyed a pleasant week here with his family and friends...The class roll of Douglass School is as follows: Berdola Boddie, Vera O. Brooks, Sophia A. Mudd, Minnie B. Thornton, Booker T. Baker, J. Elmer Bridges, Rossie W. Madison and Wm. D. Wright...Misses Cosetta and Berdola Boddie were hostesses at a social given Tuesday evening in honor of Miss Vera Brooks. Quite a large number of young people were present and spent a pleasant time…The young people, the old people, the middle aged and babes as well are longing for some one [sic] to open up a place of business where they can have a chance to resort to the delicious drinks, etc., of the season. "Don't every one start the business in the same block."

04 June 1915, pg. 3, col. 3.
"Miss Leslie Poston arrived Monday from an extended trip to Rolla, [Phelps Co.,] Mo…The friends of Mr. Sterling Alexander are in deep sympathy with him in the loss of his limbs…Mrs. Eliza Overton is spending a fortnight wither her granddaughter, Mrs. A. Reed, of St. Louis…It has been years since there were so many out of town visitors to the commencement exercises as were here last week. Mineral Point, Fredericktown, Charleston, Coffman, Bonne Terre, St. Marys [Ste. Genevieve Co., Mo.], Potosi, Herculaneum and St. Louis were well represented. The Masonic Hall, in which the exercises were held was too small for the vast crowd assembled and many were forced to go away without being able to enter. There were upwards of forty visitors present…Prof. V.E. Williams returned to Chillicothe after having had a successful school year. Some one feels lonely…Miss Zelma Swink has returned from Champagne [sic] where she has been attending school…Monday evening was one long to be remembered by those who attended the social given at the A.M.E. Church in honor of Prof. Williams and the graduates. We had one of those "Old Cad Wallikin's Times.".…Who'd a thought that those honey bees of Fredericktown would have lost the game Friday? The Bumble Bees, of Farmington, simply walked on the water and slid on the mud to a score of 13:6…Rev. Watson received the sad intelligence of the demise of his sister-in-law. Mrs. Watson was permitted to be with her when the end came…The patrons of Douglass School and friends, as well took great delight in entertaining the guests who were present at the commencement and the teachers and pupils of Douglass School desire to thank them for their generosity."

11 June 1915, pg. 3, col. 3.
"After a very brief illness at a very early hour Saturday morning, little Leonard Bridges departed this life. The remains were laid to rest Sunday afternoon[12]…Mrs. Chas. Cayce accompanied a crowd of little folks on an outing to the St. Francois River Saturday. They caught fish galore…The Juniors of Fredericktown played the Douglass boys ball on the Carleton campus Friday. Fredericktown was stung again. The score was 12-10…The members of the Eastern Star held very appropriate Esther [sic] Day services at the Masonic Hall Sunday afternoon…Rev. A.L. Reynolds will be at Fredericktown Sunday assisting Rev. Woolfolk with quarterly meeting services…Mrs. L. Kennedy

is attending to business at Charleston, Mo…Mrs. A. Simms is furnishing the delicacies of the season to the public. Make the business a success…Mrs. Jerusha Poston and son Halfred returned from Boonville [Cooper Co., Mo.], Thursday, where he has been attending the Missouri School for the Deaf. The youngster shows very readily that he is doing his grade work nicely… The King's Heralds will render their regular Children's Day program Sunday evening…We are informed that smallpox has made its advent into Bonne Terre. We hope it will not be billed for this place…Miss Dayse Baker returned Monday from a trip to Bonne Terre and Festus, having been a guest at a house party at the cottage home of Miss Louise Sides, in company with Miss Ruth B. Davis, of Springfield, [Sangamon Co.,] Ill., and Mrs. J. Nelson, of St. Louis. It was a joyful meeting and a reluctant parting…Vacation time is here for many, but your vacation will not begin until you have o.k'd with the Argus collector. Your neighbor said he'd rather you'd read your own Argus first and then his. The Argus brings joy to its readers. The subscribers feel that to do without it now would be quite a task. It is "a newsy gem, full of interest to the brim."

18 June 1915, pg. 3, col. 2.
"Harold Staten really believes there's no place like home when one is ill. He arrived Monday from St. Louis. His Condition has improved.

Mr. Geo. Meyers is makng [sic] his cottage home quite a modern one. His son, Wilson, writes from Hawaii that he is now out of the hospital, though not fit for duty.

The friends of Mr. Talbert Burns are glad to see him out again.

Good Will Lodge No. 99 is preparing to observe St. John's Day appropriately. The court and chapter will attend and aid them in making it a success.

The critical illness of Mr. James Foulk made it necessary for Mrs. P. Swink to go to Champaign to assist her daughter in caring for him.

Mr. Jno. Franks is recovering slowly.

A deal of pleasure was had by those who attended the law fete at Mr. Geo. Evans Thursday evening.

Miss Estacada Baker and Mrs. Robt. Simpson conducted the Children's Day program at the M.E. Church Sunday evening. The Heralds pleased the audience much.

Mrs. D. Buford is rallying from an operation of a fortnight ago. She is rapidly improving.

You've been wanting to "kill it," been trying to "kill it" ever since spring came, now "kill the fly." You swat it, let the children swat it, swat it anyhow.

Messrs. Wayman and Orville Chappelle, of Avon, spent Sunday here.

Miss Alice Swink is preparing to give a musical treat with her pupils at an early date.

Little Lamont Cayce has recovered from a serious illness.

Mrs. Lewis Kennedy, of Greenville, spent Saturday here transacting business.

Tonight on the parsonage lawn the King's Heralds will serve many delicacies of the season.

Mr. Chas. Baker had the misfortune to lose two fine hogs last week.

Mr. Jno. Bridges writes home that the medical treatment is doing him much good.

Mr. Lewis Murphy returned to Festus Sunday.

> The Argus notes we like to read,
> So interesting and so new;
> For truths indeed it has the lead,
> Its articles all are true;
> It costs us but a dollar, too,
> It will rest you from your labors,
> Just let us send it now to you;
> Don't bother 'bout your neighbors.
> --Dayse F. Baker."

25 June 1915, pg. 3, col. 3.

"Mrs. Lewis Murphy has for a week been the house guest of Miss Lorene Staten, of Coffman…Miss Edith Cayce was accompanied by Master Elbert Baker Wednesday on a trip to Potosi…Mrs. Geo. Blackwell received the sad intelligence Wednesday of the death of Mrs. Ollie Fulton, of Bonne Terre…A special communication to Prof. J.C. Staten informed him of the demise of Prof. A.T. Lewis[13]….Mr. Lewis Hill was bitten by a cur Sunday[14]…Miss Mattie Valle is enjoying a sojourn with home folks at Eads…Patrick Cayce was slightly burned about the face. His would are rapidly healing…Mr. and Mrs. Scott Cole had a pleasant week with relatives at Potosi…Rev. F.S. Bowles held a very successful Quarterly Meeting Sunday. At the afternoon service Rev. T.L. Watson preached a soul-awakening sermon. Rev. Watson, Mesdames Jo. Franks and Laura Kennedy, Miss Berdola Boddie and Mr. Rossie Madison attended the District Convention at De Soto this week…Tonight at the Masonic Hall, Miss Alice Swink and pupils will entertain with a musicale [sic] …Sunday afternoon, for an hour, beginning at two o'clock, St. John's Day will be observed by the Masons, the Masons' daughters, etc. The public is invited…Mr. Pyrtle Evans has arrived from Jefferson City, where he has had a successful scholastic year…The Bumble Bees hate to have it published. We're just saying it to you. Don't tell it to anyone. They went to Fredericktown Saturday and played ball with the honey bees, "and beat 'em."…The King's Heralds presented Rev. A.L. Reynolds a nice number of coins Sunday evening…An entire community sympathizes with Mrs. Mamie Foulk in the loss of her husband…Mr. Thos. Cayce enjoyed Sunday with home folks…Master Halfred [sic] Poston is having serious trouble with his eyes…One month of vacation has passed. Improve one [sic] the next two by subscribing for the Argus. Everybody wants company and longs for company in the good old summer time. Let the Argus be your company. You'll have no cooking to do for this company and no horrid dish washing; just sit in the shade and get better acquainted…Rev. A.L. Watson and Master Warner Cayce have invited the Argus to their homes."

02 July 1915, pg. 3, col. 2.
"The musical given by Miss Alice Swink and pupils was a good rendition, and was highly commended by those who attended…The Bumble Bees swarmed on the Carleton Campus Saturday with the Mineral Point team, and stung them, 9 to 5…Miss May Baker enjoyed a pleasant trip to De Soto last week… Rev. T.L. Watson is preparing for quarterly meeting which will be July 11… Mrs. Fred Chappelle, of Coffman, spent a few days of last week at the bedside of her mother, Mrs. D. Buford, who is convalescing…Mrs. Albert Simms spent Sunday with home folks…Miss Edkith [sic] Cayce and Master Elbert Baker returned from Potosi Friday…Messrs. Wm. Cayce and Wm. Kennedy left Monday en route to Mount Vernon, Ill., where they have employment… Mr. Samuel Burke has returned from a business trip in Washington County… Miss Bessie Hunt is gradually recovering…Sunday is rally day at the M.E. Church…Miss Corine Wilkins was hostess to a party of young folks at her home Saturday evening. Modern amusements were enjoyed…The little lads and lasses are glad to have Master Ambus Drew in their midst…Mrs. Jno. Franks and daughters spent Friday night with Mrs. Joseph Carson of Potosi."

16 July 1915, pg. 3, col. 1.
"Prof. J.C. Staten attended to business in St. Louis last week…Little Miss Olivia Wilkins accompanied Mrs. P. Boddie home from St. Louis, to be the guest of her grandmother, Mrs. S.O. Wilkins…Mrs. S.A. Smith went to St. Louis Friday in answer to a message announcing the sudden demise of her brother, Mr. Wm. Young[15]…The concert given Thursday night under the management of Mesdames Smith and Simms was quite a success…Rev. T.L. Watson and congregation enjoyed a splendid quarterly meeting Sunday. Rev.

A.L. Reynolds preached the sacramental sermon...On rally day at the M.E. Church the collection amounted to $52...Prof. V.E. Williams has tendered his resignation to the board and Prof. J.C. Staten has been appointed his successor...Miss Dayse Baker was presented with a beautiful set of silver teaspoons by Queen of Honor Court. This indeed brought joy to her in her hours of illness...Mr. Cornelius Cole, of St. Louis, spent Sunday the guest of his brother, Mr. Scott Cole[16]...Miss Hortense Kennedy is spending her vacation in St. Louis...Mrs. Robt. Simpson has returned to her home in Chicago...Miss Hadassah Bridges is visiting in Champaign, Ill...Mrs. Talbert received the said intelligence of the death of her son, George, at Wellington [Lafayette Co., Mo.][17]...Mrs. Carrie Burns has returned from a visit to Coffman. She was accompanied home by Mr. Walter Franks...Miss Luetta Matthias was hostess for a number of young people at an evening luncheon Monday...Mr. Henry Amonette and family and Mrs. Charlotte Clay spent Sunday at Coffman...Miss Melview Kennedy is convalescent."

23 July 1915, pg. 3, col. 3.
"Miss Alice Swink had the misfortune to scald her right hand. The wound is healing nicely...While en route to Poplar Bluffs [sic] Rev. R. Philips spent a day with his father-in-law, Leo Blackwell...Mr. Samuel Burke was one of the number who autoed to De Soto last week...Messrs. Lewis Murphy and Geo. Meyers have resumed their work at Festus...Miss Minnie Thornton is improving rapidly...Mrs. F. Poston and Mrs. C. Baker are attending the Grand Session of the O.E.S. in the city of St. Louis. The latter is representing...Mrs. Jessie Ward and daughter, Alleda, of St. Louis, are the guests of Mr. and Mrs. Geo. Evans...Mr. Alonzo Reynolds has gone to St. Louis for an extended visit...Miss Pauline Hawkins of Charleston, is the house guest of Mrs. Laura Kennedy...While visiting with her mother in St. Louis, Helen, the three-year-old daughter of Mr. and Mrs. Lewis Smith, fell into a basin of hot water and died after a few days from the effects of it. The remains were brought here for burial Sunday. Mrs. Lavada Hill and daughter, Dorothy, accompanied the mother here[18]...Despite the fact that the county went dry Saturday, we had almost a cloudburst Sunday...Mrs. Mary Taylor, of St. Louis, came down Sunday and accompanied her little son, Ambus, back to their home. He had been here for recuperation...The Clever Bees enjoyed Thursday evening with Mrs. P.M. Cayce. The menu was delightful...Mrs. D. Buford is improving rapidly. Mr. H.B. Keatts is taking a much needed rest. He expects to visit several nearby places...Miss Ethel Swink has been suffering from a blood poisoned foot, but is much better...Today is picnic day at Coffman. Many a chicken crowed his last time last night...Six more weeks of vacation. Little folks are making well of these scorching days...Rossie Madison spent Sunday

at Bonne Terre, the guest of his aunt, Mrs. Geo. Maul...Mr. Wm. Wright attended to business in St. Louis last week."

30 July 1915, pg. 3, col. 1-2.
"Master Booker Baker was struck on the head by the seat in his swing. Medical attention rendered him able to still take exercise...Some went one way, some went another, but they arrived there in large numbers to the picnic at Coffman on Friday...Mrs. Wesley Douthitt [sic] has been ill for more than a week in Doss Addition...Mrs. Eliza Overton has returned from an extended visit to little Miss Lonie V. Reed, in St. Louis...Master Melvin Overton is again able to be in the street...The continued illness of Mr. Harold Staten renders him very weak...Messrs. Chas. Baker and Moses Hunt are attending the Grand Lodge, K. of P., in St. Louis...[H?]on. B.F. Adams was the guest of [Bu]rleigh Lodge on Thursday evening...Mr. Byrd J. Wilkins is at home [illegible] recuperation...Mrs. Jane Hunt [illegible] in Fredericktown on business [du]ring the week...Take a car ride [illegible]ay to Claridy's Grove and attend [illegible] M.E. Sunday-school's annual outing...Miss Dollean Poston, of St. Louis, is spending a fortnight with relatives...Mr. Moses Hunt is sojourning in St. Louis...Mrs. Edw. Harris delightfully entertained the C.B.C.'s Thursday evening...Mrs. Lucile Martin, of St. Louis, is the guest of Mrs. Chas. Baker...Mr. H.B. Keatts is at the place he long sought, and mourned because he arrived there not—St. Louis is the place."

06 August 1915, pg. 3, col. 3.
"Mr. J.F. Sutherland returned Sunday from attending the Grand Lodge of K. of P.'s...Mrs. Jerry Bridges, of St. Louis, is here on a visit...The Bumble Bees met with defeat at a game of ball with the Jackson Boys on Carleton Campus Saturday. They were, nevertheless, able to render a program for their entertainment Saturday evening at the Masonic Hall...Miss Lorene Staten and Mrs. Mazie Lyons, of Coffman, have returned to our city. Edgar Kennedy is conducting a successful dray service...Mrs. Hildred Overton is visiting relatives in St. Louis...The death of Mrs. Jas. Cunningham, which occurred at Crystal City [Jefferson Co., Mo.], was a shock to all who knew her...Mrs. Mary Taylor brought the remains of her son, Ambus, here for interment. The remains were laid to rest Monday. Funeral was held at the A.M.E. Church... Mrs. Gertrude Oliver and daughter, Clementine, of St. Louis, are the guests of Mrs. Antoine Murphy...After a short illness, Mr. Lewis Burke, a pioneer of this place, died. He had been in Potosi for a number of months with relatives. His sister, Mrs. Sarah Amonette and son, Samuel went early to his bedside, but could only give temporary relief. The remains were brought home Saturday. The funeral services were conducted Sunday at the A.M.E. Church.

The deceased was ninety years old and had been farming even this season, thus showing his rare physical strength...Misses Dollean Poston and Roxy Douthit, of St. Louis, spent a few days of this week at Coffman...Mrs. Lucile Martin, who has been visiting here, returned to St. Louis, Saturday...Misses Edna Harris and Edith Cayce are the house guests of Mrs. Jos. Carson, of Potosi, this week...Miss Stella Poston returned to St. Louis Sunday, after having been the guest of her aunt, Mrs. W.I. Roberts...Come and see the collector and pay for your subscription. The Argus is a volume of interesting items. It dis[ca]rds gossip and deals with facts. Send it to your friend who is away on vacation."

13 August 1915, pg. 3, col. 1.
"Mr. Thos. Cayce and nephew, Master Kossuth Baker, returned from Potosi Sunday, accompanied by Mrs. Jos. Carson...Mrs. Peter Swink and children Beatrice and Sumner, have returned from Sidney, Ill., where they have been for the past month or more...Rev. R. Phillips, of Poplar Bluff, attended to business here the first of the week...Miss Dollean Poston and Mrs. Roxie Thomas have returned to St. Louis...The C.B.C.s were delightfully entertained by Miss Melview Kennedy, Thursday evening...Walter, the infant son of Rachel Moore, was badly scalded about the arms. He is doing nicely... Mrs. Chas. Douthit and daughters, Alcesta and Christina, of Coffman, spent a few days of last week here with relatives...St. Luke Sunday school enjoyed a pleasant outing Wednesday. The youths, the aged, and visitors as well, will long remember it...Miss Hortense Kennedy has returned from St. Louis... Mr. and Mrs. F. Madison have returned from a trip to Festus...The Bumble Bees, of Farmington, played the Jackson Cyclones two extensive games of ball last week. The Bumble Bees lost the first game, but crowned themselves victors the last day. The boys declare that the Jackson people spared no pains to make their stay a pleasant one...Mr. Albert Simms, of St. Louis, was accompanied home Saturday by Masters Ware and Cash Pendleton[19]...Mrs. F. Poston returned Friday from an extended trip to St. Louis, bringing Master Seward Poston to be the guest of Master Addison Roberts...Rev. Reynolds is recovering gradually from an illness of eight or ten days...Mrs. Lewis Kennedy was hostess Sunday to quite a number of persons at a dinner party served in honor of the fifty-first birthday of her husband, Mr. Lewis Kennedy. Those present were Mr. and Mrs. Chas. Baker and family, Mr. and Mrs. Scott Cole, Mr. J.P. Evans, Mr. J.F. Sutherland and Miss D.F. Baker...Rev. Reynolds and family were surprisingly visited Friday evening by members and friends who brought a large donation, of which they were very thankful. Groceries were brought galore...Mr. Geo. Meyers spent Sunday with home folks...Just twenty-four more days of vacation and then away to school. We

hope the patrons will make the opening day the banner day for attendance for all concerned."

20 August 1915, pg. 3, col. 3.
"Deep regret reigned in our hearts when we received the sad intelligence of the death of our ex-pastor, Rev. J.H. Noland, of St. Louis. His wife has our most profound sympathy[20]...Mr. Scott Cole and Master Sumner Swink are among the ill...The patterns of crocheting exhibited by the Clever Bees, Thursday at the residence of Mrs. Lewis Murphy were demonstrative of hard, earnest labor and originality, as well...Messrs. B.J. Wilkins, Lewis Hill and Moses Hunt, representing Burleigh Lodge attended the funeral of Rev. J.H. Noland, at St. Louis Monday...Miss Mae Baker is enjoying a pleasant stay in St. Louis...Mrs. Cora J. Turner, of Parsons, Kansas, is visiting relatives...Mrs. S.A. Smith attended to business in Fredericktown last week...Master Elbert Baker fell and severely injured his foot...Miss Grace Anthony has returned from Quindaro [Wyandotte Co., Kan.], where she has had a successful scholastic year[21]...Rev. Reynolds was at his post of duty Sunday with two effective sermons...Miss Anna Reynolds left Thursday for Sedalia [Pettis Co., Mo.], where she will attend Geo. R. Smith's College...Mrs. Laura Amonette accompanied Miss Mauree [sic] Madison home from St. Louis Sunday...Mrs. Wesley Douthit is recuperating from a recent illness...Mr. Lewis Murphy enjoyed Sunday with home folks...This has been the banner year for vegetation in this locality and those who had the smallest plot under cultivation, had sufficient for home use, and those who followed the pursuit on large scales had enough for market exchange. With so fruitful a yield as this we can easily subscribe for the Argus and read the time away. Mrs. Geo Evans has invented a new quilting frame. It requires no nails, no ropes or string, no hanging nor letting down, no chairs to sit around it. It's a novel, easy method. It is worth a patent."

27 August 1915, pg. 3, col. 2.
"The circus at Fredericktown Monday night was well attended by Farmingtonians, who went by auto route...Mr. Felix Poston can hardly 'spress himself about the visit with his brothers at St. Louis...Mr. Chas. Baker met with a slight accident Monday, which caused him to be crippled for several days... Nothing is more needed in Farmington than a night school. Many are anxious to attend...The cool weather certainly had its effect upon the Bumble Bees. They lost the game at Ironton with a score of 15 to 3. They left their name there; they will hereafter be known as the Giants...Miss Hadassah Bridges expects to remain in Champaign for an indefinite time...Jr. Jas. Cunningham, of Crystal City, was here on business last week...Mr. H. B. Keatts is back

at his old stand...Mother Talbert is able to be out again...Master Halfred Poston and Mrs. Lucy Mooten are on the sick list...We regret that Rev. Reynolds has had a relapse...Rev. T.L. Watson is making gradual preparations for the approaching conference...Mr. and Mrs. Scott Cole and granddaughter, Estacada Baker, spent Sunday visiting Mr. and Mrs. Jerry Bridges...During the next nine days of vacation let's begin to divest ourselves of Master Frivolity and invest ourselves with a zeal to make this a banner year for Douglass School...It's no longer a secret, everybody knows it; the old and the young are talking about it, and it has even arrested the attention of the white people. It's the neighborhood talk. What is it? The Argus."

03 September 1915, pg. 3, col. 1-2.
"After a pleasant visit of two weeks with Mrs. Laura Kennedy, Miss L. Fulks, of Charleston, has returned to her home...Rev. Chas. Wilkins ably filled the pulpit at the M.E. Church Sunday evening. He was the guest of his mother, Mrs. S.O. Wilkins...Mesdames P.S. Poston and Oscar Hunt, of St. Louis, are spending a pleasant week with relatives....Miss Bertha Cunningham, of St. Louis, was the guest of Miss Bertha Staten at the week's end...The Farmington Giants simply took the "B" out of ball with the Ironton Boys, Friday. The score was 23 to 4. At night the team was entertained at the Masonic Hall... Estacada and Booker Baker departed for St. Louis Sunday. The latter will remain for the school year with his uncle, Mr. Chas. Sutherland...Mr. Talbert Burns has returned from a visit with relatives at Coffman...The officers have their eyes open for some youths who are prone to run away. They are offering them a free ride to Boonville...Labor Day will be observed at Douglass School with an all-day session. Patrons as well as pupils are welcome... Miss Berdola Boddie has returned from St. Louis...Mrs. Jane Baker received the message Saturday of the death of her brother, Mr. Geo. Hutchinson, of Clarksville, [Montgomery Co.,] Tenn[22]...Quarterly meeting will be held at the M.E. Church, September, 11, 12...Mrs. Harry Cayce, of St. Louis, is the guest of her mother...Every reader of the Argus should preserve the article of last week's Argus, on "Thoughts of the Mouth." It is a splendid article and the writer deserves to be congratulated."

10 September 1915, pg. 3, col. 2-3.
"Miss Edith Cayce has resumed her work at Mineral Point...Mr. Henry Amonette is slowly recovering from an injured ankle...Mr. Lewis Murphy had a pleasant visit with home folks Sunday...Mesdames Oscar Hunt and P.S. Poston returned to St. Louis Monday accompanied by Mr. Oscar Hunt. While here they were entertained by Mesdames Jane Hunt, Felix Poston, W.I. Roberts and Misses Zelma and Alice Swink...Miss Estacada Baker returned

Sunday from a week's visit at St. Louis...Rev. J.D. Barksdale conducts quarterly meeting services at the A.M.E. Church Sunday...Miss Ethel Swink is visiting at Herculaneum...Misses Luetta and Helen Matthias spent a pleasant vacation at Coffman...Mrs. Fred Chappelle and daughters, of Coffman, are the guests of Mrs. David Buford...Miss Alice Swink is having a prospective visit with relatives in St. Louis...Mrs. Wesley Douthit is yet indisposed... The friends of Mr. Harold Staten deeply regret his weak condition...Sunday will be quarterly meeting day at St. Paul...Douglass School opened Monday morning, with a large enrollment. Prof. J.C. Staten, principal and Miss Dayse Baker, assistant...Mrs. Beulah Cayce and a party of young folks spent Monday angling at the St. Francois River...Rev. T.L. Watson and congregation are striving earnestly to have a complete report at the annual conference, which will convene next month...Mr. Eric Matthias has been quite a shut-in from rheumatism...The reporter wishes to have a financial revival for the Argus. If you will send your remittance in it will be highly appreciated. Several have expressed themselves as being anxious to subscribe. Do it now while you have it at interest."

17 September 1915, pg. 3, col. 2.
"Who said Dan Cupid had gone on a vacation? Not so. Mr. J.P. Evans and Miss Melview Evans quietly stole over to the residence of Rev. A.L. Reynolds last Tuesday night and 'twas then and there the rites of matrimony were performed. About forty-five persons were entertained at the home of the youthful bride at Greenville Thursday evening. Mr. and Mrs. Evans received quite a shower of gifts. The groom, in company with Elmer Bridges, departed for Jefferson City [Cole Co., Mo.] Friday, where they will attend Lincoln Institute...Mrs. Thos. Cayce attended a picnic at Mineral Point, Saturday... Mr. Wm. Wright is attending Sumner High...Mr. Onan Poston is attending George R. Smith College...Rev. A.L. Woolfolk, of Fredericktown, assisted Rev. Reynolds at quarterly meeting services, Sunday. At three o'clock Rev. Watson delivered one of his soul-stirring sermons...Mrs. T.L. Watson returned Sunday, accompanied by her sister, Mrs. M.C. Henry, of Speed, [Phillips Co.,] Kans...At the opening of Douglass School Rev. A.L. Reynolds was a visitor...The demise of Mr. Harold Staten, Sunday morning, brought sorrow to a host of friends as well as to his parents, sisters and brother. His illness was of long duration. The funeral services were held Monday at the A.M.E. Church at which time the Douglass School was closed. The out-of-town attendants were: Mrs. Eliza Cunningham and son, Mr. Clarence Cunningham, of St. Louis, Mr. Walter Franks, Misses Imogene Staten and Alcesta Douthit, Mr. Fred Chappelle and Mr. Reuben Staten...Master Jimmie Cayce is suffering from a wounded scalp...Mr. Wilson Chappelle, of Coffman,

spent Saturday in our city...Mr. Geo. Meyers enjoyed Sunday with home folks...Misses Augustine Swink and Miss Zenobia Swink were the guests of Mrs. Peter Swink, Friday...Prof. V.E. Williams is teaching at Chillicothe, his home town...Our list of new subscribers will be ready to send in within the next few days. Help us place this newsy gem in every home. Subscribe for a paper in which you can read something good that the Negro is doing and not always the deeds of the lower element."

"Society and Local Notes," 24 September 1915, pg. 5, col. 4.
"Miss Ora Hunt, of Farmington, and Prof. V.E. Williams, of Chillicothe, were quietly married by Rev. S.B. Anderson at the residence of the bride's brother, Mr. Oscar Hunt, 4148 Lucky St., Saturday, September 18. Immediately after the wedding dinner the bride and groom left for Chillicothe, Mo., where Prof. Williams is principle of Garrison School."[23]

"Marriage License," 24 September 1915, pg. 5, col. 4.
"...Virgil E. Williams..Chillicothe, [Livingston Co.,] Mo.
Ora M. Hunt....Farmington, Mo..."

01 October 1915, pg. 3, col. 1.
"Prof. and Mrs. V.E. Williams, of Chillicothe, and Mr. and Mrs. J. Jordan, of Charleston, have the wishes of this community for a long, prosperous life. Folks say this marriage affair is contagious and nothing will prevent the spread...Mrs. A. Simms accompanied her brother, Halfred, to Boonville to school. The former expects to take a few weeks' vacation at Hot Springs, [Garland Co.,] Ark., before returning...Mrs. M.C. Henrie, of Speed, Kans., accompanied Mrs. T.L. Watson home. Rev. Watson is all smiles...Mrs. Geo. Maul, of Bonne Terre, attended to business here Saturday...Quite a number of persons witnessed the literary program of the sixth and seventh grades at Douglass School, Friday.

Many were in attendance at the house social conducted by Mrs. James Cayce, a the residence of Mrs. Jordan...Dan Cupid hurled an arrow in Coffman, [sic] vicinity, and as a result, Miss Charlotte Valle became Mrs. Walter Franks. The query: who'll be next to speak a word to the pastor?...Mrs. E. Overton and Mr. Henry Amonette, who have been in disposed, are able to be out again...Miss Alice Swink and Mrs. Kossuth Robinson, are visiting in Chicago...Mr. Jas. Robinson has built a modern poultry apartment, which will enable him to make a success in the poultry pursuit...Mrs. David Buford, who is in St. Louis where she underwent a very technical operation, is reported doing nicely...Miss Bernice Hunt, of St. Louis, is the guest of her sister, Miss Bessie Hunt...Rev. H.C. Bell, of Ironton [Iron Co., Mo.], and

Rev. A.L. Woolfork [sic], of Fredericktown, are assisting in the anniversary of the M.E. Church. Rev. Reynolds is proving himself a very energetic, successful pastor. Hear his theological sermons…A very successful entertainment was given for the benefit of the A.M.E. Church, Friay, at the Greenville residence of Mr. and Mrs. Lewis Kennedy…Arlin Staten is yet quite ill…Miss Helen Matthias is a new subscriber to the Argus."

08 October 1915, pg. 3, col. 1-2.
"Great enthusiasm reigned at St. Paul from September 30 to October 3, at which time Rev. Reynolds and congregation were celebrating the forty-sixty anniversary of the church. This special occasion brought large audiences each evening. It was one of the most sociable affairs ever witnessed in our city. Thursday evening Rev. T.L. Watson delivered an able address, paying homage to the aged ones. Friday evening, Rev. Bailey preached a sermon on "The Duty of Man to the Church." Saturday evening, Rev. A.L. Woolfolk, of Fredericktown, interested a large audience on the thought of "Sacrifice." At the baby contest, little Gladys Meyers won the prize. At the guessing contest the successful ones were Misses Berdola Boddie, Alice Cayce and Madine [sic] Baker. The church was gorgeously decorated and the needle craft displayed was said to be one of rare showing. At the services Sunday morning two additions were made. The captains were Mesdames Thos. Cayce, Lewis Murphy and Gen. George Evans. Much credit is due these faithful ones. Rev. Reynolds, the able pastor, preached the closing sermon Sunday evening. Miss D.F. Baker read resolutions on behalf of the church. The total receipts of the meeting were $65.66, Mrs. Cayce being the star captain…On her return to St. Louis, Miss Katheryn Drew was accompanied as far as Bonne Terre by her grandmother, Mrs. Geo. Blackwell…Miss Charlotte Valle says Dame Rumor pronounced her marriage a bit too soon…Mrs. T.L. Watson conducted a masquerade of juniors Friday evening at which time the grown-ups as well as the little ones had mirth galore…Little Roberta Lynn Kennedy had the misfortune to have her foot smashed with an iron, from which she is recovering rapidly…Miss Sophia Mudd is enjoying the fall festivities in St. Louis this week…Mr. Lewis Murphy spend Sunday with home folks…We are sorry to hear that Mr. S. Alexander is not improving very rapidly…Master Lester Wilburn has gone to Eads to make his home with Mrs. Laura Valle…One month of school has passed. The enrolled have reached eighty. There are a few yet who are due to enroll in the higher grades…Parents, it is in your interest and to their future welfare, if even at a sacrifice to have them enroll and not only enroll, but to attend regularly…For a boy or girl to be mentally diseased in this day means some time had been abused, some hours carelessly spent. See to it that their failure to succeed does not condemn you in the least."

15 October 1915, pg. 3, col. 4.
"Sunday afternoon at three o'clock, Mr. Chas. Baker gave a brief history of
St. Paul M.E. Church, for the past two score years. It was a newsy budget
and heartily received...Mesdames S.O. Wilkins, F.D. Baker, Elizabeth Cole,
and Mr. Rossie Madison, enjoyed the St. Louis festivities last week...A large
number of persons attended the rhetorical exercises of Room No. 1, Douglass School, Friday. Interesting remarks were made by Miss Helen Matthews,
Mr. P.M. Cayce, and Prof. J.C. Staten...Quite a number of persons attended
the funeral of Mrs. Charles Swink, at Minnith [Ste. Genevieve Co., Mo.],
Wednesday...The Clever Bees were delightfully entertained at the residence
of Mrs. Chas. Baker, Monday evening...Mrs. Lewis Kennedy is quite ill at
her home at Greenville...Rev. A.L. Reynolds and congregation assembled
with Rev. Watson and congregation Sunday afternoon, to assist the latter in
the completion of his Conference year's work. Rev. Watson has had a successful year and he and his wife have a host of friends as the result of their
unassuming dispositions...The residence of Mr. and Mrs. Otis Vaughn, of
Potosi, was completely destroyed by fire Thursday...Mr. Samuel Burke spent
Sunday at Ste. Genevieve visiting old friends...Rev. Reynolds and congregation are engaged in a protracted effort to save souls...Rev. Watson and wife
and Mrs. Henrie are spending the week attending the annual Conference at
St. Paul Chapel, St. Louis...Farmington is a very prosperous little town for its
size. Very few of the Negroes rent property. They not only own their homes,
but many own cattle, hogs, etc. Few loafers are found. Most of the citizens
have paying jobs. Some have been employed by the same firm for more than
a decade. The county prison seldom has a Negro in it, and to have to arrest
one of our race is a rare occurrence. Living in such a town as this, how can
you do without the Argus?

22 October 1915, pg. 3, col. 4-5.
"Master Samuel Blackwell fell from a wagon Tuesday and injured his left
eye...Mrs. Eric Matthias is recovering rapidly...Mrs. Lewis Murphy spent
Saturday and Sunday at Crystal City...Mr. Henry Amonette took a part of
young folks out nutting last week and a good time was reported...Little Arlan
Staten is quite ill...The B.T. Washington Society of Douglass School rendered
a program Friday....The teacher and ment [sic] enjoyed an outing Friday. The
purpose of the tripe was to examine the beauties of nature produced by the
forest growth. May specimens were brought back....Mrs. Antoine Murphy
has gone to Herculaneum for an indefinite stay....The friends of Mr. Jas.
Matthias were quite surprised to hear of his death, which occurred at his
home at Fredericktown, Tuesday...Mr. Fred Madison has returned from a
trip to Sparta, Ill., Ste. Genevieve, and St. Louis...Beatrice Swink and Ethe-

81

line Cayce had like experiences the past week. Each swallowed a pin...Miss Grace Anthony is making good with her sale of household necessities..[sic] Mrs. Charlotte Clay is improving fast...Mrs. A. Simms will leave the latter part of the month for a trip to Hot Springs...Mr. Wilson Meyers writes interesting letters of his experiences at Honolulu....Much interest is being manifested in the protracted effort at the M.E. Church...Mr. [sic] pupils of Douglss [sic] Primary Depart [sic] Sterling, Alexander has been removed from the hospital to his parents at Curryville [Pike Co., Mo]. His recovery has been slow."

29 October 1915, pg. 3, col. 6 and pg. 6, col. 4.
"Mr. Percy Swink returned Monday from a trip to Mineral Point. "Going again, too," there's a reason...While engaged in athletic sport, P.J. Evans sprained his ankle. He is recovering gradually...Miss Sophia Mudd returned Thursday from a two weeks' visit with relatives in St. Louis...Mrs. Chas. Douthit was the guest of Mrs. L. Murphy Saturday...Mr. Talbert Burns has been quite ill...Mrs. Comfort Staten, of Coffman, attended to business here the first of the week...St. Luke A.M.E. Church feel very cheerful over the gift of Rev[.] Spurlock as their pastor for the ensuing conference year[24]...Mrs. Mabel Harris has the apron you lost. See her and be made happy...Mesdames E.J. Harris and P.M. Reynolds, chaperoned a party of nut gatherers Saturday in Greenville and vicinity...The town boys played Douglass boys a game of rugby Friday. The Douglass boys didn't score. The weather was too warm. Everybody knows that...Mr. Thos. Cayce had a day with home folks this week. He has a star band at Mineral Point. Farmington needs a band as much as the rosebush needs the thorn. Let some enterprising young man start the movement...The remains of Mr. Arthur Murphy were brought here from DeSoto Sunday for burial. More than forty out of town persons came to attend the funeral. There were representatives from De Soto [sic], Valles Mines, St. Louis, Bonne Terre and Coffman. Rev. M.S. Smith, of DeSoto, preached the sermon. He was assisted by Revs. Reynolds, Spurlock, and Watson. Goodwill Lodge No. 99 had charge of the remains. Besides a wife he leaves many other relatives and a concourse of friends. Little Miss Hilda Kennedy accompanied Mrs. Murphy home. Mr. Chas. Baker had business in St. Louis Sunday... Mrs. J.H. Noland, of St. Louis, is the guest of Miss Dayse Baker...Today ends two months of school work. A number of pupils need to be congratulated. They were neither tardy nor absent. The primary room issued twenty-one certificates and the secondary room issued nineteen. The attendance is good, but it can be better. Patrons are urged to help make it better."

05 November 1915, pg. 3, col. 6, pg. 6, col. 4.

"Rev. A[.]L[.] Reynolds is enjoying a vacation to points in the northern parts of the state...Miss Gracie Anthony has extended her agency to Fredericktown, where she is meeting with success...After a pleasant visit with friends of this city, Mrs. Jordan, Mrs. Jos. Jordan and Mrs. Moore, of Charleston, returned home Friday. They were also the guests of Mrs. Lewis Kennedy, of Greenville and Mrs. Chas. Douthit, of Coffman...Mrs. Fred Chappelle and daughter were the week's end guests and [sic] Mrs. David Buford. The latter is gradually recovering...Douglass faculty and students felt at home with Miss Ruth B. Davis and Miss Alice McGee, of Bonne Terre all day visitors Friday. Mesdames Jas. Robinson, Felix Poston and S.A. Smith were present during the afternoon...Sunday afternoon is rally day for St. Paul Sabbath School... Mr. Ulysses Robinson, of Poplar Bluff, had an old time handshaking and "howdy do" with home folks Saturday...Mr. Jno. Cayce is suffering from a wound of the left hand. He is doing very little meat-chopping these days... Mrs. Lewis Murphy enjoyed Sunday with home folks...Mrs. Edna Kemp, Miss Corinne McFaddin, and Miss Lulu Colwell, of Fredericktown, were the guests of Mrs. S.A. Smith last week...Miss Dayse F. Baker had a pleasant hour or so with friends in Bonne Terre Saturday...After a pleasant week in Farmington, Mrs. J.H. Noland left for DeSoto Monday to be the guest of Mrs. Alice Murphy...November has come, Thanksgiving is coming, Christmas will be here sure, but the money you owe for "The Argus" is yet to be collected. The reporter is coming your way soon. We hope you'll be at home."

12 November 1915, pg. 3, col. 3-4.
"Mr. Wesley Douthit is spending a pleasant week with home folks...St. Paul observed rally day at the church Sunday afternoon. The speakers of the evening were Rev. Spurlock, Prof. Staten, Madam Hunt and Rev. A.L. Reynolds. The little folks were in splendid regalia for the occasion...Little Misses Zanada Cayce and Nadine Baker were the collectors...Rev. Spurlock and congregation are preparing a contest entertainment for Thanksgiving. The captains are Mrs. Jno. Franks and Mr. Moses Hunt...Master Floyd Kennedy, Mrs. Wm. Kennedy, Misses Cora Meyers, Mable Meyers and Lorene Staten attended an old time fish fry at Coffman Friday evening. They had fish galore... Rev. Reynolds described his trip as being very enjoyable...Queen of Honor Court was hostess to Madam Stevens, G.M.A. at which time Mrs. Stevens delivered a splendid address. While here she was at home with Mrs. Felix Poston...Messrs. Jas. Robinson, Eric Matthias, Ulysses Robinson and Mrs. Susie Robinson had a pleasant day at Coffman...Miss Frankie Maul and Mrs. L.T. Robinson, of Bonne Terre, were the guests of Mrs. Jas. Franks Sunday... Mr. B.J. Wilkins is here this week making merry with his many friends... Little Alberta Cayce accompanied her uncle, Mr. Philip Thornton home

from St. Louis...Mrs. Antoine Murphy had a few days of business in our city last week...Mrs. Lewis Murphy will extend the Poro system into Festus. She will succeed Mrs. Geo. Robinson, who will hereafter be employed at Bonne Terre...Miss Mattie Valle has returned from St. Louis, giving a glowing account of her pleasure there. To our surprise she came back "Miss Valle"...The coming of the Argus to the homes of the Farmington people is looked forth to with joy. It is an interesting paper. When it fails to come there is a feeling of loneliness in the home, which nothing but its advent will eradicate. Do many visitors come on that day?"

19 November 1915, pg. 3, col. 4-6.
"Mrs. A. Simms writes from Hot Springs that the trip there is quite beneficial...Mr. Arvilla Wilkins and wife are enjoying a pleasant week with their mother, Mrs. S.O. Wilkins...Farmington delights in the intellectual activity of its young people. Miss Corinne Wilkins will soon assume the work of teaching in the Coffman vicinity...Mrs. P. Boddie has been quite ill[.] James Cayce, Alice Cayce, and Etheline Cayce were absent this week from school from physical inability...Mrs. Jerry Bridges was the guest of Mrs. Jas. Cunningham Sunday...The debate at the school room, Friday, was well attended by patrons and friends. The judges, Revs Reynolds and Spurlock and Miss Bessie Hunt, decided in favor of the girls by nine points. The discussion was, "Resolved, That a boy needs a higher education more than a girl." The girls represented the negative. The boys, however, stayed on the firing line...Mrs. Lewis Smith and sons have gone to St. Louis for the winter...Mrs. Talbert Burns enjoyed a pleasant trip to Coffman last week...Jack has really come to stay. Mercury tells it all...Master Scott Hunt is able to be at school again. We are glad to state that Little Arlin Staten is recovering...Rev. Reynold [sic] has organized a Research Club with the young people, which bids fair to cause them to read more anxiously than ever...News reached Mr. Eric Matthias that his brother Burrill has taken unto himself a companion. Three cheers for him! Mr. and Mrs. Lewis Kennedy, of Greenville. [sic] were the guests of the their daughter, Mrs. P.J. Evans, Sunday...Mrs. and Mrs. Edward Harris entertained some young people Sunday afternoon. Delicious refreshments were served...Thanksgiving day services will be observed by both churches. If life is spared you, take time that day to be holy lest the next one finds you elsewhere. Give honor and praise to Christ your God...Dr. F.S. Bowles will be present Sunday at the M.E. Church to conduct quarterly meeting. Rev. Spurlock will preach the sacramental sermon...We deeply regretted to hear of the death of Mr. Sterling Alexander, which occurred Sunday morning at Curryville. His mother, Mrs. Rev. Guyton, has the community's sympathy."

26 November 1915, pg. 3, col. 4.

"At Douglass School at noon Wednesday memorial services were held for our deceased hero, Booker T. Washington, with Miss Dayse Baker presiding. The portrait of this noble man was properly draped and it seemed for a period of time that even the air about was filled with solemnity. The student body sang appropriate selections. The speakers were Revs. Spurlock and Reynolds, Mr. Chas. Baker and Mr. P.M. Cayce. Mr. Samuel Burke and Miss Sophia Mudd assisted in the musical selections. Though dead we feel that he will ever live in our hearts for his great and wonderful deeds. Another epoch is added to Negro History...Miss Bessie Hunt is the guest of her brother, Leroy Hunt, of St. Louis...Mrs. Jno. Franks entertained Miss Frankie Jenkins, of Minnith, Saturday and Sunday...Mr. Benjamin Chappel, Orville Chappel and Misses Ida and Mildred Chappel attended a birthday dinner Friday which was prepared by Mr. and Mrs. Wesley Douthit in honor of their son, Mr. Wesley Douthit, Jr.[25]...Mr. Douthit returned to St. Louis Sunday...Miss Dayse Baker was relieved from duty Thursday and Friday and was given a chance to visit the schools of St. Louis. Miss Baker feels greatly benefited through such an opportunity. The teachers spoke very commendably of Vera Brooks, Wm. Wright and Booker T. Baker, ex-students of Farmington...The "Work and Win Club" had a successful concert at the A.M.E. Church Friday night."

03 December 1915, pg. 6, col. 3.

"Mrs. Fred Chappelle and daughters, of Coffman, enjoyed Thanksgiving with Mrs. D. Buford...Miss Imogene Staten was the guest of Miss Mabel Meyers, Thursday...Master Booker Baker returned to St. Louis Sunday, after spending a few days with relatives and friends...Miss Edith Cayce came home from Mineral Point where she is having a successful term's work. She spent Thanksgiving Day with home folks...The concert, given at the M.E. Church, Thursday night, was largely attended...Master J.P. Boddie entertained Master Freddie Franks the latter part of the week...Misses Berdola Boddie, Cosetta Boddie and Leslie Poston entertained for Master Booker Baker Saturday evening...Mrs. Jane Baker was hostess to Mr. and Mrs. Chas. Baker and family and Miss Edith Cayce at a five o'clock tea, Saturday...At the rally at the A.M.E. Church Sunday, Rev. Reynolds preached the afternoon sermon. Mr. Moses Hunt, captain of Work and Win Club, carried the competitive honors...The Research Club, with Mrs. P.J. Evans, is having interesting times... Rev. Spurlock entertained Revs. Baker and Oakes last week. Rev. Spurlock left for St. Louis, Monday, to accompany Mrs. Spurlock home...Miss Virgia Cayce had a pleasant visit with friends at Mineral Point and Potosi this week...Mrs. Robt. Simpson, of Chicago, is the guest of Mrs. Lewis Murphy, her mother...Mrs. Lou Long, of Herculaneum, spent the first of the week with her parents, Mr. and Mrs. Wm. McCallister...Farmington has quite a number of subscribers to the Argus and some few have decided to give the Argus as a Christmas present to their friends. It would be a present that would not have to be laid away for lack of an opportunity to use. So many times we give gifts for which the receiver never finds a use. You need not be in doubt when you give the Argus as a gift. It can always be used and well used."

10 December 1915, pg. 2, col. 2-3.
"Mr. and Mrs. Arvilla Wilkins were united in the bonds of holy matrimony according to Catholic rites by Rev. J.R. Morgan, Friday morning...Rev. Spurlock is rejoicing over the fact that Mrs. Spurlock has returned home...Prof. J.C. Staten and daughter, Miss Bertha, visited the city schools of St. Louis the first of the week...Mrs. Chas. Cayce entertained Mrs. Jos. Franks, of Coffman, last week...Mrs. Lewis Murphy has returned to Crystal City where she expects to spend the winter...Mrs. Chas. Baker entertained the C.B.C.'s Thursday night. The session and service were very enjoyable...Everybody should see "Tommy's Wife," Christmas night under the direction of Miss Cora Meyers...That Mr. P.M. Cayce is an artist is plainly seen by viewing his recently well-painted cottage...Rev. A.L. Reynolds is assisting Rev. Woolfolk this week in a protracted effort at Fredericktown. The "Little Bumpers" of Douglass Primary, defeated the "Middle Bleachers," at football last week. The score was too much to mention. These lads are coming starts for the year 1920. "Takes time."—Mr. and Mrs. Lewis Kennedy entertained quite a number of friends Thursday evening at their residence at Greenville at their twenty-fifty anniversary. The home was beautifully decorated. The gifts received were appropriate for the occasion. A community wishes them another quarter century of successful living."

17 December 1915, pg. 3, col. 1.
"Some years ago the library of Douglass School burned. An attempt is now being made to establish another one. The case has been purchased and the following persons have contributed to it: Mrs. Scott Cole, Mrs. Thos. Cayce, Master Kossuth Baker, Miss Edna Harris, Mrs. E.J. Harris, Mrs. M.P. Cayce and Miss Sue Beeson...Rev J.D. Barksdale held quarterly meeting services at St. Luke's Chapel Sunday...Miss Dayse Baker entertained the Clever Bees Monday night. The work that these ladies are doing is wonderful to see... Dan Cupid has been lurking around again and its arrow struck Farmington. Mr. Lindsey Clay and Miss Bessie Hunt were married in St. Louis and Miss Josephine Bridges and Mr. Lee Roden were also married in St. Louis...Mr. Reuben Taylor of St. Louis is here for recuperation...Mr. Robt. Simpson, of Chicago, is here shaking hands with old friend and relatives...Miss Jennie

Thornton, Mrs. E. Boddie, Mr. Jas. Cayce and Mr. Talbert Burns are among the numbered ill...Miss Corrine Wilkins and Mr. Weyman Chapel were the guests of Mrs. S.O. Wilkins Sunday...Miss Ethel Swink came back to our city Monday accompanied by Mr. Walter Franks...Mrs. Geo. Meyers visited at Crystal City Sunday...Mrs. Thos. Cayce accompanied her daughter, Miss Edith, to St. Louis, Thursday, on a business trip...Mrs. Lewis Kennedy was a pleasant visitor at Douglass School Monday. He expressed himself as being pleased with the work in general...Miss Nelson addressed pupils of Douglass primary Monday afternoon on the subject of thoughtful singing. It was highly appreciated. The pupils have an invitation to sing at the municipal tree."

24 December 1915, pg. 2, col. 4-5.
"Master Kossuth Baker is handling the prospectus of a memorial of Booker T. Washington, our deceased hero. He is having much success...Mr. Robert Simpson is recovering from slight injuries received from falling from a wagon...Mr. Owen Kennedy is able to be out on the streets...Miss Lucy Mooten is among the numbered ill...See "Tommy's Wife," at the Masonic Hall Christmas night. It will afford plenty of mirth and laughter. It will be rendered by local talent...Mrs. Antoine Murphy has returned from Herculaneum where she has had an extended visit with relatives...Miss Minnie Thornton and Mr. Rossie Madison were visitors at school last week...Rev. Baker was the guest of Rev. W.H. Spurlock Friday...Dr. F.D. Bridges is at home from St. Louis, where he has had employment...Mrs. Fred Chappelle is very sick at the residence of her mother, Mrs. Nancie [sic] Buford...Mr. Samuel Burke had business at Bonne Terre last week...Mr. Jas. Robinson, Jr. has quite a display of choice poultry at his home in South Farmington...The little folks of the A.M.E. Church, under the direction of Miss Mae Baker, are preparing to entertain the pulbic [sic] Christmas night...Mrs. Eric Matthias is slowly recovering...Mr. Talbert Burns is now able to be up in his room... With the promise of so many visitors and relatives to visit our city during the Yule-tide, it will be an old time "home coming." Such squalling of geese and quacking of ducks will be heard in this vicinity. A protest meeting of the fowls."

07 January 1916, pg. 3, col. 6; pg. 7, col. 1.
"Mr. Fred Chappelle, of Coffman, visited his wife here Monday. Mrs. Chappelle is ill at the home of her mother, Mrs. D. Buford...Mrs. Rachel Moore has returned from a visit with relatives in St. Louis...The many friends of Mr. Howard Overton were glad to see him on the streets Sunday...Mrs. Tullock and grandson were Christmas day guests at the residence of the former's daughter, Mrs. H. Amonette...Miss Leslie Poston spent the Yuletide as the

guest of Mr. and Mrs. A. Simms of St. Louis...Mrs. Lewis Murphy is making good with Pore products at Festus, Mo...Miss Mae Baker, Mr. Clarence Meyers, Mrs. P.J. Evans, Mr. Peter Swink, Mrs. E.J. Harris are among the numbered ill...Mesdames Brown, Robinson and Reed, of St. Louis, had a pleasant visit at the residence of Mrs. P. Boddie several days of last week... Rev. Reynolds and congregation are completing a successful rally on behalf of the stewards...Mrs. Spurlock entertained the choir with popular amusements Monday evening...Mrs. Felix Poston reports a pleasant visit at S. Louis. Mrs. Jos. Jordan, of Charleston, is attending to business here this week...Messrs. Ernestine Wilkins, Booker Baker, William Nught and P.J. Evans laid aside school duties and spent the holidays at home...The young folks will long remember the evening of merriment spent at the Masonic Hall last Tuesday evening...Mrs. Geo. Blackwell had an enjoyable week at St. Louis...Mrs. Antoine Murphy has been ill with a heavy attack of asthma...The pupils and teachers were quite glad to greet each other after a week of vacation. A few who are victims of la grippe are absent this week...Mrs. P.M. Cayce was hostess to the Clever Bees Monday night. The house was beautifully decorated. On the dining table stood a small pine with Christmas greetings to each club member. The menu consisted of turkey, cranberries, salads and ices. Mr. and Mrs. Cayce delight in entertaining in their beautiful cottage home...Misses Helen, Reba, Irene and Luetta Matthias attended a New Year's festival at Ste. Genevieve...Mrs. Mamie Faulk, of Sidney, Ill., is the guest of her mother, Mrs. P. Swink...Miss Zelma Swink enjoyed a few days in St. Louis...We are glad to know you resolved to quit reading your neighbor's Argus. The reported will send your name in soon and you will have this newsy paper to while away the winter gloom."

14 January 1916, pg. 3, col. 4-5.
"Lack of space makes it impossible to enumerate the ill. In some families all are ill and in others barely enough well to care for the ill. La grippe has fastened its pangs on more than two-thirds of the Colored population and as a result the school and church services are poorly attended. The slogan is: "Have you got the grippe yet?"...Mrs. Geo. Blackwell returned from St. Louis Saturday reporting a pleasant trip...Mr. P.J. Evans returned to Jefferson City Sunday after a fortnight with home folks...Mr. and Mrs. Lewis Kennedy, of Greenville, visited friends here Sunday...Mr. Clarence Meyers is ill with an attack of pneumonia...Mrs. Emma Jones and Mrs. Ada Cayce have turned to another page in the history of their lives by subscribing for the Argus. It is a panacea for la grippe...Mrs. Jos. Jordan is having serious trouble from a wound of the knee which occurred last year. At first it seemed a small matter. She is taking special treatment to try to avoid surgery...Mrs.

Lillian Chappelle recovered sufficiently to return to her home at Coffman... Miss Minnie Thornton writes interesting facts concerning the excellent work being done at Sumner High. Farmington has quite a number of pupils in the several schools of the state...Miss Anna Reynolds and brother, Alonzo, are having a successful term's work at George R. Smith College at Sedalia, Mo... Mrs. Jas. Cayce is rallying from a recent illness...Mr. H.B. Keatts had open doors for Christmas visitors who had splendid times in his "Bachelor Quarters." He's the man for merry times...Rev. A.L. Reynolds and family received a Christmas basket given by the congregation and friends, which contained groceries, drygoods [sic], jewelry and a gift in coins. There were more than two score separate articles. The rally which closed Sunday night amounted of $85.17. Miss Cora Meyers won in the contest. Mrs. P.J. Evans was second. Rev. Reynolds and family declare this the most pleasant week of holiday ever spent since they've been in the ministry...Mrs. Katie Cayce invited the Argus to her home for three months. Others are anticipating doing the same thing."

21 January 1916, pg. 3, col. 2.
"Many have been released from the clutches of la grippe and others are convalescing. A few are just now taking. "There's no use to take a trunk where a grip will hold the articles.".…Mr. and Mrs. Henry Amonette and son, Elmer, attended the funeral of Mr. Harve [sic] Carson [of] Potosi last Tuesday[26]... Skating has been the chief sport for athletes at Douglass School for several days...Principal J.C. Staten has returned to his post of duty after a week's illness...At a "Zoo Conundrum Hour," Sunday afternoon at the residence of Mrs. D.F. Baker the successful contestants were: Misses Zelma Swink, Mattie Valle and Mrs. Mamie Foulk. The ladies are to be commended for their deep thinking. A luncheon was served...The ladies of Farmington have not realized that this is leap year. Let no lady be single when the year comes to a close...Mr. Walter Franks, of Coffman attended to business here Friday... Mrs. Jos. Jordan recovered sufficiently to return to her home in Charleston, Thursday...Rev. Reynolds, and congregation were, [sic] quite glad to be able to render financial aid to a traveler, who, through ill health, found it necessary on entering the town to apply for aid. The young man was thus enabled to pursue his journey to his home in Louisiana. The King's Heralds donated the sum of one dollar and a quarter...Mr. Samuel Burke and Mr. Rossie Madison are now dealing in facts and figures[.] They are preparing for a brighter day."

28 January 1916, pg. 3, col. 1.
    "Mrs. V.E. Williams of Chillicothe, arrived Wednesday to attend to her mother Mrs. Jane Hunt who has been ill for more than a week. Her son, Mr. Oscar Hunt of St. Louis, spent Sunday here.

Mrs. F. Madison had a pleasant visit with Mr. and Mrs. Geo. Maul of Bonneterre [sic], last week.

Mrs. Maggie Burke is rallying from a recent illness.

Miss Mae baker has added her name to the list of subscribers. This is averaging a new one each week.

Miss Florence Taylor made is pleasant at her home for about sixteen people Thursday evening. Dancing was a feature.

Rev. Spurlock and congregation are preparing to celebrate "Allen Day" with appropriate exercises.

Mr. Thos. Cayce had a day with home folks this week.

The Research club had a social at the Church Friday evening. Dainty refreshments were served. An enjoyable time was spent. The Research is being conducted by Rev. Reynolds and Mrs. P.J. Evans.

Mrs. Geo. Meyers has gone to Crystal City for an indefinite stay. She will be greatly missed in our community.

Everything and everybody seem to be taking on new life. The grippe has about made its tour and its victims have been set free.

Mrs. Parnell Cayce and Mrs. Reynolds spent Sunday afternoon at Swink's Settlement the guest of Mr. and Mrs. Jerry Bridges. The former has been quite ill.

It is with deep regret that we learned of the death of Mrs. Prince Maul which occurred at Bonneterre [sic] Thursday.

Mr. T. Craig of Herculaneum had a pleasant visit with relatives here the last of the week.

Messrs. Paul Alexander and Harry Aubuchon of Bonneterre [sic] were the guests of Mr. H.B. Keats Sunday. They made the trip in a Ford."

11 February 1916, pg. 7, col. 4.
"We have all been "dark town swells" since the recent icy season has put the electric lights out of order. It has been a case of "everybody stays at home at night and father stays there, too."…Miss Ethel Swink is recovering from bruises received about the face and arms while busily engaged in cooking. Miss Swink is also a subscriber to the newsy gem, "The Argus"…Mrs. Annie Bridges, Miss Mattie Valley [sic] Mr. David Buford, Mrs. Geo. Evans and Mrs. Jane Hunt are convalescing…We are sorry to know that Mr. Jos. Cunningham, of Festus, is ill with smallpox…Mr. Felix Poston is quite busy doing the work of a horticulturist…Rev. W.H. Spurlock and congregation will observe Allen Day Sunday evening…Rev. Reynolds assisted Rev[.] Reynolds [sic] in his anniversary Saturday and Sunday…Mrs. Geo. Meyers returned from Crystal City Saturday, reporting a splendid visit…Mrs. Sara Amonette had a pleasant visit with relatives at Potosi…Mrs. Anna Yeager returned

Monday to spend the winter with her sister Mr. L. Cayce...Mr. Chas. Baker wont the flag last week that was awarded for running by "cloud-light." He's wearing it...Mrs. Jas. Cunningham was the guest of Mrs. Jerry Bridges at Swink Settlement Sunday afternoon...Messrs. Eric Matthias and Geo. Evans are stunning butchers of great repute. They have ready samples...At the M.E. Church Sunday will be patriotism-awakening time at two o'clock. Hear the gentlemen in their commemoration of Lincoln and our hero B.T. Washington...Masters Arville and Alonza [sic] Kennedy are quite well again...Mrs. Kate Cayce entertained quite a number of young folks Sunday afternoon in honor of her niece, Miss Ada Jones, who has been indisposed for several weeks...Now you surely wouldn't quit taking "The Argus," because the reporter failed to get your visit in the items! Don't blame the editor. Send a statement when you leave or return and we'll be glad to acknowledge it. The reported believes in a "square deal." This is leap year. Put up your hammer "knocking is out of style."

18 February 1916, pg. 3, col. 6; pg. 6, col.
"The cast of characters of the play rendered at the Masonic Hall Friday evening was Messrs. Reuben Taylor, Chas. Cayce, Tillman Cayce, Robert Simpson, Miss Cora Meyers and Miss Mabel Meyers. The mirth experiences by the hearers was something galore. The play was good...Mr. Jos. Robinson, Sr., has returned from a lengthy visit to St. Louis...Miss Hortense Kennedy is rallying from a recent nervous breakdown...Mrs. A. Simms has returned from Hot Springs, feeling quite as though she had been to Ponce de Leon's foundation of youth. Her many friends are glad to know she was so much benefited...Little Misses Frances Harris, Odessa Cayce and Lelia Franks are much improved...Rev. F.S. Bowles, district superintendent, will hold the fourth quarterly conference Saturday evening at the M.E. Church, followed by the quarterly meeting services Sunday...Quite a number of persons attended the program of the sixth and seventh grades of Douglass School Friday afternoon. Nothing is more encouraging to the faculty and pupils than to have frequent visits from patrons and friends...Mr. Moses Hunt is yet confined to his bedroom...Much praise was given to the following participants of the Lincoln Day Program, which was presented Sunday afternoon at the M.E. Church: Messrs. P.M. Cayce, F.D. Bridges and Chas. Baker, Misses Mabel and Cora Meyers, Mrs. J.P. Evans, Principal J.C. Staten and Revs. Spurlock and Reynolds...Mrs. Joseph Carson, of Potosi, is the guest of her mother, Mrs. Thos. Cayce...The "Seven Table Affair" at the A.M.E. Church and the valentine social at the M.E. Church Monday evening were enjoyable gatherings...Mrs. Scott Cole is still indisposed...Mr. James Robinson, Jr., is kept quite busy as a caterer. He is serving the leap year "hops."...Mrs. Geo. Meyers is in receipt

of a communication from her son, Wilson, at tal [sic] murder of one of his solider friends [at] Schofield Barracks, telling of the bru-[sic][27]...Mrs. Abraham Cayce is a recent subscriber to "The Argus." Quit visiting your neighbors so regularly on Argus day and subscribe for your own Argus with your own consent, written by your own pen, paid for with your own money, sit by your own fireside by your own gas light and read your own Argus by your own self and then you'll be right up with all the current news."

25 February 1916, pg. 7, col. 3-4.
"Mr. George Meyers of Crystal City spent Sunday here with his family... The ladies of the A.M.E. Church are busy preparing for the leap year social which will be February 29th. Each lady escorts a gentleman, takes an untrimmed hat and requires the gentleman to trim it to suit his taste...Mrs. Joseph Carson spent a pleasant week with her other, Mrs. Mary Cayce. She returned to Potosi Friday...Miss Corinne Wilkins has just closed a successful term of school at Coffman. Misses Lorinne [sic] Staten, Bernice Hunt, Laura Wilburn, Mrs. David Buford and Mr. Rossie Madison attended the exercises Saturday...Master Clarence Reynolds had the misfortune to bruise his eye while spinning tops. Medical aid rendered him able to resume his studies Monday...Rev. Bowles preached two very interesting sermons Sunday. Rev. W.H. Spurlock preached the sacramental sermon to a large appreciative congregation...Rev. A.L. Reynolds and congregation are very busy trying to finish up the conference year's work...Mrs. Harry Cayce of St. Louis is the guest of her mother, Mrs. P. Boddie...Mr. William Clay is quite ill. His condition is serious...A combined program rendered at Douglass School Monday was very largely attended by patrons and friends. Tuesday was "gala day" for the youngsters...Mr. Samuel Burke has recovered from a recent fall. His mother is yet quite ill...Mrs. Jane Hunt is gradually recovering. Messrs. Abraham Davis and John Madison of Fredericktown were Sunday visitors...Mrs. P.M. Cayce entertained with an evening tea Sunday...Mrs. Scott Cole has recovered sufficiently to resume her household duties...Mrs. Richard Occamore of Sprott was the guest of her mother, Mrs. Maggie Burke, Saturday...Master Kossuth Baker was injured about the ankle with a top. The accident rendered him unable to be at school...Mr. Weyman Chappell of Coffman attended to business here Monday...The Pythians and Calanthians hope to make March 26 a day of joy and thanksgiving...It is an evidence of spring when some folks start to work so we believe spring is near at hand."

03 March 1916, pg. 3, col. 3.
"Messrs. Geo. Williams and Lorenzo Matthias, of Cape Girardeau, attended to business here the first of the week...Master Patrick Cayce was host to

a number of young people Sunday afternoon...Mrs. E.J. Harris is yet indisposed...Mesdames Lucy Bridges and Mazie Lyons of Swink's Settlement, were Farmington visitors Thursday...At the prize contest Tuesday evening at the M.E. Church, the winners were Elbert Baker and Etheline Cayce...Mr. H.B. Keatts is an authority on diet for sick people...The Leap Year Social at the A.M.E. Church Tuesday was an affair of rare enjoyment. "Dem wimmen sho spent dey cash."...Rev. Reynolds and wife, Clarence Reynolds, and Warner Cayce had a pleasant visit with Mrs. Lewis Kennedy Tuesday at Greenville...Mrs. Jane Hunt is preparing to go to St. Louis for the remainder of the winter...Miss Ruth B. Davis found it necessary to consult an oculist while in Farmington Saturday. Conditions were in her favor...Mrs. S.A. Smith, of St. Louis, is attending to business here this week...Mrs. Geo. Meyers went to Crystal City Saturday in answer to a message announcing the illness of her husband...Miss Gracie Anthony is able to be up...Master Clifton Cooper and Le Roy Wilburn received a pleasant surprise Friday from the Busy Bee Class of Douglass Primary...Mr. Wm. Cayce is under the care of a physician...Mrs. Belle Watkins [sic], an aged woman of our community, has recently been informed that the will of the late Mrs. B. Swartz provides for her, that she may be comfortable in her declining days. Would that a few more of the whites would locate their generous spot and get busy![28]...That leap your frolic caused some folks to spark "sho nuff." Didn't mean that! That was just playing like you were courting!"

10 March 1916, pg. 3, col. 2.
"Mrs. Laura Valle, of Coffman, was the guest of her daughter, Miss Mattie Valle, the first of the week...Mr. Samuel Burke is rallying from a recent illness...Mrs. Lewis Murphy is at home for a two weeks' visit...Mrs. Mayers [sic] returned from Crystal City Saturday reporting her husband much improved...The body of the M.E. church with Rev. W.H. Spurlock and congregation as guests will banquet their pastor and family the latter part of the month...Mr. Thomas Cayce and daughter, Miss Edith, spent a pleasant Sunday with home folks...Mrs. Sara Amonett [sic] is quite improved and is able to be out...Miss Ruth B. Davis attended to business here Saturday...Mr. Weyman Chappell was a happy man with friends here Sunday...Mrs. Katie Cayce has recovered sufficiently to resume her work...Mr. Reuben Taylor is having a pleasant visit with his grandmother, Mrs. Geo. Blackwell...Miss Ada Jones, who has been ill for quite a while, enjoyed a pleasant afternoon, Sunday, when a party of young people called at her home for an hour of mirth... Mr. Wm. Cayce has been quite ill at his home in West Farmington...Mrs. Masoleat Hill, of Herculaneum, has had a pleasant visit with her father, Mr. Geo. Blackwell...Mrs. Myrtle Hunt and daughter, of Fredericktown, have

for the past week been the guests of Mrs. Jane Hunt...The many friends of Mr. J.F. Sutherland wish him a speedy recovery...Mrs. Richard Occamore and son, James, were the guests of Mrs. M. Burke last week...Mrs. Hildred Overton left for Brisco, [Lincoln Co.,] Mo., Friday for an indefinite stay... The faculty and pupils of Douglas [sic] school sympathize with Festus in the loss of its school building."

17 March 1916, pg. 7, col. 3.
"Mr. Albert Simms spent a two days [sic] vacation with his wife in their beautiful home on Franklin street...Quite a number attended the funeral of Mrs. Drusila Burns, of Coffman, Sunday. She was the mother of 12 children. Rev. A.L. Reynolds officiated...Quarterly meeting Sunday, March 19th at St. Luke A.M.E. church. You are invited to give your presence...Mr. Bird Wilkins, of St. Louis, was the week end guest of mother and sister... Grandma Fanny Simms is reported much improved. Her friends hope for her a speedy recovery...Rosa [sic] Madison and Miss Ethel Swink were quietly united in the bonds of holy matrimony last week, Rev. Spurlock officiating... Miss Ruth B. Davis spent Saturday and Sunday with Miss D.F. Baker...Mrs. Otis Vaughn, of Potosi, returned to her home Friday from attending the funeral of Mr. Frank Sutherland...Mrs. Wesley Douthit, Miss Grace Anthony and Mr. Samuel Burks are improving rapidly."

24 March 1916, pg. 3, col. 3.
"Mrs. Henry Amonette was the guest of Mrs. Julia Cook, of Bonne Terre Sunday...Mr. Wm. Clay seems to improve very slowly. His illness has been of long duration...Rev. W.H. Spurlock and congregation had a very successful quarterly meeting Sunday. Rev. A.L. Reynolds preached the sacramental sermon...An operation upon the throat of little Miss Iona Harris was quite successful...Miss Grace Anthony is still under the care of a physician...Miss Mary Cunningham, of St. Louis, is the guest of her sister, Miss Alice Meyers...Mr. Samuel Burke is able to be out again. His many friends are glad to see him out...Miss Dayse Baker was the guest of Miss Ruth B. Davis, of Bonne Terre, Saturday and Sunday...Mrs. A.L. Reynolds has quite recovered from a recent illness...Mrs. Wesley Douthit is now convalescent...Mrs. Geo. Meyers went to Crystal City Saturday to be with her husband, who is ill... Mrs. Sara Amonette has returned to her home in West Farmington...Mr. P.M. Cayce has made recent improvement on his place, which adds much to the looks...Uncle Geo. Blackwell, a well known [sic] gentleman of our town, feels himself able to cultivate his own garden. We are glad his health is improved...Mr. and Mrs. Moses Bridges are rejoicing over the arrival of little Harry Lee...Mr. and Mrs. Rossie Madison are residing with the former's

parents…The ladies of Farmington are preparing to give the gentlemen a treat next week. The boxes are going to be worth the while. The gents are anxious to attend."

31 March 1916, pg. 3, col. 3-4.
"Mrs. Alice Murphy, of De Soto,, [sic] was the guest of Mrs. Lewis Kennedy, Sunday…Mr. Alexander Anthony, of St. Louis, had a pleasant week with home folks…Miss Estacada Baker is the guest of Miss Edith Cayce, of Mineral Point…Mr. Henry Renfro, a young man of sterling habits, who is at present employed here, has decided to get in line and read the Argus…Mr. and Mrs. C. Murphy have returned to Crystal City, where the former is employed[.] Miss Ada Jones has spent a very comfortable week. She is a young lady who has given useful service to her church during her health…Miss Dola Boddie feels none the worse since she was hypnotized last Thursday. She is thoroughly convinced that it is possible. Her many friends were quite shakey [sic] until she showed signs of life…Mrs. Anna Yeager, Mr. Augustus Cayce, Little Miss Zelia Franks and Master Theodore Pugh are convalescent. The latter will undergo a slight operation later…Mrs. Jane Hunt accompanied her daughter, Mrs. V.E. Williams as far as St. Louis. Mrs. Hunt's stay there is indefinite…Mrs. Charlotte Clay received a communication informing her of the serious illness of her grandson, Master Lawrence Matthias, of St. Louis… The gallant Pythians and fair Calanthians assembled at the M.E. Church Sunday afternoon in anniversary services. Rev. A.L. Reynolds preached an eloquent sermon. Chancellor Commander Chas. Baker had a very interesting address and Mr. P.M. Cayce remembered the deceased in a very commendable manner. Rev. W.H. Spurlock offered prayer…Grand Chancellor A.W. Lloyd was the guest of Burleigh Lodge Thursday evening. Sir Lloyd has a host of friends in Farmington, who are always glad to see him. Rev. A.L. Reynolds accompanied him to the school where both delivered timely talks to the pupils."

07 April 1916, pg. 7, col. 3.
"Indeed and in truth the box social which was given by the ladies of the M.E. Church Thursday evening was one of the most enjoyable affairs ever witnessed in this place. Rev. Spurlock and wife with quite a number of their members joined in and helped to make it such. The church was beautifully decorated and more than eighty persons were served. Rev. Reynolds and family enjoyed it immensely. It was given to pay homage to them…Sunday afternoon Rev. Spurlock preached an able sermon and the rally of a fortnight closed with a total of $98.22…Rev. Reynolds left for conference Monday feeling this conference year was a glorious one to all concerned…Mrs. Margaret Glover,

of Fredericktown, was the guest of Mrs. E. Harris Saturday and Sunday. She accompanied Mrs. Scott Cole and Master Kossuth Baker to St. Louis Monday...Mr. Samuel Burke has recovered sufficiently to resume his usual vocation...Miss Alcesta Douthit, of Coffman, has come to our town for an indefinite period...The pupils of Douglass school and faculty, deeply regret the passing away of Master Laurence Matthias, whose remains were brought here from St. Louis the first of the week[29]...Miss Mabel Meyers spent Sunday in Crystal City, the guest of her mother, who while there on a visit was taken ill. She is convalescent...After a long visit with relatives in St. Louis, Mrs. Eliza Overton has returned. We are glad to know her eyesight is improved...Miss Edith Cayce has returned from Mineral Point, where she has just closed a successful term of school...Mr. Percy Swink met with a painful accident while splitting kindling. A piece of it struck him over the right eye, thus causing him to have medical attention...Mrs. Lucy Bridges is attending conference at St. Louis, this week...Mrs. Beulah Cayce has arrived from Charleston, where she has been the guest of her aunt, Mrs. Joseph Jordan."

14 April 1916, pg. 3, col. 3-4.
"Ill health has caused Miss Minnie Thornton to give up her studies at Sumner High School and come home for recreation. Miss Thornton is a young lady of rare ambition and her many friends regret the happening...Rev. A.L. Reynolds met a hearty welcome on his return to St. Paul for another conference year. Rev. Reynolds took a report to the conference that was the record breaker for Farmington. His smiles are broader than ever...The many friends of Mr. Wm. Clay regret that he is declining to rapidly. His aged mother has the community's sympathy. His sister, Mrs. A. Villars, returned to her home in St. Louis Monday...Mr. Ben. Chappelle, of Coffman, attended the lodge here Thursday...The Senior Choir of St. Paul rendered a very interesting program Sunday night...Mr. Owen Kennedy is able to be out on the streets... Gardening seems to be the chief pursuit of industry in our immediate vicinity. We are glad the change of season brought change of industry, as battling with la grippe was the past season's hobby...Mrs. Antoine Murphy is at home for an indefinite period of time...Miss Mabel Meyers went to Crystal City Thursday and accompanied her mother home...Mrs. Willa Davis, of Cape Girardeau, is the guest of her parents, Mr. and Mrs. Wm. Cayce...Douglas [sic] faculty has been re-elected for the school term 1916-1917. In view of the fact that they were re-elected without application, it was an agreeable surprise...Miss Hortense Kennedy, of Greenville, is among the ill of the week...Mr. P.L. Pratt, of Cameron, [Clinton and DeKalb Co.'s,] Mo., Grand Lecturer of the Masonic Lodge of Missouri and jurisdiction, was the guest of Goodwill Lodge No. 99, Tuesday evening. The gentlemen were well

entertained by him."

21 April 1916, pg. 7, col. 3.

"Mr. John Douthit enjoyed an auto trip to St. Louis, Saturday...Mrs. Maria Staten, of Coffman, was the guest of Mrs. Talbert Burns Friday...Mr. John Baker, and Miss Mae Baker attended the funeral of Mrs. H. Fulton at Bonne Terre, Friday...Queen of Honor Court observed Palm Sunday with appropriate services. At the election of officers Mrs. W.I. Roberts was re-elected matron. Rev. W.H. Spurlock attended to business in St. Louis last week...Rev. Reynolds and congregation observed Passion Week with nightly services... Mrs. Tulleck [sic] and grandson, and Miss Maud Cooley, of Ironton, were the guests of Mrs. Henry Amonette Sunday...Douglass School observed Arbor Day with appropriate exercises and quite a number of patrons and friends were in attendance...Miss Gracie Anthony was able to be about in the neighborhood last week...Mrs. Geo. Meyers has about recovered...Master Inman Evans certainly was a happy youngster when he celebrated his third birthday Saturday afternoon at the residence of his grandparents, Mr. and Mrs. Geo. Evans. Quite a number of lads and lassies took tea with him...Miss Ada Jones is somewhat improved since the sunny days have come...Miss Etta Jordan has returned to her home in Charleston, but she says Farmington is the town for a pleasant sojourn...Miss Laura Amonette, of St. Louis, is the guest of home folks...Mr. Reuben Taylor has returned to abide with his grandparents, Mr. and Mrs. Geo. Blackwell...Prin. J.C. Staten was physically unable to teach Monday."

28 April 1916, pg. 3, col. 3-4.

"Mr. Wm. Wright, of St. Louis, enjoyed Easter with homefolks. Messrs. Geo. Evans and Chas. Cayce put the G in granitoid at the residence of Mr. Chas. Baker...Messrs. Albert Simms and B.J. Wilkins enjoyed a pleasant sojourn with homefolks the first of the week. Both of the young men delivered short addresses at the M.E. Church Sunday evening...Mr. and Mrs. D. Buford and daughter were the guests of Mr. and Mrs. Fred Chappelle, of Coffman, Sunday...We are quite in sympathy with Mrs. M. Burke, who has lost the sight of her left eye...Mr. Weyman Chappelle and Miss Ida Chappelle, of Avon, were the guests of Mrs. Wesley Douthit, Sunday...Easter was properly observed at both churches Sunday evening...Mrs. Laura South, of St. Louis, is visiting her sister, Mrs. Abraham Cayce...Little Miss Alice Hazel Glendora Baker found a welcome at the residence of Mr. and Mrs. Chas. Baker last Thursday...Mrs. Sara McMinn, of Festus, has returned to her home after enjoying a pleasant visit with Mr. and Mrs. Scott Cole[30]...Mrs. Susie Wilkins was given a pleasant surprise at the coming from St. Louis of her son, Mr. Arville

Wilkins, who remained over a few days...The friends of Mrs. Eliza Overton are sorry to know that her eyesight is failing her so fast...Mr. Lindsay Clay and sister, Mrs. Julia Burke, of St. Louis, had the sad occasion last week of attending the funeral of their brother, Mr. Wm. Clay...Mr. W. Somerville, of St. Louis, came down Saturday and remained over until Monday. He was accompanied home by his friend, Miss Laura Amonette, who had been visiting here for quite a week...Mrs. P. Boddie is rallying from a recent illness...Mr. Jas. Robinson has made some very extended trips in his Tin Lizzie. Mr. John Douthit enjoyed another auto trip to St. Louis Sunday. He reports such trips quite air-sufficient...The reported is quite sorry that you are suffering from the disease of forgetfulness. This is April, the month your subscription is due. Some subscribers say: "I am sure to see my neighbor on Argus Day." I am sure they come to see how I am today. Believe it!"

05 May 1916, pg. 3, col. 2.
"Miss Alice Swink has returned from St. Louis, where she has been specializing in music. Miss Swink has rare musical talent...Before Rev. W.H. Spurlock and wife left for Philadelphia they were socially entertained by the members of their church...The many friends of Master Frank Drew are delighted to know that he has found employment at Uniontown, [Fayette Co.,] Pa...Mr. Fred Chappelle and family enjoyed a pleasant week end with Mr. and Mrs. D. Buford...Miss Alcesta Douthit has returned to Coffman...Mr. Samuel Burke attended to business in Bonne Terre, Tuesday...Hilda, Opal, Floyd and Ina Kennedy had a pleasant visit with their aunt, Mrs. A. Murphy, of De Soto... The friends of Mrs. Wesly [sic] Douthit are sorry to know that she improves so slowly...Mr. Chas. Baker attended to business in St. Louis last week... Little Anna Pugh, Cornelia Franks and Laurie Boddie were indisposed and absent from school last week...Messrs. Lewis Murphy and Geo. Meyers returned to Crystal City Sunday...The Farmington Giants will have the first event of baseball contact at the Masonic Hall May 11. Their uniforms will be "classy hue"...Miss Hortense Kennedy is quite ill at the home of her aunt, Mrs. J. Boddie...Mrs. A Cayce is quite ill at her home in West Farmington... Mr. B.J. Wilkins has returned to St. Louis."

12 May 1916, pg. 3, col. 1.
"Messrs. Jas. Robinson, Lewis Smith, [illegible] Matthais [sic] and John Douthit toured Ste. Genevieve Sunday afternoon [whe]re they had a pleasant time with [illegible] friends...Miss H. Kennedy is [rap]idly recovering...Miss Mattie Valle [ha]d a pleasant week with relatives at [???]ds, Mo...Mr. Thos. Cayce enjoyed [a] pleasant Sunday with home folks...[M]rs. Mazie Lyons, of Swink's Settle[me]nt, attended services here Sunday...There are five more

days of school. [M]any have registered on the visiting [???]t and a few will probably do so yet...Mr. and Mrs. John Franks and [da]ughter, Zelia, and their niece, Anna [Pu]gh, have been quite ill for a week...Mrs. Fannie Simms, the oldest [cit]izen of our community peacefully [pas]sed away Sunday afternoon, after [an] illness of many weeks. She was a [wo]man of chaste habits and during her [?]tivity was a very helpful woman to [tho]se who needed aid. Her passing [a]way serves to remind us that it pays [to] live so that when the last hour [co]mes we need have no fear to cross [th]e River of Death...Mrs. Minnie [C]ayce improves slowly...Miss Grace Anthony is quite pleased to have her many friends visit with her during her ill[n]ess...Miss Ada Jones received quite [a] number of callers last week and was [th]ereby much relieved...In a debate [at] Douglass School Friday, Resolved: "That girls are more useful to their [p]arents than boys," the affirmative [w]on. In a debate Monday, Resolved: "That cats make better pets than [d]ogs," affirmative won. The neg[at]ives stayed on the firing line...Mr. [C.?] Staten, of Coffman, had a few days [o]f business in Farmington...Mr. Rossie Madison spent a day of last [w]eek in Bonne Terre...Messrs. Henry Fulton and Samuel Townsend of Bonne Terre, spent a few hours here Sunday...Mrs. O. Smith has returned from a pleasant visit at De Soto...Mrs. Josephine Roden is visiting in Southland, [Phillips Co.,] Ark., the home of Mr. Roden...Master Leonard Cayce and little Frances Harris have been with the number ill...A few more risin's [sic] and settin's [sic] of the sun and then the Farmington Giants will measure the corners of the diamond with some team somewhere."

19 May 1916, pg. 3, col. 5-6.
"The funeral services of Mrs. Fannie Simms were held Tuesday afternoon with Rev. A.L. Reynolds officiating. Those attending from out of town were: Mr. Albert Simms, Mrs. Gertrude Oliver, Mrs. Etta Davis, of St. Louis, and Miss Jewel Cable, of Chillicothe...Mr. F. Madison spent Sunday in Bonne Terre visiting his sisters, Mesdames Geo. Maul and Mary Taylor, who were ill... Mrs. Mayme Foulk and sister, Beatrice, also Master Sumner Swink, were the guests of Mrs. Joseph Bartholomew, the first of the week...Mrs. Allie Swink, of Minnith, was the guest of Mrs. Chas. Cayce the past week...Mrs. Fred Chappelle, of Coffman, has recovered sufficiently to return to her home...Mr. Alonzo Reynolds and sister, Miss Anna, have returned from Sedalia, where they been pursuing a course at Geo. R. Smith College...The many friends of Mr. Everett Abernathy are glad to know he will complete the college course next year...Mrs. Chas. Douthit, of Coffman, visited relatives here last week. She was accompanied by her son, Roy...The ill are Mrs. Felix Poston, Miss Cossetta Boddie, and Mrs. Eliza Overton...Messrs. Samuel Burke, Luther Wilburn and Master LeRoy Wilburn enjoyed a pleasant trip to Festus Sat-

urday...Misses Jewel Cable, Zelma and Alice Swink, Helen Matthias and Mrs. E.J. Harris were entertained at the home of Miss D.F. Baker Sunday afternoon...Masters Oscar Hunt and Sumner Swink, of the primary room of Douglass, received certificates for perfect attendance...Mr. P.M. Cayce has made quite a deal of improvement on his place in the last week...

> "Lives of great men all remind us,
> We can made [sic] our lives sublime
> And in paying for the Argus
> We can read it all the time."

26 May 1916, pg. 3, col. 3-4.

"Miss Edith Cayce attended to business at Mineral Point last week...Misses Ruth B. Davis, and Susie Waide, of Springfield, Ill., and Miss Lora Robinson, and Mr. Paul Alexander, of Bonne Terre, autoed over from the latter place Sunday and enjoyed the afternoon with friends...Mr. Scott Cole is the guest of his brother, Mr. Cornelius Cole, of St. Louis, who is indisposed... Indeed Douglass School had a quiet closing. The entertainment was postponed indefinitely. Everybody was afraid of the "man and the yellow flag"... Rev. Reynolds and wife, Miss Anna Reynolds, Mr. Alonzo Reynolds, Miss Cora Meyers, ands Mrs. James Cunningham were entertained at Oak Grove Friday, the guests of Mrs. Jerry Bridges...Mrs. Mayme Foulk visited relatives at Coffman last week...Mr. Wm. Cayce is at home for a short stay...Mrs. Emma Sommers has gone to St. Louis to reside...Master Inman Evans spent the week's end with his mother, Mrs. J.P. Evans...Mr. Lewis Murphy returned to Crystal City Monday...Miss Jewel Cable returned to Chillicothe Friday. Miss Cable is a young lady possessing a pleasant disposition and has many friends in Farmington[31]...If the Farmington Giants' suits don't fit it won't be because they did not get measured. The heaviest weight has the most suit... Mrs. Mazie Lyons, of Oak Grove, entertained with a dinner Sunday. The guests commended the well prepared menu...J.E. Bridges, of Lincoln Institute, writes of a successful year's work and commends the faculty very highly. Young Bridges is a lad who is pushing to the front despite difficulties...Mr. Samuel Burke had a pleasant trip to Ste. Genevieve one day last week...Miss Beatrice Swink is recovering from an electrical shock received while visiting Fredericktown...Mrs. P.M. Cayce was hostess to the Socialists last Monday night.

> "Let us then be up and doing
> With a heart for any fate;
> Just keeping reading our own Argus,
> Tell your neighbor he'll have to wait."

02 June 1916, pg. 3, col. 2-4.

"Miss Helen Mathias [sic] was hostess to a number of ladies Sunday afternoon in honor of Mr. Mayme Foulk...Messrs. Columbus Staten and T. Bias, of Fredericktown were visitors here Friday...Rev. and Mrs. W.H. Spurlock have returned from a pleasant trip to Philadelphia, and other points...The families of Mr. Jno. Franks, Mrs. R. Harris and Mr. Felix Poston have banished the yellow flag...Mrs. Harry Cayce enjoyed a visit from her husband Sunday. Mr. Cayce returned to St. Louis Monday...The Farmington Giants are kept busy answering challenges for games. Better practice, you who come to play these stars...from [sic] a recent purchase, Mr. and Mrs. Geo. Evans have made their cottage home quite farm-like...After a lengthy visit with home folks, Mrs. Mamie Foulk returned to her home in Sidney, Ill...The friends of Miss Cossetta Boddie are glad to know she is rapidly improving... The friends of Mrs. W.H. Davis are sorry to learn of her recent illness...The Stewardess Board entertained socially at the M.E. Church Friday night...Mr. James Cayce is the man that put "F" in fish...Mr. Scott Cole has made modern improvements on his home in East Farmington...Messrs. W. Chapell and R. Staten were visitors here Saturday...Mr. Peter Swink had a narrow escape from a broken neck, when he slipped from a load of brick and received only slight injuries...After nine months of hard teaching, Miss Dayse F. Baker departed Saturday for Los Angeles, Cal. Before returning home she expects to visit in Springfield, Jefferson City, and many other points. We know Miss Baker needs rest and hope for her a pleasant vacation...Mr. Reuben Staten left for St. Louis to visit his home folks."

09 June 1916, pg. 3, col. 1.

"Prof. John Staten is indisposed...Messrs. Ed. Harris, Henry Booker, Ed. Alexander of Bonne Terre, Mr. R. Staten, and Chas. Douthit, of Coffman, were visitors of the K. of P. lodge Thursday...The stork visited Mr. and Mrs. Robert Simpson, Friday morning, and left a fine boy...Mrs. Will Davis, of Cape Girardeau, is home for a short visit...Messrs. Oran Poston, A.L. Reynolds, and son had a pleasant trip to the river Friday. They had fishermen's luck... After a successful year at Lincoln Institute, Mr. James P. Evans returned home Saturday to spend the summer...Miss Berdola Boddie is visiting her cousin, Miss Alcesta Douthit, of Coffman...Hurrah! The Giants will play their first game of ball Wednesday...Mr. and Mrs. Abe Cayce returned home from Festus, where they have been visiting a few days...Miss Bernice Hunt is convalescing...Mr. and Mrs. Scott Cole were called to Potosi to the beside of their aunt, Mrs. Rachel Bryant."

16 June 1916, pg. 3, col. 2.

"Mrs. J.P. Evans and Mrs. Bessie Clay of St. Louis, are visiting their sister, Miss Bernice Hunt...Fredericktown vs. Farmington, played an excellent game of baseball, last Wednesday. Score 8 to 0, favor of Farmington. Mr. Elmer Bridges has returned from Lincoln Institute with a greater determination to reach higher grounds...Misses E.O. Cayce, Cora Meyers and children of the M.E. Church rendered an excellent program, Children's Day. Mrs. J.S. Evans entertained the Social Engineer Club, Monday evening...Miss Augustine Swink was a visitor here the first of the week...Miss Grace Anthony and Miss Ada Jones are doing nicely...Mr. Talbert Burns has returned from Coffman, Mo. He was accompanied by his brother, Mr. Walter Franks...Miss Alcesta Douthit is visiting her cousin, Cossetta Boddie...Miss Essie Mayfield, of Minnith, is visiting her aunt, Mrs. Augusta Cayce...Mr. Frank Lewis, of St. Mary's Mo., is visiting here."

23 June 1916, pg. 3, col. 2.

"Mrs. Estella Robert and son are visiting friends in Indiana...Mrs. Eliza Overton, Emma Boddie and Miss Corsetta [sic] Boddie are attending the A.M.E. Sunday-school convention at Charleston, Mo., this week...Mrs. Booker Baker and Mr. Williams Wright have returned from Charleston, where they have been attending school...Mr. Chas. Cayce is employed at Bonne Terre...Miss Alcie [sic] Swink entertained a number of friends in honor of her cousin, Miss Augustine Swink, last Monday evening...The Old Folks concert, given by the members of the M.E. Church, was quite a success...Rev. and Mrs. Spurlock gave a banquet for the A.M.E. Church choir, last Tuesday...Mrs. Lula Maule passed through this city enroute to Charleston, Mo...The sight of the Argus will cure the worst of sore eyes. It behooves us all to subscribe."

30 June 1916, pg. 3, col. 1.

"Mrs. Bolduke, of Festus, Mo., was the guest of her sister, Mrs. L. Anthony a few days ago...Miss Lillie Swink passed through this city a few days ago en route to Coffman, Mo., her home...Mesdames Leo Lewis and Sylvester Swink of St. Mary's, Mo., were visitors here last week...Mrs. Nancy Buford and her daughter, Miss Laura, have returned after a pleasant visit at Coffman with her daughter, Mrs. Fred Chappell...The Allies and Germans are struggling hard for the great rally day at the M.E. Church, the second Sunday in July. The Germans will win without ammunition. Mesdames Ada Cayce and Nellie Evans are the captains...The Giants played St. [sic] Genevieve last Sunday and won. The score was 10 to 1. Who's next...Mrs. Lewis Kennedy was hostess to a number of friends last Friday night...Miss Cora Meyers spent last Thursday at Oak Grove...Prof. J.C. Staten is a little indisposed at this writing...Mrs. Laura Valley [sic] passed through this city last week."

21 July 1916, pg. 3, col. 1.
"Miss Dayse F. Baker, who has been taking a special course at a beauty parlor in St. Louis for a few weeks, was home Friday on a business trip. She returned to the city Monday morning...Mr. Luther Valley [sic], of Coffman, was a Farmington visitor...The Farmington Giants and St. [sic] Genevieve Rustics played an interesting game of base ball [sic] Friday. The Rustics wet down in defeat. Score 9 to 5...Mr. Frank Lewis, of St. [sic] Genevieve, was the guest of his old friend, Mr. Onan Poston. He reports a delightful visit...The M.E. Church will have their Sunday-school picnic July 28th...There will be a ball game between Farmington and Jackson...Mrs. A. Simms departed Wednesday for St. Louis...Mrs. Susie A. Smith is indisposed. Her many friends wish her a speedy recovery...Miss Irene and Rheba Mathews, of Minnith are the guests of their sisters here this week..."Fishing is fine, but reading the Argus for mine."

28 July 1916, pg. 3, col. 1.
"Quite a number of Farmington people motored to Bonne Terre, Mo., last Friday...Prof. J.C. Staten, who has been ill, is convalescent...Mrs. Geo. Evans left last Friday for St. Louis, where she will be the guest of her sister...Mrs. Estelle Roberts and son returned to the city last Thursday. They were accompanied by Mrs. Roberts' nephew, Stewart Poston...After spending a very pleasant vacation with home folks, Rev. Preston Overton returned to his home in Kansas, last Friday...Mrs. William Cayce is visiting her daughters at Cape Girardeau, Mo...Mesdames Mayman [sic] Chapel and Bud Blake were visitors here this week...Mr. Chas. Baker is attending the Grand Lodge, at Macon, [Macon Co.,] Mo., also Mr. John Douthit...Miss Lucille Cherry of Champaign, Ill., is visiting relative[s] and friends here...Mr. Cayce was at hom[e] last Saturday...Mr. Owen Kenned[y] and John Baker are employed at Festus, Mo."

04 August 1916, pg. 3, col. 1.
"Miss Merideth [sic] of Fredericktown, Mo., was the guest of Mrs. John Franks, a few days ago...Mr. Z.P. Evans, superintendent of the M.E. Sunday-school assisted by Miss E.O. Cayce and Miss Cora Meyers, rendered an excellent programme [sic] Friday evening...The picnic given by the M.E. Sunday-school was quite a success...Quite a few Farmington people motored to DeSoto [sic], Mo., last Saturday...Miss Beulah Nelson is the guest of Miss Anna Reynolds...Rev. A. Galvin preached an interesting sermon, Saturday night...Mrs. Martha Villiars [sic] of St. Louis arrived here last Monday[32]...

Mrs. George Evans has returned home...Mrs. Emma Harris was very happy to see her sister, Mrs. Lena Brown of Cleveland, [Cuyahoga Co.,] Ohio[33]... There were many visitors from Fredericktown, last Friday. Messrs. Chas. Baker and John Douthit have returned from the Grand Lodge...Mr. Lewis Murphy was at home Saturday and Sunday."

15 September 1916, pg. 3, col. 1-2.
"...COFFMAN, MO...Miss Mattie Valle, of Farmington, Mo., left for Parsons, [Labette Co.,] Kans., to make her future home..."

27 October 1916, pg. 3, col. 1.
"Mrs. W.H. Brown, of De Soto, is conducting revival services at St. Paul M.E. Church. Her sermons are quite strengthening to all who hear them...Little Samuel Blackwell is confined to his room with a broken leg, caused from playing Rugby...Mrs. L. Kennedy is yet quite ill at her home in Greenville... Mrs. Jerry Bridges is indisposed, suffering from a wounded limb...Misses Ruth B. Davis and Alice McGee, teachers of Attuck's School, of Bonne Terre, were the guests of Miss D.F. Baker, Saturday...Miss Hortense Kennedy and Mrs. P. Boddy entertained an auto party from De Soto Sunday...Mrs. Mamie Thornton, an ex-pupil of Sumner High School, is here for recuperation... Mrs. Thos. Cayce went to Potosi, Friday in answer to a message announcing the illness of her daughter, Mrs. Jos. Carson...Mrs. D. Buford has returned from Coffman from a visit to her daughter, Mrs. Fred Chappell...Mrs. Geo. Meyers is spending the fortnight with relatives at Crystal City...Mrs. and Mrs. Chas. Baker, Mr. and Mrs. Talbert Burns. and Mrs. Chas. Cayce had a pleasant time at Festus Sunday...Mr. J.P. Evans, of Jefferson City, brought his wife home ill, Friday...Rev. Spurlock and wife attended the annual conference at Poplar Bluff last week...Rev. Reynolds is yet substituting for Principal Staten, who has been ill for several months. He is gradually improving... Mr. Wm. Cayce and family moved to Cape Girardeau...Miss Corine [sic] Wilkins has resumed her work in the schoolroom at Coffman...Mrs. W. Douthit is improving...Mr. P.M. Cayce is making his home a modern place by placing in it things that will comfort his family...The wives, daughters and sweethearts of the voters are singing "Hughes." Let it be worth the while singing by casting the right bal[lot]. Make use of our privilege."

03 November 1916, pg. 3, col. 2.
"Rev. Spurlock conducted regular services at his church Sunday...Mr. P. Boddie has arrived and feels quite young again...Dr. J.R. Crossland delivered a very able political speech at the Masonic Hall Thursday night...Mr. Samuel Burke, of Crystal City, enjoyed Sunday with home folks...Principal J.C.

Staten has recovered and is back in the schoolroom...Miss Ethel Cayce has recovered sufficiently to resume her work at Mineral Point...Rev. Reynolds and family were the happy recipients of a generous donation Friday night. Estacada Baker and Edna Harris were heading the line of march...Produce is so high in Farmington that many are proclaiming that "fasting and praying" are worth the while...Messrs. L. Hill, Chas. Baker and F. Paston [sic] were busy campaigning in Fredericktown, Monday...Mrs. W.H. Brown returned to De Soto Saturday, after having held services at the M.E. Church a week... Remember to subscribe for the Argus now, as it means a saving of fifty cents, and to pay your back subscription means that you want to see the Argus succeed. See the reporter at once and compensate accordingly."

10 November 1916, pg. 3, col. 2.
"At the A.M.E. Church Hallowe'en was celebrated with a bazaar. At the M.E. Church, with a dress masquerade...Mesdames Henry Burke, Elvira Mc[G]ee an Miss Marie Anderson, of St. Louis, spent the first of this week as guests of Mrs. C.C. Clay. Mrs. Clay [h]as been indisposed, but is now able to be out... Mrs. Kemp and Miss C. McFadden, of Fredericktown, were the guests of Miss Lucy Mooten, Sunday...The painting of the M.E. Church is [q]uite an added attraction. Rev. Reynolds and his officers are striving to [b]eautify the church property in gen[e]ral...Messrs. Jno. Franks, H. Amon[e]tte and Chas. Baker were campaigning [a]t Coffman Saturday. The latter spent Monday in St. Louis...Mr. Jno. Douth[i]t spent a social evening at Coffman, Friday... Mr. Walter Franks is suf[f]erring from the loss of his eye. The [a]ccident occurred several weeks ago...Mrs. Wm. Kennedy and Mrs. David Buford are new subscribers to the Argus...Mrs. J.P. Evans is impr[o]ng rapidly...Miss Edith Cayce spent [t]he last week at home trying to recup[e]rate...Mrs. S.A. Smith, of St. Louis, [a]ttended to business here this week."

17 November 1916, pg. 3, col. 2.
"Mrs. Henry Amonette entertained Sunday with a "possum" dinner, in honor of her husband's birthday. The affair was quite enjoyable...Messrs. Thos. Cayce, Geo. Meyers, Lewis Murphy and Robert Simpson were at home Tuesday...Miss Edith Cayce returned to Mineral Point Sunday...Miss Ruth B. Davis, of Bonne Terre, spent a pleasant visit with Miss Dayse F. Baker, Saturday...The congregation of St. Luke Chapel have added more illumination to their church. This is quite an improvement to the interior...Mrs. Jane Baker received a message Sunday announcing the death of her brother, Mr. Q.M. Hutchetson [sic], of Utica, [Ness Co.,] Kansas. Death was due to paralysis... Mrs. David Buford entertained in honor of Mrs. S.A. Smith Sunday. Mrs. Smith returned to St. Louis Monday...Mr. Fred Chappelle, of Coffman vis-

ited his family the first of the week...Mr. W. Chappelle attended to business here Friday...Much credit is due the little folks of the M.E. Church, who labored so zealously to make their entertainment of Friday evening a success... Miss L. Amonette, of St. Louis, is enjoying a few days' vacation here. Every reader of the Argus is kindly requested to take advantage of the November offer and the one who has been reading his neighbor's so long is requested to take advantage also."

24 November 1916, pg. 3, col. 2-3.
"If you were at the feast of Belshazzar, or if anyone related the incident to you, then that's the kind of feast that was spread by the St. Louis corps of teachers on Friday evening at Sumner High. It was quite a demonstration of the Domestic Science...At the A.M.E. Church Sunday evening Messrs. J.C. Staten and Chas. Baker entertained with timely talks...Mrs. Geo. Meyers is at home for a short stay...Mr. Elmer Galvin accompanied Clarence Meyers home, where he enjoyed a pleasant week's end...Mrs. Josephine Roden, of St. Louis, is the guest of her mother, Mrs. Jerry Bridges, who has been suffering from a wounded limb...The entire family of Mrs. Cayce has been indisposed for several weeks...Mr. W. Douthit is enjoying his vacation with home folks. As a hunter he is proving himself a champion...Mrs. James Robinson entertained Sunday in honor of Mr. Wesley Douthit and Misses Mildred and Ida Chapelle [sic]...Mrs. Robert Simpson and son, Eugene, have gone to Crystal City, where they will spend the winter...It is a foregone conclusion that those wedding bells will soon ring in our little city...Miss Imogene Staten has returned to her home at Coffman...Miss Dayse F. Baker attended the State Teachers' Association at St. Louis last week and reports one of the most interesting sessions of the body. While you are preparing for Thanksgiving, prepare to settle your account with the Argus reporter."

01 December 1916, pg. 3, col. 4.
"Mr. Thos. Cayce attended to business here the latter part of the week...Miss Edith Cayce has resumed her work at Mineral Point...Mrs. Geo. Meyers has returned to Crystal City...Mr. Chas. Douthit and son, Fielding, were up from Coffman Saturday...Mr. Lindsey Clay, of St. Louis, visited here the first of the week...Ye bachelor girls and maidens, the leap year is nearly gone!... Miss Hortense Kennedy is spending her vacation with home folks at Greenville...Glendora, the babe of Mr. and Mrs. Chas. Baker, has recovered...Your neighbor might as well pay half of the subscription as to read your paper all the time...The remains of Mr. Henry Burke, a former resident of this place, were brought here Monday, accompanied by the wife, Mr. Sherman Burke and Mr. Thomas Burke. His brother, Mr. Samuel Burke, of Festus, was pres-

ent at the funeral, which was conducted by Rev. A.L. Reynolds at the M.E. Church[34]...Mr. Jerome Valle has decided that a winter without the Argus would be too lonesome a season...Mr. H.B. Keatts has succeeded in organizing a young men's social club, which will be a source of pleasure for the young men...Mrs. Jane Mitchell, Mrs. Ferd Madison, Mrs. Rossie Madison and son visited Douglass School Friday...We are quite thankful that the list of subscribers is increasing. May many more decide to read this newsy budget."

08 December 1916, pg. 3, col. 1.
"Mrs. Vergie Pugh and children, Theodore and Anna and Mrs. P. Swink spent Thanksgiving Day at Coffman[35]...Mrs. Mamie Foulk, of Champaign, Ill., is at home for a visit of five weeks...The visitors from out of town were many last week. Those from St. Louis were Misses Anna and Blanche Matthias, Mrs. Kossuth Robinson, Mr. and Mrs. Harry Cayce, Wm. Taylor, Booker Baker, Wm. Wright, B.J. Wilkins and G.H. Powers...From Bonne Terre were Mr. Alexander and son, Henry, Artie and McKinley Fulton, Frank Baker, Sam Townsend, Harry Aubuchon and John Booker also Mr. James Creath, of Pocahontas, [Randolph Co.,] Ark...Miss Mary McCallister enjoyed Thanksgiving with relatives in Festus...Last Wednesday evening Miss Mabel Meyers and Mr. Samuel Burke were quietly married at the residence of the bride... Mrs. Mary Cayce went to Potosi Thursday to be at the bedside of her daughter, Mrs. Joseph Carson, who has been quite ill...Misses Alcesta Douthit, Augustine Swink, Corinne Wilkins, Mildred Chappelle, Messrs. Ferris Franks, Wilson Chappelle, Roy Douthit, Eddie Staten and Sylvester Swink were up from Coffman Thursday...Mr. P.M. Cayce attended to business in St. Louis Monday...Mr. Percy Swink was the conductor of a ball at the Masonic Hall Thursday night...At the M.E. Church Thanksgiving morning Rev. A.L. Reynolds preached a soul-stirring sermon. At evening the boys of St. Paul Sabbath school rendered a program. At the A.M.E. dinner and supper was served...At the marriage of Mr. J. Somerville [sic] to Miss Laura Amonette Saturday evening at the M.E. Church Rev. A.L. Reynolds officiated. Miss Estacada Baker played the strains of music to which little Misses Parnella Cayce and Audelle Cayce led the way, bearing baskets of carnations. The ushers were P.M. Cayce and F.D. Bridges. A reception was served at the residence of Mr. and Mrs. H. Amonette[36]...Chauncey Bell arrived home Monday...Lucretia Staten fell on a stove and severely burned her arm...We are so glad that the increased rate time has been prolonged. Thanks to the Argus force."

15 December 1916, pg. 3, col. 3-4.
"Mrs. Moses Hunt has returned from a visit with relatives at Festus, Mo... Mr. Lewis Smith is away on a hunting expedition...Mr. Rossie Madison at-

tended to business at Bismarck Tuesday...The M.E. Church has replenished its light force and has also purchased a new instrument...Dr. F.S. Bowles conducted quarterly meeting services at the M.E. Church Sunday. The meeting was a financial success...Rev. W.H. Spurlock conducted quarterly meeting services at Fredericktown Sunday...Mr. Jerry Bridges will welcome the Argus to his home this week...Miss Hortense Kennedy entertained a few friends at a dinner party Tuesday...Mesdames Felix Poston and W.I. Roberts attended the cooking school last week. They will demonstrate to their many friends at Yuletide some of the latest dishes...Miss Lucy Mooten has been among the ill of the week...Mrs. Lewis Burke has recovered sufficiently to be about her usual vocation...Rev. F.S. Bowles addressed the student-body at Douglass School Monday much to their delight...Hear the concert at the M.E. Church Thursday evening. The characters are all of rare participation... Burleigh Lodge had election of officers Thursday night and Masoleat Court Friday night. Both orders are quite progressive...Just seven more days for you to tell Santa what to bring your sweetheart for Christmas. He could bring no better gift than the Argus and Santa knows the Argus headquarters. He makes frequent visits there."

22 December 1916, pg. 3, col. 2.
"Rev. A.L. Reynolds assisted Rev. A.S. Woolfolk in quarterly meeting services Sunday at De Soto, Mo...Mrs. W.H. Spurlock is training a class in Domestic Science...Rev. Greenlee, of Bonne Terre, was present with Rev. Spurlock Sunday at quarterly meeting services. He was accompanied by his wife[37]... Mrs. Robert Simpson and son, Eugene, are the guests of Mrs. L. Murphy... Mrs. Tulleck [sic], of Pilot Knob, [Iron Co., Mo.,] was called here the early part of the week to attend her daughter, Mrs. Henry Amonette, who has been quite ill. Her little grandson, Kirmen [sic], is with her...Mr. Talbert Burns is visiting in Ste. Geneieve [sic], Mo...Mesdames Jerry Bridges and Mazie Lyons were the guests of friends here Sunday...Miss Mattie Valle has returned from parsons, Kans., where she has had employment...Mrs. Moses Hunt is convalescent...Master Samuel Blackwell is now able to walk upon the limb that was broken some weeks ago...Chauncey Bell has returned to St. Louis for the winter...Farmington will be alive with festivities during the Yule tide. Many of the home folks, who are away are expected in. If you have not got the Argus in the home to greet them they'll see you are just behind the times. You would be more able to converse about the current happenings were you a subscriber."

05 January 1917, pg. 3, col. 2-3.
"This is a new year that has dawned upon us. May we seek to live it to some

108

great end…"Where there's a will there's a way." There's going to be a matrimonial breeze in the Farmington air ere long…Mrs. Henry Amonette has recovered sufficiently to resume her usual duties…Mr. and Mrs. Geo. Meyers, Robert Simpson, Clarence Meyers and Lewis Murphy, of Crystal City, spent Christmas here…The Martin-Murphy minstrel had two evenings here last week…Mr. and Mrs. James Robinson, of Detroit, Mich., are here for the remainder of winter…A new instrument has been placed in the M.E. Church…No greater joy could Mr. and Mrs. Fred Chappelle have than to be blessed with a baby girl…Booker Baker, James Hill, Wm. Wright and Leo Powell, of St. Louis, enjoyed a week of pleasure here…Rev. Reynolds and son, Clarence, and Miss Dayse Baker, were guests at a dinner at the residence of Mrs. Ed. Harris Monday evening…Mrs. Reynolds and son, Junior, are visiting at Warrensburg…Mrs. R. Phillips and son were the guests of Mr. Geo. Blackwell, the first of the week…Miss Corinne Wilkins and Edith Cayce have returned to their respective schools…Mr. J.P. Evans of Jefferson City, had a pleasant sojourn with his family…Mrs. P.M. Cayce was hostess to a number of persons at a social Monday evening…Mr. John Cayce has returned from St. Louis, where has had employment…Mrs. V.E. Williams, of Chillicothe, will enjoy an indefinite stay with her mother, Mrs. Jane Hunt… Miss Helen Matthias visited Coffman last week and Miss Luetta Matthias at Bonne Terre…Farmington had visitors from all sections last week…Mr. and Mrs. James Sampson were the guests of Mrs. Katie Cayce Monday. They have returned to their home in East St. Louis…Prof. J.C. Staten received the holy baptism at the M.E. Church Sunday morning…Mrs. Wesley Douthit has been quite ill for several days."

12 January 1917, pg. 3, col. 1.
"Mrs. Rosa Parker, of St. Louis, returned home Tuesday…Mrs. Annie Yeager and Mr. Abe Cayce, accompanied Mrs. Cayce to St. Louis Wednesday, where she will remain for a while for medical attention…The friends of Mrs. James Somerville are sorry to learn of her illness…Allen Schaffer has returned from a visit with relatives and friends in Festus, Mo…Mrs. Laura Jordan and daughter Lelia have returned to Charleston…Miss Anna Reynolds accompanied her mother and brother home from Warrensburg, [Johnson Co.,] Mo., Saturday…Mrs. Antoine Murphy is among the numbered ill of the week… Mr. Peter Hill, of Herculaneum, attended to business here this week…The young people of the M.E. Church, have organized a sewing club and will soon give a bazaar…Miss Mattie Valle is enjoying the week with home folks at Coffman…Mr. B.J. Wilkins, of St. Louis, was a welcome visitor here last week…The cooking class conducted a pie social at the A.M.E. Church Friday night. The pies were quite salable…Farmington is much in need of a ladies'

social club. All who think so begin to talk it around from fireside to oven. The beautiful home of Mr. and Mrs. P.M. Cayce, of Farmington, Mo., was a scene of beauty on New Years' Eve, when they entertained twenty-five of their friends in honor of their sister, Mrs. Rosa Parker, of St. Louis; the evening was spent in music and games, after which a delightful luncheon was served...All departed at a late hour, pronouncing Mrs. Cayce a charming hostess."

19 January 1917, pg. 3, col. 1-2.
"Mrs. Eliza Overton is able to be up and about her house...Mr. Arvilla [sic] Wilkins, of St. Louis, is the guest of his mother, Mrs. S.O. Wilkins...The friends of Miss Zelma Swink are glad to learn of her recovery...Mrs. Sarah Amonette has been quite ill at her home in West Farmington...Mrs. Mary Taylor and daughters, Katheryn and Mary, of St. Louis, were the guests of Mrs. Moses Bridges the first of the week...Miss Minnie Thornton is recuperating...Mr. Jim Cunningham, of Martin Settlement, was the guest of home folks Sunday...Mr. Onan Poston had a few hours of business out of town last week...Rev. W.H. Houston, of Poplar Bluff, was the guest of A.L. Reynolds last week. He preached a very interesting sermon Wednesday evening...Mrs. Chas. Douthit has been employed as mail carrier on the Coffman Route. We are glad of his success...Saturday was doughnut day at the residence of Mrs. W.H. Spurlock...Mr. Arville Wilkins addressed the children of the M.E. Sunday school, Sunday. Mr. Wilkins is one of the many Farmington boys who has had success...Mr. and Mrs. Occamore, of Sprott, were here attending to business Saturday...Mr. Wm. Kennedy is employed at Bonne Terre for an indefinite period...Principal J.C. Staten was unable to teach last Tuesday because of illness...The reporter will appreciate having all items as early as Monday noon of each week."

26 January 1917, pg. 3, col. 1-2.
"The Chapter O.E.S. held memorial services for Sister Lucinda Day Sunday at Castle Hall. Mrs. Felix Poston presided. Mesdames Jane Hunt, Emily Boddie and Mr. Scott Cole addressed the body...Mr. Rossie Madison enjoyed a visit to Coffman last week...Master Homers Meyers was host to a number of youth Sunday afternoon in his ninth birthday celebration...Mrs. Robt. Simpson has returned to Crystal City...We are sorry to know that Miss Mae Baker is a victim of smallpox...Mr. Wesley Douthit was a welcome visitor to our town last week...Mrs. Mamie Foulk has returned to Champaign, after a visit of a couple of months...La grippe has made its annual visit to our town and it has many guests in its domain...Mrs. Jas. Robinson attended to business in Bonne Terre, Friday...The community is grieved over the loss of Dr. Ricketts, of St. Joseph, [Buchanan Co.,] Mo[38]...The ill of the week are:

Theodore Pugh, Mrs. Dave Buford, Mrs. W.J. Roberts, Mrs. V.E. Williams and Mrs. Sallie Taylor...Master Lewis and Oscar Smith have gone to New Madrid to live with their grandmother. We regret to erase their names on Douglass roll...Miss Mildred Chappelle, Mr. Arville Chappelle and Mr. Sylvester Swink, of Coffman, were Farmington guests last week."

02 February 1917, pg. 3, col. 2.

"Mr. Chas. Baker was in St. Louis Saturday, attending business...Miss Edith Cayce, teacher of Mineral Point, accompanied by one of her pupils, little Miss Lora Lee LeMarqua enjoyed Saturday and Sunday here...A number of young men from Potosi exhibited their comedy at the Masonic Hall, Thursday night. A large crowd attended...Mrs. Lewis Murphy is spending a few days at Crystal City...Rev. A.L. Reynolds anointed Mrs. M. Lyons with baptismal rites Sunday...The congregation is rejoicing over an increase in membership...Master James Cayce was accidentally cut Sunday by falling against a knife, which cut an ugly gash in his thigh...The teachers' meeting at the A.M.E. Church each Friday is quite largely attended and much interest is being manifested...Saturday was rice pudding day with the domestic science girls economy in cooking...Miss Corinne Wilkins has been asked to teach another month. This will be quite beneficial to pupils, as well as the teacher... Mrs. Virgia Pugh, Mrs. Dave Buford and Master Scott Hunt are among the ill of the week...Mr. and Mrs. Jerry Bridges and Mrs. Mazie Lyons, of Swink's Settlement, were Farmington visitors Sunday."

09 February 1917, pg. 3, col. 3.
"Mr. Dave Staten, of Coffman, an honored citizen and a progressive farmer, departed this life Sunday, after having suffered intensely from pneumonia. His daughters, Mrs. Mazie Lyons and Miss Lorene Staten, arrived there quite a few days before the demise, and were thus able to assist in administering to his needs[39]...Mr. Jim Cayce is now able to be around his room...Mrs. Cecilia Cunningham has as her guests her daughter, Miss Irene, of Chicago, and son, Mr. J.B. Cunningham, of St. Louis...While teaming last Thursday, Mr. Ellis Taylor froze two fingers...Mrs. Virginia Pugh, Misses Dola and Laurine Boddie, Minnie Thornton, Master Inman Evans and Wm. Baker are among the ill...Mrs. Geo. Meyers, of Crystal City, is the guest of her daughter, Miss Cora Meyers...Saturday was "peach cobbler" day with the domestic science class. On Washington's birthday it wiill [sic] be "cherry pie" day...Mrs. Moses Hunt sprained her ankle, which has caused her a deal of pain...Lincoln Day will be observed at the M.E. Church...Mrs. Annie Bridges has about recovered."

111

16 February 1917, pg. 2, col. 2-3.

"Mr. Fred Madison surprised his family by placing a player piano in the home...Mrs. P. Boddie has been seriously ill at her home in South Farmington...News was received here Friday of the serious illness of Mrs. Laura Jordan, of Charleston...Mrs. A. Simms spent the first part of the week here attending to business...Mrs. Wesley Douthit is confined to her bed with inflammatory rheumatism...Mr. Henry Amonette is dealing extensively in poultry as the result of incubator service...Mr. Peter Swink is recovering from a recent illness...Mr. Henry Renfro has returned to Libertyville for an indefinite period...Miss Mae Baker has recovered and is at her usual vocation... Messrs. Wm. Wright and Leo Powell, of St. Louis, had a visit of a few hours here Sunday...Miss Luetta Matthias visited friends in Bonne Terre Sunday... Quite a number of persons attended the funeral of Mr. Dave Staten, at Coffman, Tuesday. Burleigh Lodge was well represented...After a visit of several months Mr. and Mrs. James Robinson have returned to St. Louis, enroute [sic] to their home in Detroit...Principal Staten, and pupils observed Lincoln Day with appropriate exercises...Mrs. Jerry Bridges was the guest of Mrs. E.J. Harris Sunday...Mr. and Mrs. Lewis Kennedy, of Greenville, were the guests of Mrs. P. Boddie Sunday. Mr. A. Simms was a Farmington visitor Monday... Mrs. Geo. Meyers has returned to Crystal City, after a visit of a week...You say you miss the Argus, well, it will be sent to you upon request and subscription advanced."

23 February 1917, pg. 2, col. 3-4.

"Rev. T.A. Hermon, accompanied by an automobile party from Fredericktown, preached to a well-filled church at the evening service Sunday. The party returned home later the same evening...Mr. James Robinson had a fall, which left him quite lame...Mrs. Mary Cayce and Estacada Baker attended the entertainment at Mineral Point Friday. Miss Edith Cayce conducted the same...Mr. Hward [sic] Overton, of St. Louis, is here for an indefinite stay... At the masquerade ball, Wednesday evening, Miss Cosetta Boddie won first laurels and Mr. J.P. Evans, second. Many out-of-town guests were present... Mrs. Ben Chappelle, of Coffman, is at the bedside of her sister, Mrs. Wesley Douthit, who has been quite ill for several weeks...Rev. W.H. Spurlock was called to the bedside of his father at Columbus, Ohio...Mr. Clarence Meyers returned to Crystal City, Monday...Mrs. Celia Cunningham accompanied her daughter to Chicago, where she hopes to remain for an extended visit. Miss Irene had a pleasant sojourn here...Announcement has been made of the engagement of Miss Anna Nora Reynolds, of this city, to Mr. Jasper Briscoe, of Holden, [Johnson Co.,] Mo. Girls, get busy...Dr. F.D. Bridges is busy as a book agent...Mr. and Mrs. Ben Chappelle have purchased an auto. This is typical of modern farm life...Little Odessa Cayce is visiting her mother, Mrs. Harry Cayce, of St. Louis...Miss Berdola Boddie is a guest at the home of Mr. and Mrs. Artie Reed, of St. Louis, who are rejoicing over the advent of a little son...Mrs. Laura Jordan, of Charleston, is yet quite ill...School was dismissed for Washington's Day, Thursday, and both churches commemorated the birth of a nation's first president."

02 March 1917, pg. 5, col. 4.
"Miss Sophia Mudd was hostess to the Art Club, Monday evening, at which time delicious refreshments were served...Master Clarence Reynolds entertained a number of his friends at his home Saturday evening, with games and luncheon...The friends of Mr. Fred Madison are very sorry to learn of his serious illness. His sister, Mrs. George Maul, and niece, Mrs. Rossie Madison, of Bonne Terre, visited him Sunday...Rev. Spurlock was successful in reaching his father's bedside before he passed away. In the absence of the pastor the congregation enjoyed a sacred program, Sunday, rendered by the young people...At the Washington Social, Thursday evening, Mrs. Antoine Murphy won the can of cherries...Mrs. and Mrs. Chas. Baker enjoyed having their son, Booker, spend the week's end with them...Mrs. Susie Smith, of St. Louis, attended to business here Saturday and returned home Monday... Miss Cosetta Boddie is quite ill at her home in South Farmington...A number of ladies went to Bonne Terre Friday in answer to the announcement of the demise of Mrs. Greenlee, wife of Rev. Greenlee. The remains were taken to Omaha, Neb., Saturday morning...Mrs. Charlotte Clay received the news that her grandson, James Hill, of St. Louis, got his foot broken while running an elevator...The A.M.E. Church observed Washington Day with a tea party...There are only fifty-five more days of school. Avail yourself o the opportunity to visit school...Mr. and Mrs. Gabriel Cayce have returned from St. Louis where the latter has been taking medical treatments...Mrs. David Buford, and daughter, Laura, enjoyed a week's visit at Coffman, the guest of Mr. and Mrs. Fred Chappelle...Mr. Weyman Chappelle attended to business here Saturday...Miss Edith Cayce spent the week's end with home folks and returned to Mineral Point Monday...Mrs. Scott Cole and Master Kossuth Baker are the guests of Mrs. Lucile Martin, of St. Louis...Mr. Onon [sic] Poston has employment in St. Louis...Regardless of the high cost of living, Cupid is busy. Somebody's hope chest is being replenished."

09 March 1917, pg. 2, col. 2.
"After a delightful visit of two months with her mother, Mrs. V.E. Williams has returned to her home at Chillicothe, Mo...Mr. Peter Swink has returned from a visit with relatives at Coffman...Mrs. Scott received a message last

week announcing the death of her brother, Mr. Frank Scott, which occurred at St. Louis. The remains were brought to Horine [Jefferson Co., Mo.] for interment[40]...Mrs. Geo. Meyers is at home preparing to move to Crystal City. We regret to lose this family from our midst...Mr. and Mrs. Lewis Murphy were here from Crystal City Saturday to attend to business matters...Misses Luetta and Helen Matthias entertained the Industrial Club, Monday evening at the residence of Mrs. W.H. Spurlock, where they proved themselves quite splendid hostesses...Rev. A.L. Reynolds is assisting Rev. A. Poston in a meeting at Festus, Mo...Mr. Sylvester Swink was seen on our streets last week... Mrs. Felix Poston returned from St. Louis, Friday, where she had a delightful visit with relatives...Rev. W.H. Spurlock was at his post of duty Sunday evening...Little Virginia Burks is ill with pneumonia...Mr. J.H. Fulton, of Bonne Terre, was in our midst Sunday...Mr. Percy Swink has accepted work at Bonne Terre, Mo...Mrs. Wesley Douthit has recovered sufficiently to be about in her home...The Argus will serve quite a friend to you during this H.C. of L., for in it you see some of the advantages of saving the dollar that was already earned."

16 March 1917, pg. 3, col. 3.
"Prof. Madarikan Diniyi delighted [a] large audience at the M.E. Churc[h] Tuesday evening with a lecture concerning his African home...Miss Ethel Taylor, of St. Louis, was the guest of Miss M. Baker Saturday and Sunday... Rev. C. Wilkins preached [a] very able sermon at the 11 o'clock service at the M.E. Church Sunday. Rev[.] F.S. Bowles conducted the Quarterly Meeting services, at which time much interest was manifested by all in attendance. Rev. Bowles was the guest of Mr. E. Harris...Mr. M. Fulton, of Bonne Terre, has been commonly seen in our town...The cooking class, chaperoned by Mrs. Spurlock, enjoyed making peach roll Saturday...Rev. A.L. Reynolds returned from Festus Saturday greatly inspired from his delightful[l] trip... Mrs. G. Meyers returned to Crystal City Saturday...Mr. Scot[t] Cole has resumed his labor as a black smith [sic]...Miss Ruth Boddie is absent from school on account of illness...To night [sic] (Saturday) the ladies of the M.E[.] Church will give a miscellaneous[s] shower for Miss Annie Reynolds, at which time dainty refreshements will b[e] served...Miss M. Madison and Mrs[.] R. Madison entertained the Industrial Club at the residence of Mrs. Madison Monday evening...Miss C. Boddie has recovered from a recent illness...The Pythians and Calanthians are preparing to make the anniversary service at the A.M.E. Church a success, the 25th. Rev. Spurlock will preach the sermon...Mr. C. Baker has had improvements made around his place, which gives it a spring-like appearance...Misses Mary McAllister and Willie Jones visited Douglass School last week. There remain forty-five days more

you may avail yourself of the opportunity to come.

23 March 1917, pg. 2, col. 4-5.

"Mrs. Cora J. Turner of Parsons, Kansas, arrived Saturday night to be the guest of relatives for an indefinite period...Mr. O. Poston of St. Louis enjoyed Sunday with home folks...Rev. J.D. Barksdale conducted Quarterly meeting services at the A.M.E. Church. The meeting was a success financially as well as spiritually...Mr.s Charlotte Clay received injuries from a fall Sunday...Mr. Lewis Kennedy was the successful captain at the rally Sunday at the M.E. Church; Mrs. T.L. Cayce was second; Mr. P. Cayce, third; Mrs. E. Harris, fourth. The receipts were forty dollars. This was a sacrificial rally; each member was allowed to give as the spirit moved him...Miss Cora Meyers, Mrs. Lula Kennedy and Homer Meyers enjoyed Sunday with relatives at Crystal City...Master George L. Burke is very ill with pneumonia...One of the most beautiful scenes that ever graced the M.E. Church was that exhibited Saturday evening at the miscellaneous shower. The presents were gorgeous and wholesome. The display of needle work was surprisingly splendid... The visitors present were Misses Luetta and Helen Matthiasano [sic], Misses Zelma and Alice Swink, each presented beautiful gifts. Miss Edith Cayce of Mineral Springs [sic] was present. The gentlemen who were present added much to the interest of the occasion. Refreshments were serviced and each one left feeling that it was good to have Cupid so near...Mrs. C. Swink and Mr. Staten of Coffman attended to business here last week...Misses Cozetta [sic] Boddie and Hortense Kenney entertained the Industrial Club Monday evening at the residence of Mrs. P. Boddie. This club is doing some very pretty needle work under the supervision of Miss Kennedy...Miss Loraine Staten has recovered sufficiently to be up and out...Mrs. Boddie received the sad message of the death of little Oscar, the infant son of Mr. and Mrs. Artie Reed, of St. Louis[41]...Mr. Fred Chappell came up Thursday and finished moving his household goods to Coffman...Mr. Antone [sic] Murphy has recovered from a recent injury received while gardening."

30 March 1917, pg. 2, col. 5-6.

"Three car loads of young people attended an entertainment at Bonne Terre Monday evening. They report one of "Aunt Dolly's Times"...Mr. Turner, of Parsons, Kans., has joined his wife here for a short visit with relatives...Mr. and Mrs. J. Robinson were spectators at the American in St. Louis Saturday...Quite a number of persons were here from Coffman Sunday to witness the anniversary of the Knights of Pythias at the A.M.E. Church. Rev. Spurlock preached a very appropriate sermon...Mrs. Ellen and Dora Carson, of Potosi, were the guests of Mrs. M. Cayce, Saturday and Sunday...Mr. and

Mrs. E. Williams are the guests of Mrs. Lewis Burke...Mrs. Eliza Overton will discontinue house-keeping. She will rent her home in East Farmington, and live with relatives...Miss Mamie Burk is among the ill of this week... Misses Alice and Telma [sic] Swink were hostesses to the Industrial Club Monday evening. They proved themselves quite equal to the occasion...Mrs. A. Sims [sic] is spending a few days with her mother, Mrs. J. Poston...The little misses at the cooking school, made light bread Saturday...Rev. A. Poston, of Festus, attended to business here Monday. He reports a successful conference year...The Queen of Honor Court, under the supervision of Mrs. W.I. Roberts, will hold its Palm Service at Castle Hall Sunday...The O.E.S. held a chapter of sorrow, Sunday afternoon, for Dr. O.M. Ricketts, who recently passed away...Misses Dola Boddie and Odessa Cayce arrived from St. Louis Monday."

06 April 1917, pg. 3, col. 2-3.
"Palm Sunday was well observed by the Queen of Honor Court, at the Masonic Hall Sunday afternoon. The annual address by the matron, and the paper by Miss H. Kennedy were splendid numbers. A collection was taken for the Masonic Home...Miss Edith Cayce, of Mineral Point, attended to business here Saturday...Mrs. L. Murphy had a visit to relatives at Crystal City this week...Mr. and Mrs. Turner were compelled to return to their home at Parsons, Kan., earlier than they had planned. They left a feeling, however, that Farmington is a nifty little town in which to visit...The many friends of Mrs. A.L. Reynolds are glad to know that she is convalescent...Mr. T. Cayce left early Sunday morning to accept a position in the railway service... Sunday will be the last Sunday for Rev. A.L. Reynolds in this conference year, and it will be a busy day at St. Paul's Chapel. The Easter program will be rendered Sunday afternoon...Messrs. McKinley, Artie Fulton, Roger Alexander and Samuel Townsend were over Friday evening seeing the lasses... Mr. F.D. Bridges and Mr. Frank Cayce have opened a poultry enterprise with incubator attachment...Mr. Geo. Myers [sic] was down the first of the week crating his household goods, preparing to move to Crystal City...Floyd Kennedy has accepted a position at Festus[42]...Misses Sophia Mudd and Florence Taylor entertained the Industrial Club Monday night at the residence of the former...Mr. Talbert Burns is improving...Mr. Percy Swink enjoyed Sunday with home folks...Little Edna Harris was attacked by a furious cow Saturday, and barely escaped what might have been a fatal happening, by having presence of mind to dodge the blow."

13 April 1917, pg. 3, col. 1-2.
"Mr. and Mrs. Samuel Burke have moved to East Farmington...Mr. Henry

Renfro has returned for the summer...Mr. Chas. Cayce has employment in Festus...Mr. Geo. Burns has returned from Fredericktown, where he has been working for some time...At Douglass School, Friday, trees were planted, and the remainder of the afternoon was given to the rendition of an appropriate program...Friday morning, Douglass primary enjoyed an Easter egg-hunt, conducted by Cornelia Franks, Opal Kennedy, and Theodore Pugh...Mr. Byrd J. Wilkins had a pleasant sojourn with relatives Easter...Miss Luetta Matthews and Mr. Leo Powell spent Easter I Coffman...Miss Helen Matthews spent Sunday in Bonne Terre...Mr. Felix Poston is greatly improving his place...Miss Alice Swink was the guest of Mrs. Boddie the first of the week...Miss Alice Swink is attending to business in St. Louis this week... The following visitors were here Sunday: Roy Douthit, and Farris Franks, of Coffman, and Paul Alexander, of Bonne Terre...Master Allen Schaffer visited in St. Louis last week...St. Paul is boasting of a conference year of financial success never before so reported. The receipts of the year were $833.29. When the secretary announced the figures, showing that the pastor had been paid, the congregation branded [?] their voices in singing, "Praise God From Whom All Blessings Flow"...Rev. Reynolds and his daughter, Miss Anna, left on the early train Monday morning for Sedalia, where Miss Anna, and Mr. Jasper Briscoe, of Holden, were united in the bonds of holy matrimony. Miss Reynolds is very accomplished...A large number of persons attended the ball at Bonne Terre Monday night...Edgar Cayce made a business trip to St. Louis this week...The earthquake shock was felt at Douglass School Monday; the children rushed out, and in the panic several were nerve-stricken."

20 April 1917, pg. 3, col. 3-4.
"Mrs. Jerry Bridges has returned from a visit to St. Louis, the guest of her daughter, Mrs. Roden...Mr. P.M. Cayce has made recent improvements on his place, and has also purchased more property, which shows that Mr. Cayce has an eye for business...Queen of Honor Court held memorial services for the recent departed and much loved Alice O. Jones at the Masonic Hall...At the recent election of officer of the Queen of Honor Court, Mrs. P. Bodie was elected Matron to succeed Mrs. W.I. Roberts...Mr. Fred Madison was stricken with paralysis Sunday afternoon while at work. He was conveyed to his home in West Farmington, where he remained unconscious until death came about nine o'clock the same evening[43]...Miss Lorinne [sic] Staten served a bounteous dinner Sunday to a number of her lady friends...Mrs. Lewis Kennedy was the guest of Mrs. Geo. Evans Sunday for dinner...The middle-age members of St. Paul rendered a program at St. Paul Sunday evening, much to the delight of the audience...Mr. Tillman Cayce was here the first of the week...Miss Cora Myers [sic] enjoyed the day Sunday with relatives at Crys-

tal City…There are only twenty more days of school. Have you registered on the visiting list, or will the close of the year find you on the "I intended" list?…Mr. Lewis Hill was among the ill of last week…On returning from the funeral of Mr. Fred Madison at Bonne Terre Tuesday, Barleigh [sic] Lodge received a message telling of the death of another member, Mr. Harry Jacobs, which occurred at Ste. Genevieve, Mo."[44]

04 May 1917, pg. 3, col. 3.
"Little Miss Stella Clark was hostess to a number of young people at her home Sunday afternoon in commemoration of her twelfth birthday…Miss Helen Mathias [sic] went to Ste. Genevieve Sunday to be maid of honor at the marriage of her sister, Miss Bertha Mathias [sic], to Mr. Lemmie Ambrough… Mr. Talbert Burns is visiting old comrades at Coffman…Miss Alice Swink entertained a number of young people at her home Tuesday evening with delicate refreshments and popular amusements…Mr. and Mrs. Jerry Bridges and Mrs. Mazie Lyons were guests of Mr. and Mrs. P.M. Cayce Sunday… Miss Lorene Staten has returned from a business trip to Coffman…Master Allen Schafer was pleased to entertain his father, Mr. Albert Schafer, of Crystal City, the latter part of the week…Mrs. Lewis Murphy and Floyd Kennedy were with home folks Sunday…Little Louise, daughter of Mrs. Mabel Harris, has been quite ill for several days…Mrs. W.H. Spurlock is preparing some little misses for a May drill which will be announced later…Douglass School is preparing for commencement exercises…Mr. Howard Overton has returned to St. Louis…Miss Mary McAllister is among the numbered ill of this week…Cupid has been hurling his darts around our vicinity and first and last some one [sic] is going to step off."

11 May 1917, pg. 3, col. 2-3.
"Messrs. Chas. Cayce and Tillman Cayce enjoyed Sunday with home folks… Mrs. Laura Somerville, of St. Louis was the guest of her father, Mr. Henry Amonette, the first of the week…Mr. J.P. Evans had a business trip to Bonne Terre last week…Mr. Freeman Bridges has accepted employment at Crystal City…Mrs. P.M. Cayce and daughters Theola Parnella and Etheline are the guests of the former's sister, Mrs. Rosa Parker, of St. Louis…Miss Cora Meyers has gone to Crystal City for an indefinite stay…Miss Hortense Kennedy went to St. Louis Tuesday for optical treatment…Mr. Lewis Smith visited friends in St. Louis last week…Miss Stella Poston, of St. Louis, is again in our little city…Mr. Chas. Douthit and daughter, Alcesta, of Coffman, visited Mrs. Thomason last week…The many friends of Miss Ruth B. Davis, principal of Attucks School at Bonne Terre, extended sympathy to her in the loss of her father, which occurred at Springfield, Ill., last Tuesday…Mother's

Day will be observed at the M.E. Church Sunday afternoon. [sic] with an appropriate program, conducted by Mr. J.P. Evans and Mrs. Robert Simpson... Mr. Jno. Franks has made modern improvements on his place, which makes his home look quite attractive...Mr. Robt. Simpson returned to Crystal City Wednesday after a day with home folks...Little Johnnie Wilburn, of Coffman, is the guest of his uncle, Mr. Henry Wilburn...Douglass Primary will have exercises at the Masonic Hall Thursday, May 17. Graduating exercises will be held Monday, May 21. The graduates are Clarence Bridges, Luetta Matthias, Helen Matthias and Estacada Baker."

18 May 1917, pg. 3, col. 1-2.

"Mrs. Geo. Blackwell went to St. Louis Tuesday in answer to a message informing her of the serious illness of her daughter, Mrs. Mary Taylor...Mrs. Jno. Bridges has been suffering from an enlarged ankle...Mr. Weyman Boddie chaperoned a party of friends on a tour here from St. Louis Sunday. While here they were the guests of Mr. and Mrs. P. Boddie...Mrs. S. Burke visited at Sprott Sunday...Mr. Wm. Kennedy will leave shortly for work in Illinois... Mrs. Rhida [sic] Harris stuck a nail in her foot Sunday, and Mrs. Kate Cayce happened with a like accident Tuesday...The Industrial Club entertained the class of '17 Monday evening at the residence of Mr. and Mrs. Jno. Franks... Measles invaded our community, leaving some quite speckled...Mrs. Minnie Cayce, Mrs. Minnie Wilburn, Mrs. Nancy Buford and daughter, Mrs. Anna Yeager, Misses Florence Taylor, Mamie Burke, and Mr. and Mrs. Williams attended the funeral of Mrs. Belle Burke at Herculaneum Saturday. Mr. Henry Amonette spent several days there...Rev. J.H. McCallister was present to take charge of the services at the M.E. Church Sunday. In the afternoon, "Mother's Day" was observed with a program. The children presented mothers with carnations. It was a scene of beauty...The program of Douglass Primary will be rendered tonight (Saturday)...Mrs. Geo. Maul was the guest of Mrs. Madison Sunday. She returned to Bonne Terre Monday...Miss Lottie Simms attended to business here Saturday...Mr. Ernest Wilkins favored Douglass School with circulars on the subject of sanitation, which have been read in every home in the community. Mr. Wilkins is now residing in Illinois...Mrs. Lucy Mooten was quite ill last week. She is much improved. Mrs. J.P. Evans and Miss Cosetta Boddie were the guests of Mrs. Maggie Kennedy, of Greenville, Sunday...Another school term has expired. The question comes to the parent now: "What shall I do with my boy or girl?" The answer is, let them have playtime, let them have plenty of recreation, but above all things, have them labor some each day. Teach them that you are expecting them to do a child's share. See to it, mothers, that you do not send them to the neighbor's house to play in order to be at ease yourself. Have them reverence the home, and make it earth's dearest habitation."

25 May 1917, pg. 3, col. 3-4.
"The primary exercises of Douglass School were held Saturday evening at the Masonic Hall and the commencement exercises Monday evening. There were visitors to these exercises from St. Louis, Festus, Crystal City, Fredericktown, Bonne Terre, Coffman and Eads. The pupils did credit to themselves in every number...The funeral of Mrs. Mary Green, of St. Louis, was held here Sunday afternoon at the A.M.E. Church, with Rev. W.N. [sic] Spurlock officiating, assisted by Rev. J. McCallister. Masoleat Court had charge of the remains. Mrs. Green was the daughter of Mrs. Blackwell, who, with three other children and a husband, survive her. Her death occurred in St. Louis from an illness of a few days[45]...Mesdames Antoine and Lewis Murphy attended to business in St. Louis the first of the week...The exercises of the Mineral Point School, of which Miss Edith Cayce is teacher, will be held tonight (Saturday)...Little Richard Hunt, the grandson of Mrs. M. Thornton, is critically ill with pneumonia...Viletta, daughter of Mr. and Mrs. Henry Wilburn, is so stricken with rheumatism that she cannot use her lower limbs...Mrs. Talbert Burns is among the ill of the week...Mrs. Thomason and baby have returned to St. Louis. The sojourn in Farmington was quite beneficial to her...Rev. W.N. [sic] Spurlock addressed the class of '17 and teachers Sunday night in a beautiful manner. Much praise is due this worthy pastor. The sermon was quite appropriate...Mrs. Laura Somerville, of St. Louis, came down Thursday and accompanied her little son, Politte, home. He had been the guest of Mr. and Mrs. Henry Amonette...Ester Day will be observed by the O.E.S. the first Sunday in June."

01 June 1917, pg. 3, col. 1-2.
"Mr. Lindsey Clay is enjoying his vacation here this week...Mrs. Mazie Lyons is visiting home folks at Coffman, Mo...Farmington was well represented at the commencement exercises of Attucks School at Bonne Terre, Mo...A party from Farmington attended the exercises at Mineral Point Saturday... Messrs. Weyman and Arville Chappelle motored home in their new machine Monday...Mrs. McCallister and son, Russell, have joined Rev. McCallister here and are well pleased with the surroundings...O.E.S. will observe Esther Day tomorrow at Castle Hall...Miss Leslie Poston is convalescent...Misses Alice McGhee and Ruth Davis were guests of Miss D.F. Baker the first of the week...Master Richard Hunt is improving rapidly...Mrs. Spurlock chaperoned a party of young people, who enjoyed a day of fishing Friday at Greenville Miss Clara Kennedy was hostess to the party. All reported having spent a pleasant time...Mrs. Thos. Cayce accompanied her daughter, Miss Edith,

home from Potosi, a few days ago...Misses Estacada and Nadine Baker returned from Mineral Point Sunday...Mr. Immanuel Jackson, of Festus, spent a few days here this week...Mrs. Jane Hun[t] was called to Fredericktown, on business last week. She returned Sunday...Miss Sophia Mudd, Lethia Taylor and Florence Taylor visited friends at Mineral Point and Potosi last week... Quarterly Meeting services will be held at St. Paul June 9 and 10."

08 June 1917, pg. 3, col. 3.
"Miss Ruth Boddie is visiting relatives at Charleston, Mo...Miss Corinne Wilkins was hostess at a dinner party given in honor of Miss Ruth B. Davis, of Springfield, Ill., and Miss Alice McGhee of Festus, Mo., guests of Miss Dayse Baker, last Wednesday...Master Elbert Baker and Miss Edith O. Cayce were the guests of Mr. and Mrs. J. Carson, of Potosi...Mrs. Geo. Meyer has returned to Crystal City after a week's visit with Mr. and Mrs. Samuel Burke...Mrs. Rosa Cummings of St. Louis, was the guest of Mrs. Augustine Cayce, Thursday...Mrs. Rossie Madison and son, Jessamine returned from Herculaneum, Thursday...Mrs. Mahalia Madison was the guest of Mr. Geo. Maul of Bonne Terre, last week...Mrs. A. Simms attended to business here Thursday, returning Friday, to St. Louis...Mrs. Susie Smith of St. Louis was busy here last week, organizing a camp of the American Woodmen... Mrs. Emma Summers and grandson, Politte of St. Louis, accompanied Mrs. Chas. Moore and family here, where they will reside indefinitely...Mr. Felix Poston received the sad news of the rapid declining of his niece, Mrs. Roxy Thomason of St. Louis...Rev. W.H. Spurlock was the guest of Rev. Greenlee at Bonne Terre, Thursday...Mr. and Mrs. Lewis Kennedy of Greenville, were the guests of Mr. and Mrs. J.P. Evans, Sunday."

15 June 1917, pg. 3, col. 1.
"Mr. Lewis Kennedy is convalescent...The remains of Mrs. Roxy Thomas, of St. Louis, were brought here Sunday. The funeral services were from the M.E. Church, conducted by Rev. J.H. McCallister, assisted by Rev. Spurlock and Dr. Rivere. Those accompanying the remains were: Mrs. Mary Poston, mother of the deceased; Mesdames Sneed, Yarbrough and Bell Poston, Miss Dollean Poston and Mr. Cornelius Cole; also the baby of the deceased, little Stella[46]...Dr. Rivere held Quarterly Meeting services at the M.E. Church Sunday, at which time splendid sermons were delivered by him. He received a hearty welcome by the church at large...Mr. Robt. Simpson spent the day with home folks a few days ago...Mrs. Dave Buford and daughter, Laura, returned from Coffman Monday, accompanied by Mr. Wilson Chappelle... Miss Marie Hogan White, G.W.L. of O.O.C., was the guest of Masoleat Court No. 127 Monday evening at which time she delivered a very interest-

ing address and clearly demonstrated the ritualistic part of the work in full. While here she was the guest of Mrs. Antoine Murphy...Children's Day services will be held at the M.E. Church Sunday...Mr. and Mrs. J.P. Evans are perfectly happy over the advent of little Stewart...Quite a number of out-of-town visitors attended the ball given by Mrs. James Robinson last Thursday... Rev. W.H. Spurlock is busy preparing for the Sunday school convention at Cape Girardeau, Mo. Miss Bertha Staten is the delegate...Mrs. Talbert Burns has recovered from a serious illness...Mrs. Marie Lyons has returned from a pleasant visit with relatives at Coffman...Mr. Jas. Cunningham went to St. Louis Monday, on account of his brother George's illness...Master Halfred Poston is at home from Boonville for his usual vacation."

22 June 1917, pg. 3, col. 3.
"Mrs. Eliza Overton has been quite ill at the home of her daughter Mrs. P. Bodice [sic]...Misses Luetta and Helen Matthias were hostesses to the Industrial Club Monday evening...Miss Cora Meyers has returned to Farmington for an indefinite period...Mr. Geo. Meyers and Mr. Sam Bisch were guests of their other, Mrs. Belle Matkins Sunday...Mr. Cooley brought an auto party here for a Sunday trip, returning to Ironton late in the evening...Miss Jewel Cabble and Mrs. V.E. Williams, of Chillicothe, are the guests of Mrs. Jane Hunt...Mrs. Geo. Burns is visiting in St. Louis...Miss Alice Swink and pupils are engaged in a rehearsal for their annual recital...Little Miss Lelia Franks has been recently elected organist of the A.M.E. Sunday school...Mr. Raymond Boise, of St. Louis, enjoyed Sunday here...Mr. Philip Bridges returned to St. Louis Tuesday much improved...Miss Pearl Mayfield of Eads, Mo., is the guest of Mrs. Augustus Cayce...Prof. J.C. Staten has been confined to his bed for several days, but is now convalescent...Mrs. Sara Amonette has returned from a visit at Herculaneum...Thursday afternoon from 3 to 4:30 the official staff of the M.E. Sunday school entertained the younger pupils with a social. Other appropriate amusements were features of the occasion...Rev. J.D. Barksdale will conduct quarterly meeting services at the A.M.E. Church Sunday, June 24."

29 June 1917, pg. 3, col. 2-3.
"Mr. and Mrs. Fred Chappelle and daughter, of Coffman, were the guests of Mr. and Mrs. Dave Buford last week. Mrs. Chappelle was up for dental care...Mr. Thos. Cayce has made modern improvements on his home recently...Mr. Samuel Burke has accepted employment at Crystal City...Mrs. Annie Bridges is custodian of some beautiful crocheted articles...Booker T. Baker has returned from a year's work at Sumner High, to which school he gives great praise...Mrs. S.A. Smith will perfect the organization of the Mod-

ern Woodmen, with the assistance of the commander, July 2...Mr. Robert Simpson returned to Crystal [City] Monday...The Beehive rally of the M.E. Church is in full progress. The queens are Mesdames E.J. Harris, Chas. Baker and Robt. Simpson. Every dollar raised will be one gallon of honey. The hive will contain one hundred gallons. The rally will close the latter part of July... Mrs. Jane Hunt attended to business at Fredericktown last week...Rev. W.H. Spurlock, Mrs. Clara Poston, Mrs. Jane Hunt, Miss Bertha Staten and Miss Mae Baker are attending the Sunday school convention at Cape Girardeau this week...The club, of which Mrs. Simpson is queen, will make honey July 4...Miss Hortense Kennedy was hostess to sixteen persons at her home at Greenville, Monday evening...Mr. Alex Anthony, of St. Louis, is attending to business here this week."

06 July 1917, pg. 3, col. 3.
"Mr. Chas. Sutherland of St. Louis, was the guest of his mother, Mrs. Scott Cole, Sunday. Mr. and Mrs. Henry Amonette were pleased to entertain a party of friends from Ironton, Sunday...The Kindergarten Musical conducted by Miss Alice Swink, was a splendid affair and very largely attended...Master Elbert Baker accompanied Miss Edith Cayce home from Potosi Sunday... Little Miss Hilda Wagner is spending a few days with Mrs. Robert Simpson, who returned Tuesday from a visit to Crystal City. Her son, Eugene Hartman accompanied her...Mr. Lewis Murphy enjoyed a pleasant vacation here the first of the week...The friends of Mr. Onan Poston are lamenting his serious illness...Commander Knox of the M.W. of A. was present Monday night at the Masonic Hall, to assist Mrs. S.A. Smith in the organization of a camp. He will make another official visit to our town soon...Miss Ruth Boddie has returned from Charleston accompanied by Little Miss Lora Fulks... Miss Hortense Kennedy entertained a crowd of young people at the beautiful country home Wednesday...Mrs. J.H. McCallister is convalescing...Mrs. Mamie Foulk of Champaign, Ill[.] arrived Tuesday for an indefinite time. Glenard, the oldest son of Mr. and Mrs. Chas. Cayce injured his foot by cutting it on glass, and has thereby been a cripple for several days...Dr. Frederick Bridges has accepted a position at Fredericktown...Master Patrick Cayce has suffered intensely with a muscular throat affection for a couple of weeks... Messrs. Chas. Cayce, Tillman Cayce, Freeman Bridges, Walter Mathias [sic] and Moses Bridges are employed at Crystal City."

12 July 1917, pg. 3, col. 1.
"Mrs. Thos. Cayce chaperoned some young people on a trip to St. Francois River, last Tuesday...Rev. A. Poston, of Festus, Mo., was the guest of his brother, Mr. Onan Poston, Saturday...Mr. Lewis Smith chaperoned a party

of sixteen youths on a fishing expedition, Wednesday…Miss Imogene Staten, of Coffman, Mo., visited her sisters, Miss Lorene Staten and Mrs. Mazie Lyons, a few days ago…Rev. and Mrs. W.H. Spurlock and Miss Berdola Boddie attended the Quarterly Meeting at Bonne Terre, Sunday…Mesdames Susie Smith and Susie Robinson attended the picnic at Festus, Wednesday…Mrs. Talbert Burns is quite ill at her home on Columbia St…Mrs. Geo. Meyers is ill at Crystal City, Mo…Mr. and Mrs. Gabriel Cayce have returned from a fishing trip…Mr. Wm. Kennedy is employed at Mt. Vernon, [Jefferson Co.,] Ill…Commander J.B. Knox of the American Woodmen will lecture at the M.E. Church, Monday night, during which time some of the best local talent will render choice selections…Mrs. J.H. McAllister is able to be out again after a brief illness."

20 July 1917, pg. 3, col. 4.
"Miss Alice Meyers has gone to Chicago, Ill., where she expects to make her future home…Mesdames Beulah Cayce and Laverghe [sic] Smith, of St. Louis, spent a few days here last week…Messrs. Chas. Cayce and Samuel Burke returned to Festus Sunday…Good Will Lodge had the pleasure of initiating Joe Carson, Ed Carson, Chas. Carson, Jerome Valle, Henry Renfro, Weyman Boddie, Julius Johnson and Joseph LaMarque Saturday night…Mrs. S.A. Smith attended to business at Coffman last week…Camp No. 11 of the Order of American Woodmen perfected its organization Tuesday night, following a lecture by Commander B.J. Knox, last Monday night, at the A.M.E. Church. Refreshments were served each night. Mr. Hy. Wilburn was chosen Presiding Officer of the Camp…Miss Mattie Valle has gone to Michigan to spend her vacation…Mr. J.P. Evans has been elected Sunday school delegate to the convention, which will convene at Springfield, Ill., August 1…Dr. Weber and Dr. Watkins performed a successful operation on Mr. Onan Poston last Wednesday. The patient is doing fine. He was visited by his brother, Rev. A. Poston, of Festus, Mo., last Thursday…Miss Luetta Matthias was the guest of Mr. and Mrs. L. Armoureux at Ste. Genevieve last week…Miss Helen Matthias was the guest of Mrs. George Robinson, of Bonne Terre, Sunday… Mr. Geo. H. Powers, of St. Louis, was the guest of Miss Alice Swink a few days ago. While here he was entertained at the home of Mr. and Mrs. Jno. Franks…Among the out-of-town people to join the American Woodmen Camp No. 11 were Mr. Gus. Lyons and Miss Alcesta Douthit."

27 July 1917, pg. 5, col. 4.
"Mrs. Artie Reed of St. Louis is the guest of her mother, Mrs. E. Boddie. Mr. Thomas Cayce had a pleasant sojourn at home this week. Mr. Chas. Baker is attending the Grand Lodge of K. of P.'s, at Hannibal.

Mr. Felix Poston is spending his vacation with relatives in St. Louis. Howard Smith is enjoying a short stay with home folks.

Rev. E.L. McCallister of Sturgeon visited his parents Rev. and Mrs. J.H. McCallister the past week. Sunday night he preached to a very large appreciate audience. Rev. McCallister is a graduate of George R. Smith College, also of Gammon Theo. Inst. at Atlanta, Ga.

Mr. Perry Swink, of Bonne Terre, was a visitor here last week.

Mr. Lewis Smith went to New Madrid Monday in answer to a message announcing the demise of a brother from the result of being shot.

Messrs. Robert Simpson, Lewis Murphy, Moses Bridges and Samuel Burke of Festus spent Sunday here.

Mr. Elmer Bridges is expected home from Jefferson City within a few days. Just thirty five days more of vacation and then the youths will hie [sic] away to the call of the school bell."

03 August 1917, pg. 3, col. 3.
"Mesdames Katie Hunt and Mahalia Madison are visiting relatives at St. Louis...Mrs. Geo. Evans, J.P. Evans and son, Edward, are on the sick list this week...The rally collection of the M.E. Church Sunday amounted to $60.39. Mesdames E.J. Harris, Fannie Baker and L. Simpson were queens. Mrs. Simpson Led...The choir of St. Luke's Chapel entertained with dainty refreshments Sunday afternoon with Mr. Sylvester Swink, Mrs. Artie Reed, Miss Jewell Cabbell, Rev. J.H. McAllister and wife as visitors. This entertainment was complimentary to Rev. and Mrs. Spurlock...Mr. Felix Poston is convalescing...Mr. Chas. Baker returned from Hannibal, Mo., Sunday. Mr. Lewis Smith returned from New Madrid, Mo., Tuesday, much grieved over the death of a brother and the serious illness of another brother and his mother...The residence of Mr. and Mrs. Dave Buford caught fire last Saturday. The flames were extinguished before much damage was done...Mrs. Artie Reed and daughter, Lonie, were the guests of Mr. and Mrs. Lewis Kennedy, of Greenville, Sunday...Quite a large number of people attended the musical at the M.E. Church, Monday evening. Miss Alice Swink, Directress...Bonne Terre, Mo., was well represented a the musical, by some of the leading young men of that city...Mrs. Samuel Burke and son are visiting at Festus, Mo... Mrs. Geo. Meyers was called to St. Louis, on account of the illness of her daughter."

10 August 1917, pg. 2, col. 4.
"Mr. Henry Renfro received the sad news of his mother's death Wednesday afternoon. He departed for St. Louis Thursday morning...Those who attended the outing at St. Marys [sic] and DeSoto, Mo., August 4, report a

delightful time...The musical given by Miss Alice Swink's pupils was quite a success and much credit was reflected upon their excellent teacher...Mrs. Velma Reed and daughter returned to their home at St. Louis last Thursday... Mr. J.P. Evans is on the sick list...Mr. Onan Poston is still improving...Mesdames Kate Hunt and Madison returned home from St. Louis a few days ago. They report a pleasant visit...Mrs. Frank Harris returned home from Festus, Mo., last Wednesday...Mr. Peter Swink spent the day with home folks, last Sunday...Messrs. Percy Swink and Henry Fulton, of Bonne Terre, Mo., were visitors in this city last Thursday...Mr. Felix Poston has returned from St. Louis. He reports a pleasant visit...Mrs. Jno. Franks entertained Mrs. Charlotte Clay at dinner last Sunday."

17 August 1917, pg. 2, col. 4 and pg. 3, col. 1.
"The American Woodmen added two new members to their camp last Monday evening in the persons of Mrs. D. vans and Miss Maude Burks... Mrs. Bolduke, of Festus, Mo., visited her sister of this city, last week...Mrs. C.L. Anthony and Laurine Boddie are visiting relatives at St. Louis...Mrs. Geo. Blackwell entertained Mrs. Charlotte Clay at dinner last Sunday... The A.M.E. Sunday school will have their picnic Thursday, August 30. All are invited to attend...Mrs. Eliza Overton and granddaughter, Miss Ruth Boddie, will leave for Detroit, Mich., to visit Mrs. Overton's daughter, Mrs. James Robinson...Mr. Alph Washington, of Bonne Terre, Mo., was a visitor in Farmington last week...Miss Dayse F. Baker left for St. Louis Tuesday morning...Mr. Chas. Douthit and son, of Coffman, motored to Farmingotn Saturday. Miss Cosetta Boddie accompanied them home...Mr. Jerry Bridges is visiting relatives at St. Louis...Little Miss Theola Cayce is spending the week with her aunt. [sic] Mrs. Jerry Bridges at Swinks Grove...The many friends of Mrs. Rosy Parker were glad to learn of her approaching marriage, which will take place Thursday, August 16, to Mr. B. Blake, of Festus, Mo... Mrs. Mabel Burks has been spending a few days visiting her husband, Mr. Samuel Burks of Festus, Mo. Mrs. Burks and son returned home Monday... Miss Cora Meyers has been visiting her parents at Festus, Mo...Mr. and Mrs. Fred Chappelle, of Coffman, Mo., spent a few hours here Saturday...Mrs. Buford and mother spent a few days in Coffman as the guest of her daughter, Mrs. Fred Chappelle...Mr. Onan Poston is much improved...Mrs. Talbert Burns entertained Mr. Wayman Chappelle and Mrs. Eliza Overton at dinner Sunday...Mr. Jas. Cayce spent last Sunday at St. Louis...Miss Birdola Boddie will leave Sunday for Kete, Mo., to visit her sister, Mrs. Dorothy Overton... Mrs. Jno. Franks and daughters Zelia and Cornelia will leave Sunday to visit friends and relatives at St. Louis...Prof. J.C. Staten and daughter, Miss Vivian will visit friends at St. Louis this week."

07 September 1917, pg. 3, col. 1.

"Mrs. Julia Burke, of St. Louis, is the guest of her mother, Mrs. Charlotte Clay...Mr. Raymond Boise, of St. Louis, was a visitor here a few days ago... Mrs. Jas. Robinson entertained a few friends in honor of Mrs. J. Johnson and daughter, Selma, of St. Louis. Mrs. Johnson returned home Monday...Misses Corsetta [sic] Boddie and Hortense Kennedy entertained the Industrial Club at the residence of the Misses Boddie, Monday evening. Miss Alcesta Douthit, of Coffman, was among the guests...Miss Zelma Swink is very ill at her home...Mr. Booker Baker returned to St. Louis, where he will resume his studies at Sumner High School...Estacada Baker and Elmer Bridges left Wednesday morning for Jefferson City, where they will attend Lincoln Institute...The entertainment given by the American Woodmen, Monday evening, was one of the best ever given in this city, and was largely attended. Visitors were present from many nearby towns. Music was furnished by the Festus Orchestra...Mrs. Jane Hunt visited Fredericktown, last week... Mr. and Mrs. Arvella Wilkins have returned to St. Louis, after a pleasant visit with relatives...Miss Minnie Thornton and Mr. Russell McCallister will leave Monday for Sedalia, Mo., to enter George R. Smith College...Mr. Wm. Wright was the guest of his mother, Mrs. Louisa Anthony, last week...Douglas [sic] School opened Tuesday with a large enrollment. Rev. J.H. McAllister visited the school Tuesday."

14 September 1917, pg. 2, col. 3.

"Howard Smith, Edgar Kennedy and John Baker motored to Ste. Genevieve Sunday...Mesdames Charlotte Clay, Eliza Overton and Nellie Evans are ill... Messrs. J. Ernest Wilkins and B.J. Wilkins were the guests of their mother, Mrs. S.O. Wilkins, this week...Misses Luetta Matthews and Lorene Staten are enjoying a vacation at Coffman...Mr. and Mrs. Blake of Festus were the guests of Mr. and Mrs. P.M. Cayce Sunday...Messrs. Earl Wright, Henry Fulton and Percy Swink were here from Bonne Terre Sunday...Mr. Jerome Valle, Mr. Philip Thornton, Miss Mae Baker and Miss Jewel Cabbel [sic] enjoyed Sunday at Ste. Genevieve...Mr. G. Oliver of Fredericktown visited here Sunday...Laurine Boddie arrived home Saturday after spending a pleasant fortnight with Mr. and Mrs. Weyman Boddie of St. Louis...The friends of Mrs. Marshall Curtaindoll of 2941 Pine St., St. Louis, are sorry to learn of her recent illness[47]...Rev. J.H. McCallister is the guest of his son, Rev. E. McCallister, of Sturgeon, [Boone Co.,] Mo...Mrs. Geo. Meyers and grandson, Homer, of Festus, were here the first of the week...Mr. L. Murphy and R. Simpson returned to Festus Monday...Mrs. A. Simms is spending a few days with Rev. A. Poston and wife of Festus...Master Allen Schaffer is now residing with Mr. and Mrs. Lindsey Clay of St. Louis...Quarterly meeting services will be held at St. Luke's Chapel Sunday...Mr. Orran Poston attended to business in St. Louis this week...Mr. Leroy McCallister of Springfield, Mo., was the guest of his parents, Rev. McCallister and wife, the first of the week. The former addressed the pupils of Douglass School Tuesday... Goodwill Lodge initiated Messrs. Ulysses Jennings, James Johnson of Potosi and Paul Alexander of Bonne Terre Saturday night. Messrs. Geo. Robinson of Bonne Terre, Joseph, Ed and Chas. Carson of Potosi, attended the meeting also...Mr. J. Ernest Wilkins of St. Louis delivered a very timely talk at the M.E. Church Sunday night...Be present Sunday night at the M.E. Church and hear the Senior program."

21 September 1917, pg. 2, col. 3.
"Many people went to Ste. Genevieve, Sunday to witness the ball game played with St. Mary's vs. Farmington Giants. The scores were 5 to 6 in favor of Farmington...The picnic at Mineral Point was largely attended last Saturday. A delightful time was spent...Mr. and Mrs. Fred Chappelle of Coffman and daughters Mary, Lavada and Alta, returned home Monday...Mr. Frank Lewis of Ste. Genevieve was a visitor here Monday...Mrs. Charlotte Clay is quite ill at her residence in South Farmington...Mr. Sylvester Swink visited relatives here Saturday...After a few months search, Mrs. Eliza Overton received the sad news of the death of her son Howard in St. Louis, last Monday. Mr. Overton had suffered during early spring from a peculiar nervousness which no doubt caused his death...Miss Mattie Valle has returned from a pleasant visit in Michigan...Mr. Felix Poston is visiting relatives in St. Louis, this week...Mrs. Anna Yeager accompanied Clara, Anna and Willie Taylor to visit their mother, Mrs. Ellis Taylor...Mrs. Minnie Cayce visited friends at St. Louis, this week...Mrs. Scott Cole is spending the week at Festus, as the guest of Mrs. McMinn a former resident of this city...Mrs. Rossie Madison and son, Jessamine are visiting at Coffman...Mr. Arville Manning of Minnith, Mo., visited here last week...Mrs. Lewis Murphy went to Sedalia Monday. She was accompanied as far as St. Louis, by Mrs. Robert Simpson and son, Eugene. Mrs. Murphy will be the guest of Mr. and Mrs. Antoine Murphy... Rev. J.D. Barksdale conducted services at the A.M.E. Church, Sunday...Rev. W.H. Spurlock and congregation are making extensive preparations for the Annual Conference, which will convene at Poplar Bluff."

28 September 1917, pg. 2, col. 4; pg. 3., col. 1.
"Miss Cosetta Boddie was hostess at a delightful birthday party last Monday...Rev. W.H. Spurlock was agreeable surprised last Saturday evening when a number of friends assembled to remind him of his birthday...Rev. U.R. Rivere [sic] conducted quarterly meeting at the M.E. church Sunday. In the

afternoon Rev. W.H. Spurlock preached to a large audience...Mrs. Jane Hunt is visiting friends at Fredericktown this week...Miss Alice Swink had charge of the successful musicale [sic] given at Masonic Hall, Tuesday evening...Mr. and Mrs. Chas. Douthit motored to this city on business Monday...Mrs. Esther Williams of St. Louis, is the guest of home folks this week...Miss Thelma Swink is convalescent after a brief illness...Messrs. Owen Kennedy and Granville McGhee of Festus, were the guests of Mr. and Mrs. Talbert Burns, Saturday...Miss Luetta Matthias was the guest of friends at Festus Sunday afternoon...Miss Helen Matthias will leave for St. Louis in a few days where she will spend the winter...Mrs. James Cayce was the guest of relatives at St. Louis last week...Mr. Myrt Hunt was the guest of Mrs. Jane Hunt Saturday. He returned to St. Louis Monday...Mrs. Albert Simms has returned after a pleasant visit at Festus...Mrs. Geo. Evans is able to be up, but is unable to resume her duties...Mrs. W.J.[?] Roberts and son, Addison, are visiting relatives in St. Louis, this week...Mrs. Eliza Overton and granddaughter, Ruth Boddie, left Thursday for Detroit, Mich."

05 October 1917, pg. 2, col. 4.
"Miss Hortense Kennedy visited in St. Louis Tuesday...Mrs. Anna Yeager accompanied her mother, Mrs. Sarah Amonette to Herculaneum Tuesday... Mr. Phillip Thornton returned home from St. Louis Sunday accompanied by little Miss Alberta Thornton...Mrs. Jessie Ward and Miss Bethel Cayce were the guests of Mrs. Geo. Evans Sunday...Mr. Chas. Douthit of Coffman, was in the city Sunday and was accompanied by his daughter, Alcesta, who is affected with rheumatism...Mr. and Mrs. Talbert Burns, Misses Lorene Staten, Luetta Matthias and Mattie Valle were entertained at a dinner party Sunday at the home of Mr. and Mrs. Jerry Bridges...Prof. J.C. Staten and daughters, Lucretia and Vivian, were the guests of Mr. and Mrs. Peter Hill at Herculaneum, Sunday...Cards are out announcing the engagement of Miss Alice Swink to Mr. G.H. Powers...Messrs. Weyman Boddie, Alex Anthony and A. Reed of St. Louis, chaperoned a party of gentlemen on an auto expedition here Sunday...Mrs. Wm. McCalister and son Edward, Mrs. Chas. Cayce and sons Glennard and Robert, visited relatives at Festus Sunday... Mr. Wm. Murphy, of Valles Mines, visited friends here Sunday...Mr. Henry Renfro went to St. Louis Monday where he will spend the winter...Floyd Kennedy is enjoying a few days with home folks...Mr. J. Bartholomew and son Joseph are the guests of Mrs. Peter Swink and family...Miss Cora Meyers and Mrs. Wm. Kennedy spent Sunday at Festus...Edgar Cayce returned to St. Louis Wednesday...Mrs. Anna Steiger, Mr. and Mrs. Frank Villars, Mr. Ed. McFadden and daughter, Mrs. Georgia Bigsby of Fredericktown, visited I the city Sunday."[48]

19 October 1917, pg. 2, col. 3.

"Mrs. Sara Occamore and sons, Cecil and Marion, have moved to Madison, Ill...Rev. W.H. Spurlock left Tuesday morning for the annual conference which is in session at Kirkwood, [St. Louis Co.,] Mo...Miss Edith O. Cayce, of Mineral Point, attended to business here Saturday...The miscellaneous shower given at the residence of Mrs. F. Poston, Thursday, for Miss Alice Swink was largely attended. The gifts were beautiful and useful...Little Miss Olivia Wilkins has entered Douglass School. She will reside with her grandmother, Mrs. S.O. Wilkins...Mr. B.J. Wilkins had a pleasant visit with homefolks this week...Mrs. Louisa Anthony and granddaughter, Miss Virginia Matthias are spending the week in St. Louis...Mrs. R. Phillips, of Poplar Bluff, and her three children are spending the week with the former's father, Mr. George Blackwell...Misses Hortense Kennedy and Cosetta Boddie entertained the Industrial Club, Monday night...Mrs. Harry Cayce, of St. Louis, is visiting relatives...Roy Douthit, Miss Alcesta Douthit and Miss Imogene Staten visited here Sunday...Mrs. Maggie Burke has moved to the southern part of town...Mrs. Eric Matthias and daughter, Elizabeth, visited Fredericktown last week...Mr. John Douthit and Miss Mary McCallister, Mr. Arville Chappelle and Miss Hortense Kennedy motored to Fredericktown Sunday...Miss Florence Taylor and Mrs. James Cayce visited at Festus Sunday...Mr. Owan [sic] Poston has accepted work at Collinsville, [Madison Co.,] Ill. He will leave here Sunday...Miss Mayme Burke is employed at Festus...Mrs. Henry Wilburn, Mrs. F. Poston, Mrs. Geo. Evans and Mrs. Wm. Kennedy were among the ill of last week...The Fortnightly Club presented Douglass School with the contents for a medicine chest of which the school and faculty are thankful."

26 October 1917, pg. 2, col. 3.

"Elmer Amonette is ill with typhoid fever...Quite a large number of persons attended the entertainment at Bonne Terre Saturday night...Mesdames Peter Hill and Amile Nelson of Herculaneum were the guests of Mrs. Antoine Murphy Sunday...Mrs. Jerry Bridges is ill at her home at Swink's settlement...Mesdames Katie Cayce and Chas. Cayce attended a birthday dinner at Valles Mines, Sunday...Mr. John Cayce has arrived from St. Louis well and happy...Mrs. Jane Hunt is attending to business at Fredericktown this week...Mr. Geo. Meyers and daughter, Miss Cora, arrived from Festus Sunday night...Dr. F.D. Bridges is attending to business in St. Louis this week...Misses Jewel Cabble, Telma Swink and Alice Swink went to St. Louis Saturday...Mrs. Gus Villars is in the hospital in St. Louis with complicated illness...Messrs. Jno. Baker, Howard Smith and Onan Poston left for St. Louis...Mr. Samuel Burke is at home for recuperation...Mr. and Mrs. James

Cunningham spent Sunday with Mr. and Mrs. Jerry Bridges…Miss Bertha Staten lacerated her finger almost to the bone Friday while opening a can of fruit…Miss Minnie Thornton was compelled to return home on account of illness. She is improving…Mrs. P. Boddie had a pleasant trip to St. Louis last week…Rev. W.H. Spurlock has been assigned to Booneville [sic] [Cooper Co., Mo.] for the ensuing year and Rev. Greenlee to this place…The friends of Mrs. S.A. Smith are sorry to learn of her illness…Miss Dorice Villars has returned to St. louis [sic]…As sure as the grass grows round the stump, we buy coal in Farmington by the lump."

02 November 1917, pg. 2, col. 4; pg. 3., col. 1.
"Mr. William Wright has returned for the winter…Mr. Chas. Douthit and son, Roy, and Miss Corinne Wilkins, motored to Farmington Sunday…Mrs. Geo. Evans is still very ill…Mr. Ulyses [sic] Robinson, of Poplar Bluff, Mo., visited Mr. James Robinson last week…Rev. R. Phillips passed through our city last week en route to Charleston…Elmer Amonette is convalescent… Mrs. M.P. Cayce and Miss Mamie Giessing addressed the pupils of Douglass school [sic], Monday, on the conservation of Food. Quite a number of pupils signed the pledge…Miss Dola Boddie has arrived for the winter…Misses Zelma Swink and Jewel Cabbel have arrived from St. Louis. They witnessed the marriage of Mr. G.H. Powers and Miss Alice Swink at Kirkwood Sunday, October 21. Rev. W.H. Spurlock performed the ceremony. They are at home to their many friends at 1011 Newstead Ave., St. Louis, Mo…Mrs. Louisa Anthony entertained three lady missionaries at her home this week…Miss Sophia Mudd was hostess to a number of friends Sunday at a tea given in honor of Mr. Tillman Cayce, who with Mr. Walter Matthias departed for St. Louis Monday, en route to Camp for training…Mr. Servis Smith has undergone a successful operation…Rev. Greenlee filled his pulpit for the first time here Sunday…Rev. and Mrs. Spurlock left for Booneville [sic] Wednesday."

09 November 1917, pg. 2, col. 4.
"Mr. Lewis Murphy enjoyed Sunday with home folks…Mr. R. Phillips and children left the first of the week for their new home at Charleston, Mo…Mr. and Mrs. James Robinson chaperoned a party of young people Sunday at a persimmon hunting…Mr. Baker of Festus and Mr. Murphy of Valles Mines, visited here Sunday…Miss Cosetta Boddie is quite ill…Mr. Moses Hunt attended a football game at Perryville Saturday…Mrs. David Buford and daughter Laura had a pleasant visit at Coffman last week…Rev. Green was here Saturday enroute [sic] to Coffman…The friends of Miss Charlotte Valle are glad to hear of her marriage to Mr. Walter Franks of Coffman…The residence of Mrs. Eliza Overton was damaged by fire Monday. Elmer Amonette

is still improving...Mr. Thomas Cayce is able to resume his work...Mrs. Leora Simpson and son Eugene are visiting in Festus...Mrs. Jerry Bridges has recovered from a recent illness...At the anniversary held at the M.E. Church Sunday, Rev. Charles Wilkins and Mr. Albert Simms of St. Louis, Prin., J.C. Staten, Mr. P.M. Cayce and Mr. Chas. Baker were the principal speakers... Rev. McCallister is quite actively engaged in preparing for Thanksgiving... Mrs. P. Boddie, who has been quite ill in St. Louis arrived Tuesday...Miss Lorene Staten is indisposed. Mr. Rossie Madison visited at DeSoto Sunday... Mrs. Fred Chappelle and children are visiting relatives here...Scarlet fever is gaining a rapid headway in our community...Miss Hortense Kennedy spent a pleasant fortnight at the old homestead at Greenville...Master Alonzo Kennedy and little Miss Parnello [sic] Cayce are able to be at school again... Master Kossuth Baker had the misfortune to have his bicycle stolen from one of the public highways."

23 November 1917, pg. 2, col. 3.
"Mrs. Lewis Kennedy accompanied Mrs. Geo. Evans home Saturday from St. Louis. Mrs. Evans is improving...Mr. Lee Roden, of St. Louis, was the guest of Mr. and Mrs. Jerry Bridges Sunday...Miss Cosetta Boddie remains quite ill. Her many friends are anxious for her recovery...Mrs. Geo. Blackwell is visiting in Fredericktown...Rev. Green, of St. Louis, preached at the A.M.E. church Sunday night...Mesdames Thomas Cayce and Ed. Harris are conducting the Thanksgiving Festivities at the M.E. church. Preaching services will be held at ten-thirty that day...Dame Rumor says "Some one [sic] will soon wed in our town." Not much left now but a few old bachelors and a couple or so [of] old maids. Get busy...Mrs. Mahalia Madison visited in Bonne Terre last week...Mr. Jerome Valle is suffering from a nervous breakdown. His many friends wish for him a speedy recovery...Mrs. Tullock, of Ironton, was the guest of her daughter, Mrs. Henry Amonette, last week... Mr. Wilson Chappelle, of Coffman, attended to business here Thursday... Mrs. Jerry Bridges is rapidly improving...Miss Lorene Staten, of Coffman, was in our city one day last week...Rev. Greenlee and congregation are preparing for Thanksgiving enjoyment...Mr. John Cayce, of St. Louis, is the guest of his brother, Mr. Frank Cayce...We have only one blind person in our community, i.e., Mr. Matt Bridges. As you meet him, help him. He will appreciate it and God will bless you abundantly...Mr. Rossie Madison was in DeSoto Sunday...Instead of giving so many gifts at Christmas, let's try and help the Y.M.C.A. and thereby reach millions."

16 November 1917, pg. 2, col. 3.
"Mrs. Josephine Roden is the guest of her mother, Mrs. Jerry Bridges. Mrs.

Lewis Murphy and Mrs. Lewis Kennedy accompanied Mrs. Geo. Evans to St. Louis, where the latter will take a special treatment...Mrs. Harry Cayce visited at Coffman Saturday. Mrs. H. Overton and son, Melvin of Okete, Mo., are the guests of Mrs. P. Boddie...Mr. Wesley Douthit of St. Louis is having a pleasant vacation with home folks here...Miss Lorene Staten has gone to Coffman for recuperation. Miss Cosetta Boddie is yet quite ill...Mrs. Booker T. Baker and Mr. and Mrs. J.A.K. Ficklin of St. Louis motored here Sunday and were the guests of Mr. and Mrs. Chas. Baker...Rev. Oaks was in our city Saturday...Mrs. Jane Hunt is convalescent. Mesdames Katie Cayce and Ada Cayce visited in Valles Mines Sunday...Mrs. Geo. Burns arrived from St. Louis Saturday...Mr. Sylvester Swink of Minnith attended to business here Friday...The young people of the A.M.E. Church are actively engaged in preparing for a program to be rendered soon...A letter from Mr. Tillman Cayce states that camp life is not bad after all. He likes to be with the Sammies."

30 November 1917, pg. 2, col. 3.
"Mrs. Ella Merrill and daughter, Nadine, of Champaign, Ill., Messrs. Edgar Cayce, F.D. Bridges, Moses Cayce of St. Louis, Mr. and Mrs. Wm. Cayce and daughters, Mrs. Juanita and Lamont of Cape Girardeau, attended the funeral of John Cayce which was held Monday afternoon. While at work Saturday afternoon, Mr. Cayce fell dead. He was a prosperous butcher and an esteemed citizen. Rev. J.H. McCallister officiated at the funeral...Mr. Clark Tullock and wife of Ironton, were the guests of Mr. and Mrs. Henry Amonette the first of the week...Mr. B.J. Wilkins, of St. Louis, and Miss Corinne Wilkins, of Coffman, were the guests of their mother, Mrs. S.O. Wilkins, Sunday... Mrs. Lewis Kennedy and Mr. and Mrs. J.P. Evans were out persimmoning Sunday...Messrs. Weyman Chappelle and Roy Douthit, were up from Coffman in their cars on business last week...Mrs. Felix Poston is visiting relatives in St. Louis...Miss Cosetta Boddie is some what [sic] improved. Miss Alcesta Douthit of Coffman visited her last week...Mrs. Geo. Evans is critically ill... Mrs. Antoine Murphy is among the ill of the week...Mr. Wesley Douthit bagged thirteen rabbits while hunting at Coffman, and they accompanied him to St. Louis for sight seeing [sic] Thanksgiving. Believe it?...Misses Mildred and Ida Chappelle of Coffman, were the guests of Mrs. T. Burns last week."

07 December 1917, pg. 2, col. 5; pg. 3., col. 5.
"At the Thanksgiving ball St. Louis, Festus, Bonne Terre and Coffman were well represented. The ball lasted till early Friday morning. It was no doubt one of Aunt Dolly's times...Mrs. Eliza Blackwell has returned from a visit to Fredericktown...Mrs. Emily Boddie accompanied her daughter Cosetta

to St. Louis Saturday for medical aid...Miss Marie Hogan White, G.L. of O.O.C., addressed Masoleat Court Wednesday evening. She also addressed a large audience at the M.E. church Thursday morning. Both addresses were interesting and well delivered...Mr. and Mrs. Lewis Kennedy entertained Rev. J.H. McCallister and wife at dinner Thanksgiving...Master Kossuth Baker appeared on the program at an entertainment at Mineral Point, Thursday evening, which was conducted by Miss Edith O. Cayce. Miss Cayce spent the week's end with homefolks. Miss Minnie Thornton went to St. Louis Monday to accept a position...Mr. and Mrs. Percy Swink visited here Thanksgiving. Mr. Swink has returned to Bonne Terre where he is employed...Mr. Lewis Murphy returned to Crystal City Sunday...Mrs. Alice Powers, of St. Louis, visited home folks last week...Mr. and Mrs. O. Vaughn, of Potosi, were the guests of Mr. and Mrs. Ed. Harris last week...Miss Mary McCallister accompanied Miss Marie Madison to St. Louis, Sunday afternoon. Miss Mae Baker and Mr. John Baker went to [one line illegible] Mrs. James Robinson and Miss D.F. Baker chaperoned Misses Leslie Poston, Hilda Kennedy, Edna Harris and [several words illegible] to Bonne Terre Sunday...Quarterly meeting services will be held at the M.E. church Sunday and at the A.M.E. church the third Sunday. Rev. Greenlee will preach at the M.E. church Sunday afternoon. Dr. Rivere will conduct the services...Mr. Felix Poston attended to business at Crystal City Sunday...Little Miss Anna Pugh is convalescing... You will admit you are lonesome without the Argus, then why not subscribe for it and read what the Negro is doing, can do and will do. It tells it all. It is a paper worth the while...Mrs. Louisa Anthony was called to Fredericktown Saturday to be with her cousin, Mr. Geo. Villars, who is critically ill from a blood poisoned hand...Send the Argus to a boy at Camp Funston. He'll appreciate it."

14 December 1917, pg. 2, col. 3.
"Rev. H. Overton, of Okete [Lincoln Co., Mo.], preached an excellent sermon at A.M.E. church, Sunday...Rev. Greenlee preached at the M.E. church Sunday afternoon. Dr. Rivere conducted quarterly meeting...Edith O. Cayce, of Mineral Point, is at the bedside of her mother, who has been very ill...Little Miss Vee Occamore is visiting at Detroit, Mich...Mr. Ferris Douthit, of Coffman, was the guest of Mrs. T. Burns, Sunday...Quarterly meeting will be held at St. Luke's Chapel, Sunday in the afternoon, and the sacramental sermon will be preached by Rev. J.H. McCallister...Mr. and Mrs. P.M. Cayce entertained Saturday in honor of their daughter Parnelia's eighth birthday...Miss Florence Taylor is visiting Mr. and Mrs. Fred Chappelle at Coffman, Mo...Mrs. Jane Hunt was a business visitor at Fredericktown last week...Mrs. Mayme Foulk has returned to Champaign...Mrs. Felix Poston

has returned from an extended visit in St. Louis...Christmas is ten days off. You could not give your friend a better present than the Argus for a year. Husband, present it to your wife; young man, present it to your lady friends."

21 December 1917, pg. 2, col. 2.
"The Pie Social given at the A.M.E. Church Friday night was a financial success...Mrs. Percy Swink has gone to Bonne Terre where she and husband will reside...Miss Cosetta Boddie is improving after a successful operation... Mrs. Geo. Evans is convalescent...Rev. J.H. McCallister and congregation worshipped with Rev. Greenlee, Sunday afternoon and a splendid service was had...Mr. James Robinson visited at St. Louis Sunday...The friends of Mrs. Ellen Busch are sorry to know that her eyesight is failing...For some reason it is not generally known that Rev. J.E. Edwards, a former pastor has passed to the Great Beyond...At the election of officers of Masole [sic] Court Friday night Prof. J.C. Staten was elected worthy counsellor [sic]...Mr. and Mrs. Henry Wilburn are rejoicing over the arrival of a bouncing baby boy."

18 January 1918, pg. 2, col. 3-4.
"Miss Sophia Mudd is recovering from a recent illness...Mr. Peter Swink is enjoying a visit with home folks...Mr. Chas. Baker has been duly appointed vice chairman of one of the committees of Thrift Stamp and War Certificates of this county. The other members are Felix Poston, James Robinson, Mrs. Susie Robinson and Miss Dayse F. Baker...Mrs. Lucy Bridges received the said intelligence of the demise of her brother, Lewis Cunningham of St. Louis who has been ill for some time. Her sister, Mrs. Allie Magness of Oklahoma City spent a few hours here Thursday[49]...News reached here last week announcing the death of a fo[rmer] resi[dent] of thi[s] place in the person of Mr. Luther Cayce...The friends of Mr. Walter Matthias are glad to know that he is up and able to make his daily hike at Camp Funston...A letter from J. Elmer Bridges at Lincoln Institute states that the school year is a busy and interesting one...The severe weather caused the percentage of attendance at Douglass School to run lower than it has for years. This was due to the fact that the majority of pupils live the greater distance away...Mrs. Henry Wilburn and little son, Henry Lewis are getting along nicely...Mrs. Mary Cayce has fully recovered...We are informed that Clarence Meyers is quite ill at Crystal City...Mrs. J.H. McCallister and Mrs. Jane Hunt entertained guests in their homes last week...St. Paul M.E. Church will hold memorial services in remembrance of the splendid service rendered by Dr. R.E. Gillum, ex-dist. supt. By his works shall we ever remember him."

25 January 1918, pg. 2, col. 4.

"Mr. [illegible] Taylor of Bonne Terre, attended to business here Wednesday...Miss Bertha Staten, Mrs. Jane Hunt, Mrs. Eliza Blackwell and Mrs. J.H. McAllister are among the ill of this week...Miss Irene Matthias of Coffman was the guest of Mrs. Thomas Cayce, Saturday...Mr. Sherman Overton, of Okete is the welcome guest of Mr. and Mrs. H. Overton...After and [sic] absence from school of five or six weeks on account of scarlet fever, Anna Pugh has returned...Mr. and Mrs. Percy Swink of Bonne Terre were in our city on a business jaunt Monday...Despite the fact that there is such a scarcity of fuel both churches held their usual services Sunday...Mr. James Robinson Sr. has returned from a pleasant visit with friends in St. Louis... Prof. J.C. Staten was installed W.C. of Masoleate [sic] Court Tuesday night... Unless the fuel supply is greatly replenished within the next few days, there will be much suffering in and about our city. The supply has been so meager that those who had money could not purchase it at any price...Mr. Thomas Cayce is quite ill at his home in the eastern part of town...Mrs. Louisa Lee is recovering slowly."[50]

08 February 1918, pg. 3, col. 4-5.

"Miss Alcesta Douthit has accepted a position [illegible] and we are glad to have her in [illegible] community...Miss Zelma Swink entertained Rev. Greenlee and Miss Bertha Staten at dinner Sunday...Master Kossuth Baker was the captain of the number who gave Rev. J.H. McCallister such a pleasant surprise Saturday...Miss Edith Cayce of Mineral Point visited her parents who are ill...Mr. Henry Amonette had a slight attack of pneumonia but is convalescent...Mrs. Lewis Murphy has returned from a visit at Crystal City...Rev. Logan passed through the city last week...Miss Cosetta Boddie has returned to the hospital where she is undergoing special treatment... The reporter enjoyed a pleasant visit in St. Louis, last week where she visited some of the city schools and found the schools well equipped and in splendid working order...Laura Wilburn, a pupil of Douglass school [sic] is ill at her home in West Farrington [sic]...Messrs. Sherman and Hildred Overton, left Thursday for their home at Okoto [sic]. The former is in Class A of the next draft...Mr. Thos. Cayce has recovered sufficiently to resume his work...More and more do we feel the necessity of having a charitable organization to which we might appeal when help is needed...Mr. J.P. Evens [sic] is quite ill...Miss Florence Taylor is visiting at Crystal City...Miss Lorene Staten is spending the week at her home at Coffman, Mo...Quite a number have bought thrift stamps and many more will buy. The citizens have and will ever be loyal to their government."

15 February 1918, pg. 3, col. 4.

"Prof. A. Coffin was in the city this week arranging for Blind Boone's concert which will be Feb. 21, at the Monarch...Mr. Henry Wilburn was called to Crystal City Saturday on account of the serious illness of his sister, Mrs. Jennings. Mrs. Jennings was formerly Miss Arna Wilburn of this city and a very admirable young lady...Messrs. Witt, Wright and Maul of Bonne Terre were in the city Sunday...Mrs. George Blackwell is able to be out...Mr. Lewis Kennedy is suffering from the result of frozen ears...Mr. and Mrs. Talbert Burns entertained in honor of Rev. T.H. McCallister and wife with a bounteous dinner, Sunday...Mr. Artie Fulton of Bonne Terre was here on business last week...Miss Corinne Wilkins has returned from Coffman where she has just finished a successful term of school...Miss Mamie Burke is visiting at Festus...Mrs. Jane Hunt is recovering rapidly...Rev. J.H. McCallister and congregation are preparing for the Annual Conference, which will convene at Hannibal [Marion Co., Mo.]...Much ado is being made by way of co[?????] tion of food. It was not a task [illegible] [m]any of us to Hooverize for it had been our plan through dire necessity. While we as a community are feeling very much the effects of the high price of fuel and food, we have learned a greater lesson of saving. Notwithstanding the times are hard, many are buying Thrift Stamps in order to aid in this time of government need."

01 March 1918, pg. 3, col. 4-5.

"Mrs. Geo. Blackwell attended to business in Bonne Terre last week...Mr. Felix Poston has returned from St. Louis where he has had optical treatment for several days...Mr. James Cunningham had the misfortune to have several ribs broken while farming. He is recovering slowly...Mesdames Lewis Murphy, Mazie Lyons and Lucy Bridges were entertained at the home of the reporter Sunday afternoon...Mrs. Cora J. Turner of Saginaw, [Saginaw Co.,] Mich., was an admirable visitor at Douglass School Monday. Mr. and Mrs. Turner will soon move to Grand Rapids, [Kent Co.,] Mich...Mr. Chas. Baker was master of ceremonies at the Lincoln celebration Sunday afternoon at the M.E. Church. Prin. J.C. Staten and Rev. J.H. McCallister were the principal participants. The choir furnished special music...Mr. Wm. Wright has returned from a visit with friends at St. Louis...Mrs. Dorothy Overton and son, Melvin, have returned to their home at Okete...Mrs. James Cayce is visit[ing] [line illegible] Messrs. Arville, Weyman and Wilson Chappelle, of Coffman, were visitors here last week...Quarterly meeting services will be held at the M.E. Church, March 10 and at the A.M.E. Church March 17... Miss Leslie Poston had a pleasant week the guest of Rev. Poston and wife, if [sic] Festus...Ruth Boddie has returned from Detroit, [Wayne Co.,] Mich., to be with homefolks...Mrs. Eric Matthias entertained in honor of Mrs. Cora

J. Frias Sunday...Mrs. Dorothy Overton, Mrs. Beulah Cayce and Miss Dola Boddie were entertained by Mrs. Maholia [sic] Madison Friday...Almost the Colored population to a unit attended the Boone Concert Thursday evening, which was grand. Mr. Boone made an everlasting impression on all who heard him."

08 March 1918, pg. 3, col. 3.
"Messrs. Rossie Madison and Charles Cayce are spending the week in St. Louis...Mrs. Gabriel Cayce is able to be up and around. Miss Mamie Burke and Mrs. Richard Occamore visited at Festus last week...Elmer Amonette is nursing a blood poisoned hand...Mr. Phillip Thornton has returned from St. Louis, where he attended to important business...Laura Wilburn is able to be out again...Mr. Lewis Hill was badly bruised about the face while trying to rope a cow. He says he likes other jobs better...Mrs. Belle Matkins, one of the oldest citizens of our community is ill and needs cheery visitors near her... Mrs. Georgia Franks, has recovered from a serious illness of a fortnight... Sunday will be quarterly meeting day at St. Paul. Dr. Rivere will conduct the services. Rev. Greenlee will preach the sacramental sermons. Mrs. Anna Jennings died at Festus Sunday after an illness of many months. Her brother, Mr. Henry Wilburn, left Tuesday to attend the funeral. Mrs. Jennings was a splendid woman and lived in our community for many years."[51]

22 March 1918, pg. 3, col. 2.
"Mrs. Lewis Murphy is at home for recuperation...Mesdames Geo. Maul, Mary Robinson, Gordon Taylor and Luther Taylor, of Bonne Terre, attended Quarterly meeting at the A.M.E. Church Sunday...Mr. and Mrs. Gabriel Cayce have moved to their new home in East Farmington...Sunday will be Anniversary Day for the [line illegible] M.E. Church. At two o'clock a programme [sic] will be rendered...The residence of Mr. Tim Murphy was damaged by fire last Sunday evening...Messrs. Henry Wilburn and Dave Buford accompanied Mrs. Buford and daughter, Laura home from Coffman, Sunday...Mr. Henry Amonette visited in St. [sic] Genevieve Sunday...Mr. Weyman Chappell of Coffman was a Sunday visitor...Mr. P.M. Cayce has accepted a new position with an increase of salary...Mrs. Esther Williams is quite on the decline at her home in West Farmington...Mrs. Leah Evans Wilkins and her daughter, Olivia, returned to St. Louis Monday after having had a pleasant visit with Mrs. S.O. Wilkins and family...Mr. N. Cunningham visited relatives here last week...Mrs. J.H. McCallister is able to be out again...The young people of the A.M.E. Church are preparing to render a play Good Friday evening which bids fair to be a good one. All of the participants are local talents...Queen of Honor Court No. 38 will observe

Palm Sunday with an appropriate program with Mrs. P. Boddie, Matron...
Principal J.C. Staten and wife are rejoicing over the advent of a baby girl. Mr.
and Mrs. Antoine Murphy have like pleasure at their home at Sedalia, [Pettis
Co.,] Mo. Mr. Murphy is employed by Civil Service at Kansas City, [Jackson
Co.,] Mo...Mrs. Sarah Amonette has returned from a visit with relatives at
St. Louis...Mrs. Belle Matkins, who is more than four score years has been
quite ill at her home in East Farmington."

29 March 1918, pg. 3, col. 3-4.
"Regardless of the high cost of living and the scarcity of things we have
measles, mumps and smallpox galore...Mr. Walter Matthias is at home from
Camp Funston looking "spick and span" in his uniform and is enjoying a fur-
lough which will last quite a few days...Miss Augustine Swink, of St. Louis,
visited relatives here Sunday...Prof. Wise and Mr. and Mrs. Percy Swink, of
Bonne Terre attended the Pythian and Calanthean anniversary Sunday...Mr.
Arthur Cayce, of Potosi, Mo., was the guest of Mr. Scott Cole the first of the
week...Mesdames Mahalia Madison and Katie Hunt en [sic] and Mrs. James
Cayce are comfortable situated in their new home...Mrs. joyed [sic] Sunday
at Bonne Terre...Mr. [sic] Alice Powers, of St. Louis, is he guest of homefolks...Mrs. Chas. Baker has been among the ill of the week...Mr. Floyd
Kennedy is at home for recuperation...Miss Edna Harris has recovered from
a recent illness...Mrs. Rebecca Bridges is suffering from rheumatism so much
that she is unable to be at her usual vocation...Easter will be appropriately
observed by both churches [illegible] J.H. McCallister and congregation are
busy preparing for conference...Mr. Lewis Murphy returned to Crystal City
Monday...Mr. James Robinson, Sr., went to Iron Mountain Lake on a fishing
expedition...Mr. Wm. Baker had the misfortune to have his left hand badly
bruised while drawing ice at Schramm's plant Monday...Mr. and Mrs. Lewis
Murphy visited at Coffman last week. Mr. Gabriel Cayce has been quite ill
at his home in East Farmington...Mr. Jesse Koehn of Herculaneum was the
guest of his sister-in-law, Mrs. Rossie Madison, Sunday...Room No. 2, of
Douglass School was dismissed Wednesday on account of illness in the principal's home...Miss Edith O. Cayce, principal of the school at Mineral Point
enjoyed Sunday with homefolks...Mr. Moses Cayce of St. Louis attended to
business here the first of the week...Mr. Sylvester Swink, of Coffman, visited
here Sunday...Mrs. Esther Williams is confined to her bed now and is quite
ill...Mrs. Charlotte Clay is able to be out of doors after a very serious illness."

05 April 1918, pg. 3, col. 6-7.
"Rev. F.P. Greenlee was host to a large number of persons at a reception at
the A.M.E. Church Monday evening...Mrs. Bettie Meyers of Crystal City,

enjoyed Easter Sunday with home folks…Mrs. S.A. Smith, of St. Louis, attended to business here this week…Mr. B.J. Wilkins, of St. Louis, was in our midst Sunday…Miss Berdola Boddie is visiting relatives in Festus this week…Mr. Howard Smith of Festus spent Easter with relatives…The play rendered by the local talent of the A.M.E. Church, Friday evening was largely attended…Mr. Walter Matthias and his niece Virginia, are the guests of Mr. and Mrs. O. Vaughn, of Potosi this week…Mrs. Leora Simpson and son Eugene of Crystal City, are the guests of Mrs. Lewis Murphy…Rev. J.H. McCallister will end the conference year's work Sunday. He has had a successful year and has proven to be a worthy pastor…Mr. and Mrs. Fred Chappelle and family of Coffman, were the guests of Mrs. Buford this week…Gardening is the chief occupation in our community. Every available spot is being tilled… Mr. Thomas Cayce is enjoying a visit with home folks. He is [illegible] ailing with rheumatism…We have just thirty more days of school. Have you visited the school? Where [two words illegible] is there should you go at some time [illegible]. We solicit your presence."

19 April 1918, pg. 3, col. 3-4.
"Mr. Henry Wilburn has been ill for several weeks…Mr. Tine Murphy purchased a house and lot in West Farmington this week…Mrs. Esther Williams is seriously ill…Mr. Peter Hill of Herculaneum is the guest of relatives here… Miss Winston and Mrs. F.S. Weber addressed Douglass School Thursday in the interest of the Third Liberty Loan. The school furnished patriotic music for the occasion…Mr. Weyman Chappelle and mother and Mrs. Chas. Douthit and family and Miss Imogene Staten of Coffman attended services here Sunday…Rev. J.H. McCallister is home from Annual Conference, introducing himself as St. Paul's new pastor, of whom we are ecstatically proud… Mrs. Rebecca Bridges, Mrs. Chas. Baker, Mrs. Henry Amonette and Mrs. Lucy Mooten are among the ill of the week…The members of St. Paul's worshipped with Bro. Greenlee and congregation Sunday, at which time the reverend preached two inspiring sermons…As the result of a sprained ankle Mr. J.P. Evans was a cripple for several days this week…The old homestead of Mrs. Ridder Harris and family, which is no doubt one of the oldest residences in this county, was torn down this week, with the likelihood of a new one being erected…Mrs. Sara Amonette, an aged resident of this place, succumbed to an illness of nine days Monday afternoon at the residence of her daughter, Mrs. Minnie Cayce. She was a Christian woman and much beloved by all who knew her. The funeral services were conducted by Revs. J.H. McCallister and Greenlee Wednesday morning at the M.E. Church. The remains were taken to Caledonia, [Washington Co.,] Mo., for interment…Miss Estacada Baker and a number of young people will soon render a drama of her own

composition...The organization of the Young People's Social Club was held March 31 and from all appearances it will be just the thing for these youths... There are 20 more days of school. Have you visited this year? Should you have done so? Will you? We solicit your presence."

03 May 1918, pg. 3, col. 1.
"While doing some repairing on a business house last Thursday Mr. Gus Cayce fell from a porch and cut an ugly gash in his arm, thus disabling him for several days...Mr. Mert Hunt of St. Louis came down Friday night just to say "good-by" before leaving for Camp Funston...Mrs. Stella Roberts entertained the Stewardess Board at her residence Monday evening...Dainty refreshments were served after the business session...Miss Ida Chappelle of Coffman was here on business Tuesday....Miss ...Edith Cayce has been much indisposed this week...Mrs. James Cayce is enjoying a visit out of town... Mr. Rossie Madison is at home from St. Louis for a visit with home folks... Miss Bertha Staten's illness caused her father to be absent at Douglass school Wednesday...Mr. Henry Wilburn is able to be at work again...The Community Club entertained Monday at high noon for Freeman Bridges, Robert Clay, John Baker and Henry Renfroe, who were leaving at 1:12 for St. Louis en route to Camp Funston. The Colored population was out en masse. Prof. J.C. Staten was master of ceremony. Revs. Greenlee and McCallister spoke very befittingly to the boys. Douglass school rendered patriotic selections. Dinner was served for the boys and their nearest relatives. The line of procession, with Douglass school in the front, extended from the Masonic Hall to the street car depot and from thence to De Lassus. Several autos were in line. There the boys joined others who were on the train bound for U.S. service. The dinner was one like Aunt Dolly used to serve when Uncle Tom and all his relations came on New Year's Day."

10 May 1918, pg. 3, col. 1.
"Rev. Greenlee, Mrs. Clara Poston, Mrs. Mahalia Madison and Mrs. Katie Hunt attended services at Coffman Sunday...Mr. Leroy Pitcher of St. Louis was a visitor here Sunday...Mrs. Tulleck [sic] and grandson of Ironton visited Mrs. Henry Amonette last week. Mrs. Amonette is recovering slowly...Mr. Scott Cole has made some recent improvements on his place [illegible] it is quite a cozy [illegible] how in East Farmington [several words illegible] will be rendered at the Masonic Hall the 24th inst. Tickets are now on sale... Mr. Jerry Bridges renews his subscription to The Argus, saying: "I feel lost without it," and so do you. Don't put off today for tomorrow. You need it for yourself, and then you need to send it to the boys in camp after you've read it...The sad intelligence of the death of Mrs. Talbert, mother of Mrs. A.L.

Reynolds, came to this community as a terrible shock. Mrs. Talbert was loved by all who knew her and her spotless life made her the idol of our community during her stay here…Mr. Fred Chappelle attended to business here one day last week…Mr. Wayman Chappelle and Miss Mildred Chappelle of Coffman enjoyed Sunday here…Mrs. Dave Buford and daughter Laura returned from Coffman Sunday, where they had visited Mrs. Fred Chappelle, who is ill… Mr. Lewis Murphy returned to Crystal City Sunday…Mrs. Vergia Simms is recovering from a recent illness…Rev. J.H. McCallister will attend George R. Smith College commencement exercises and his son Russell, who has been a student there this year, will return with him…Quarterly meeting will be held at St. Paul, June 8-9…Mrs. Jane Mitchell has recovered from a recent illness…News has reached us that Harry Aubouchon, Immanuel Jackson, Paul Alexander, and Frank X. Lewis are "over there." "God bless our noble boys." They write that they are well and happy "over there."…Five days more of school and then the lads and lassies will be begging mother and father to give them some work to do…Mr. H.B. Keatts is taking in the sights of Ringling Bros. in St. Louis this week. He is also looking after business matters."

17 May 1918, pg. 3, col. 3.
"Mr. Booker Baker of St. Louis was the guest of home folks the first of the week…Mr. Wilson Chappelle of Coffman attended to business here this week…Mr. Henry Amonette is spending the week in St. Louis having his eyes treated. His wife is slowly recovering from a nervous attack…Mrs. Charles Cayce visited in Festus Sunday…Mr. Howard Smith of Festus enjoyed Sunday here…Miss Zelia Franks is expecting to spend the summer in and about St. Louis…Miss Elizabeth Alexander of Chicago arrived Saturday to be the guest of her aunt, Mrs. Sallie Taylor, and her cousin, Mrs. James Robison… Douglass primary will have their closing exercises at the Masonic Hall, Saturday evening, May 18…Mrs. Jerry Bridges and Mrs. Mazie Lyons of Swink's Settlement visited here this week…Mr. and Mrs. Percy Swink of Bonne Terre were the guests of Mrs. Peter Swink Sunday…Mrs. George Burns is visiting in St. Louis…Rev. F.P. Greeblee and Mr. Harvey McCallister enjoyed a pleasant day fishing in Greenville vicinity last week…Mr. Lewis Smith is still having serious trouble with his arm, which was operated upon some months ago…"

24 May 1918, pg. 3, col. 3.
"One of the largest assemblies at the Masonic Hall ever was that of Saturday night, when the program of Douglass primary was rendered. Quite a large number of out-of-town persons were in attendance. In song and sentiment those clever lads and lassies tried their best to "kill the Kaiser."…Messrs. Ed

Cayce and Arthur Proctor returned to St. Louis Monday. The latter had a thrilling experience while out fishing. To his great surprise he found himself down under the water where the bullfrogs live. He didn't tarry long... Miss Corinne Wilkins entertained in honor of Miss Elizabeth Alexander last Thursday evening. Miss Leslie Poston paid her the same compliment Monday night...Russell McCallister has arrived from Sedalia where he has been attending George R. Smith College. He reports a very splendid commencement...Mrs. Celia Cunningham has arrived from Chicago, where she has been for more than a year. She will spend the summer here...Roy, Ora and Owen Kennedy of Crystal City were the guests of Mrs. Talbert Burns Saturday...Mrs. Robert Simpson and baby have returned to Crystal City...Mrs. Louisa Anthony is visiting at Festus this week...Miss Edith Cayce and Estacada Baker returned from Potosi Tuesday...Miss Helen Bartholomew of Fredericktown was the guest of Miss Beatrice Swink this week...Rev. J.H. McCallister met Halfred Poston at St. Louis and accompanied him home on his return from Fulton School for Deaf Mutes...Ancel Douthit and William Taylor have gone to St. Louis to reside...The entertainment of seven tables was enjoyed by many at the A.M.E. church, Friday night. Quarterly meeting services will be held there Sunday, May 26...Miss Mayfield of St. Mary's is the guest of Mrs. Augustus Cayce...Miss Lora Robinson, Miss Thelma Alexander, Carl and George Robison motored here Saturday night from Bonne Terre...Mr. Be[n] Ransom of Bonne Terre was the guest of Mr. Scott Cole Sunday...Mr. H.B. Keatts has returned from an extended visit in St. Louis... The Red Cross Drive is on this week. Do more than your bit."

31 May 1918, pg. 3, col. 5.
"Rev. J.D. Barksdale conducted quarterly meeting services at the A.M.E. church Sunday...Mrs. Biddie Evans of St. Marys was the house guest of Mrs. Lewis Murphy Saturday...Mr. Chas. Douthit and son Fielding, Sylvester Swink, Mr. D. Staten, Mr. Walter Franks and Miss Imogene Staten of Coffman visited here Sunday...The play "Lost and Found" which was exhibited at the Masonic Hall Friday evening, was well attended and well rendered... Mr. Thomas Cayce enjoyed a visit with home folks last week...Mrs. Esther Williams is very ill and enjoys having her friends step in with words of comfort and cheer...Mrs. Henry Amonette has recovered from a long illness... Decoration Day was observed as requested by President Wilson and much good is expected as a reward for the faithful...The entertainment given by "The Misses" at the A.M.E. church Monday night, was quite a success...Mr. Robert Clay writes his mother from Camp Funston that the training is doing great physical good and that he rather likes the military work...Children's Day exercises will be held Sunday night at the M.E. church, to be conducted

by Misses Edith Cayce and Estacada Baker...Mr. and Mrs. J.P. Evans and children, Inman and Earl Stewart, enjoyed Sunday at Greenville with Mr. and Mrs. Lewis Kennedy and family...Mr. Philip Bridges of St. Louis visited his parents here the last of the week...An automobile party chaperoned by Mrs. Edna Kemp of Fredericktown, passed through here Sunday...A contingent of 142 boys (white) left here Tuesday en route for some training camp...Mrs. Jane Baker has recovered from a recent illness...The reporter is the recipient of an invitation to the commencement [exer]cises of the Champaign (Ill.) Hi[gh s]chool, of which Miss Lucile Cherry is a member of the graduating class...Mr. and Mrs. James Robinson have had their cottage wired, and are enjoying more and better light...Many gave to the Red Cross last week and many did not. This is our time as well as the other fellow's time to do more than our bit to help win the war for our grand old U.S.A."

07 June 1918, pg. 3, col. 3.
"Rev. J.D. Barksdale conducted quarterly meeting services at Coffman Sunday...Prof. J.C. Staten delivered the address at the commencement exercises of Potosi School of which Mrs. Alice Jenkins is principal...Mrs. Eliza Overton has returned from Detroit, Mich., for a summer's stay...Mesdames Chas. Cayce and Katie Cayce visited relatives at Festus Sunday...Mrs. Melissa Mc-Callisle of Herculaneum, is the guest of Mrs. Jno. Franks...Mrs. Eliza Blackwell and granddaughter, Mary, visited in Bonne Terre Sunday...Mrs. Susie A. Smith of St. Louis, made her usual trip here to be present at Decoration Day to join her relatives and friends on this Memorial Day. She returned Tuesday...Union services were conducted at the M.E. Church by Revs. Greenlee and McCallister Decoration Day...Mrs. Wesley Douthit is quite ill at her home in Boss[?] Addition...Messrs. Lewis Murphy and Geo. Meyers visited home folks this week...Mrs. P. Boddie is among the ill of the week...Mrs. Howard Smith has returned to Festus...The Rosebud Club had a picnic on the parsonage lawn Friday evening. It was a financial success...Mrs. Rebecca Bridges has recovered sufficiently to resume her usual vocation...Miss Alcesta Douthit is visiting in Festus...Mr. and Mrs. Lewis Kennedy of Greenville, attended the picnic Friday."

21 June 1918, pg. 3, col. 4.
"Mr. Fred Chapelle, of Coffman, was here Monday...Mr. Thomas Cayce is installing city water on his place...Mr. and Mrs. Buford and daughter, Laura, visited at Coffman Sunday...Mrs. Lewis Murphy spent the week's end at Crystal City...Booker T. Baker arrived from St. Louis Monday to be at home for the summer. Little Miss Nadine Baker is visiting at Potosi...Miss Baker entertained Mr. Powell of Arkansas the first of the week...Mr. Eric Matthews

is summering in St. Louis...Mr. Clarence Bridges is a recent subscriber to the Argus. He says he is simply "at home" when he has it with him...Mrs. Esther Williams is very ill...Mrs. Susie O. Wilkins attended the commencement exercises of the Champaign, Ill. University last week. She was the guest of her son, M[r.] Ernest Wilkins, who was a graduate of this year from the mathematical division...Mr. Henry Wilburn has been ill for several weeks, but is convalescing...Mr. Moses Cayce is touring the northern states with Hallerberg's Circus Co...Mrs. Harry Cayce, of St. Louis, [was] he guest of her mother, Mrs. P. Boddie...Messrs. Weyman Boddie, Stubbs, and Jno. Franks motored to Coffman Monday for a few days of fishing...Miss Elizabeth Alexander has returned to her home in Chicago...Mrs. Eliza Overton spent last week at Greenville...Mrs. Wesley Douthit does not improve very rapidly... Mr. Jack Blackwell and Mr. Kennett Yeager are the boys from this town in the last contingent...Farmers are now offering advanced prices for farm hands. It looks as though the women will be compelled to don a pair of overalls and join the wheat harvest...Mrs. Jane Mitchell is able to be out...Mr. Philip Bridges has returned to St. Louis after a visit with parents...Miss Willa Jones was seen out Sunday after a few weeks of illness...Mr. Elmer Bridges has accepted a position in St. Louis. He left Thursday. The Rosebud Club regrets his departure and yet the members are glad he was so successful."

28 June 1918, pg. 3, col. 3.
"Mrs. Blake, of Festus, was a visitor of Mrs. Mahalia Madison, Saturday...Mr. B.F. Wilkins, of St. Louis, is enjoying a vacation at home...Miss Mattie Valley left Sunday for her home at Eads, Mo. where she will spend her vacation... Mrs. Whitfield, of St. Louis, is the guest of Mrs. Emily Boddie...Messrs. Wayman, Boddie, Frank Stubbs and John Franks brought home bass, squirrel, cat fish from their expedition to Coffman...Miss Pearl Galvin returned home Sunday...Mrs. Ada Murphy and Mrs. Carrie Burns enjoyed a delicious Sunday dinner at the pleasant country home of Mr. and Mrs. Jerry Bridges... Mr. and Mrs. Rossie Madison, of Bonne Terre, visited in Farmington last week...The Rosebud Club entertained on the parsonage lawn Friday evening...The officers are: President, B.F. Baker; vice-president, Estacada Baker; secretary, Edna Harris; treasurer, E.O. Cayce...Miss Zelma Swinks [sic] will be the guest of her sister, Mrs. Alice Powers, of 1011 N. Newstead, St. Louis, Mo., for an indefinite period of time...Mr. Thomas Cayce returned to St. Louis Friday after a few days at home...Misses E.O. Cayce, Corine Wilkens, Edna Harris, Estacada Baker, and Messrs. B.F. Wilkins, Booker Baker, Clarence Bridges, Russell McCalister [sic] were entertained at the home of Miss D.F. Baker Sunday afternoon."

05 July 1918, pg. 3, col. 4-5.
"Mr. Nelson Hunt, of Kansas City, is visiting his brother, Mr. Moses Hunt... Mrs. Dave Buford and daughter, Laura, are spending a few days with her daughter, Mrs. Fred Chapple [sic], of Coffman, Mo...Mrs. Harry Cayce and Mrs. Whitfield visited Mr. and Mrs. Lewis Kennedy, of Greenville, Saturday and Sunday...Mrs. Georgia Harris and Mrs. Etta Cayce are spending a few days at Festus, Mo...Master Harry Cayce, of St. Louis, is visiting James Cayce this week...Mrs. Mayme Foulk, of Champaign, Ill., is visiting her mother, Mrs. Jennie Swinks...Miss Daysie F. Baker left Friday for a few days visit at S. Louis, Mo., after which she wills spend the rest of her vacation at Washington, D.C...Miss Corine Wilkins has been ill for a few days. Her many friends wish to see her out soon...Messrs. Sylvester Swinks, Wayman Chapple [sic], of Coffman, were visitors here Saturday and Sunday...Mr. and Mrs. Lewis Kennedy, of Greenville, attended church Sunday evening...The many friends of Mrs. Chas. Baker are glad to hear of her improving and hope that soon she may be able to mingle with them...A jolly crowd of young men from Ironton, Mo., drove here Sunday...Rev. Greenlee held services at Coffman, Mo., Sunday...A lawn social was given by the members of the A.M.E. Church on Mrs. Felix Poston's lawn Saturday evening. Quit a number attended...[two words illegible] Swinks, of Bonne Terre, Mo., was a visitor here Monday... Mrs. Cora Meyers is visiting her mother, Mrs. George Meyers, of Crystal City, Mo...Save your pennies, nickils [sic], and dimes and buy War Savings Stamps."

19 July 1918, pg. 2, col. 5 and pg. 3, col. 4.
"Mr. Chas. Baker was a business visitor at Festus, Sunday...Mrs. Fred. Chappel is the guest of her sister, Mrs. Eliza Doughit [sic]...Mrs. Jane Hunt visited at Fredericktown, last week...Mr. Wilson Chappel, of Coffman, was in the city last week...Messrs. Wayman Body and Harry Cayce, of St. Louis, are visiting home folks...Mrs. Georgia Harris, who is employed at Crystal City, Mo., visited her children Saturday and Sunday...Those who are ill are: Mrs. Clara Poston, Mrs. Ada Cayce, Mrs. Fannie Baker and Misses Corine Wilkins and Willa Jones...Mr. Purnell Cayce and son, Patrich [sic] Cayce, visited at St. Louis, Sunday...Mrs. Susie Robinson and Boyd Wilkins were entertained at the home of Mr. and Mrs. Fred Chappel, of Coffman, Mo."

26 July 1918, pg. 6, col. 3.
"Mr. Charles Baker left Sunday for Sedalia, Mo., to attend the Grand Lodge K. of P...Mr. William Wright is visiting home folks...Miss Martha Tullock of St. Louis was the guest of her sister, Mrs. Effie Amonette...Mr. and Mrs. Percy Swinks of Bonne Terre were visitors here Saturday and Sunday...Mr.

Charley Cayce, who is employed at St. Louis, Mo., is at home for a few days...Miss Golda Maul was the guest of Miss Beatrice Swinks last week... Mrs. Charley Doughit [sic of Coffman, Mo., make a business trip here Monday...Mr. Talbert Burns has gone to Crystal City for a few days...Mr. and Mrs. Robert Simpson and son of Crystal City, Mo., are here for a few days... Mr. Booker Baker is at home again for a week filling the position of his father at the Bank of Farmington...The R.B. Club gave an entertainment Friday evening which was a great success...Mr. Henry Amonette, who has been in St. Louis, Mo., having his eyes treated, returned home Sunday."

02 August 1918, pg. 2, col. 5.
"Mr. Cornelius Cole of St. Louis, Mo., is visiting his brother, Mr. Scott Cole... Mr. Clarence Bridges has gone to St. Louis for a few days...Mrs. Betty Meyers of Crystal City, Mo., visited her daughter, Miss Cora Meyers Sunday... Miss Zelma Swink who has been visiting her sister, Mrs. Alice Powers of St. Louis, Mo., has returned...An excellent program was given at the A.M.E. Church last Friday evening by the primary class of the Sunday School. A large crowd attended...Mrs. Effie Amonette and Miss Martha Tullock are visiting their mother, Mrs. Malinda Tullock of Pilot Knob, Mo...Miss Ora Hunt Williams entertained the board No. 2 Tuesday evening July 23 at her home. While there the engagement of Miss May Baker to Mr. W.H. Powers of Pocahontas, Ark., was announced...Mr. Peter Swink visited home folks Sunday...Mrs. Ester William [sic] who has been sick for several months died at their [sic] home Wednesday evening, July 24. The funeral services were conducted Friday afternoon at 2 o'clock by Rev. Greenly [sic] after which the remains were laid to rest in the Masonic Cemetery. The News joins in extending sympathy to the bereaved."

09 August 1918, pg. 2, col. 3.
"Mr. Charlie Sutherland of St. Louis, Mo. is visiting his mother, Mrs. Elizabeth Cole...Msr. [sic] Thomas visited home-folks Wednesday and Thursday...Rev. Greenley [sic] held services at Coffman, Mo., Sunday...Mr. and Mrs. Arvella Wilkins of St. Louis, Mo. are spending a few days with home folks...Mr. Henry Amonette and son Elmer, were called to Ironton, Mo. Thursday, to attend the funeral of his nephew...Mrs. Percy Swinks and Sameul [sic] Burks left Thursday for the training camp at Camp Funston, Kans...The R.B. Club gave a social Friday evening on the beautiful lawn of Mr. Purnell Cayce. An enjoyable evening was spent by of [sic] Crystal City, Mo. visited home-folk Saturday and Sunday...Mrs. Maggie Kennedy of Greenville, Mo[.] passed through Sunday enroute [sic] to St. Louis...Mrs. Mary Cayce accompanied her husband to Columbia, ker [sic] made a busi-

ness trip to Festus, Mo. Sunday…A number of Farmingtonians attended the picnic at St. Mary's Saturday."

15 August 1918, pg. 2, col. 3.
"Mr. Phillip Bridges of St. Louis is the guest of her [sic] mother Mrs. Jerry Bridges…Mrs. Irene White of St. Mary's, Mo. visited Mrs. Sophia Mud last week…A party was given last Tuesday evening at the residence of Miss Corine Wilkins in honor of Mr. and Mrs. C. Wilkins and Miss Josephine Banks of St. Louis…Mrs. G. Harris has moved her family to Crystal City, Mo., where she has been employed for several weeks…Miss Myrtle Thorton [sic] of St. Louis, Mo[.] is the guest of her mother, Mrs. Maggie Thorton [sic]…Mrs. Melvina Evans and two sons are spending a few days at Greenville, Mo., visiting home folks. Miss Lizzie Cayce of Cape Girardeau, is visiting home folks this week…An entertainment was given Friday evening by the members of the A.M.E. Church. A large crowd attended. Mrs. Alice Cunningham of Festus, Mo. visited Mrs. Ada Cayce last week[.] Mrs. Jernahy [sic] Poston is visiting her son Rev. A. Poston of Festus, Mo. Messrs. Chas. Baker, John Franks, and Moses Hunt attended an initiation of a member in the K. of P. at Festus, Mo., Saturday evening. Mrs. Velma Need [sic] and children are guests of her mother, Mrs. Emily Boddie."

23 August 1918, pg. 2, col. 4.
"Mr. Thos. Cayce enjoyed a few days of last week at home[.] Miss Edith Cayce is enjoying a pleasant vacation at Potosi. She is the guest of Mr. and Mrs. Joseph Carson. Misses Cora Myers and Hilda Kennedy are the guests of relatives at Crystal City this week…Mrs. Lewis Murphy, Mrs. Robert Simpson and son Eugene returned from Crystal City Sunday. Mrs. Dollean Alexander of St. Louis is enjoying a pleasant vacation here. Quite a tribute was paid to Mr. Phillip Thornton Wednesday evening at the Masonic hall, prior to his leaving for camp the next day. Miss Hortence [sic] Kennedy, mistress of ceremony performed her duties very creditably. Miss Sophia Mudd visited at Festus, this week…Prof. J.C. Staten has accepted a position in St. Louis and is already for duty…Misses Mae Baker and Flossie Bridges have returned from a visit to Bonne Terre. Mr. George Evans has returned from his usual vacation on the lakes…Mrs. Eliza Overton attended to business here Monday…Douglas School will open Monday, September 9…Mrs. Lewis Kennedy has returned from a business trip to St. Louis…Mr. Henry Wilburn will be pleased to have his friends near him during his illness…Mr. Augustus Cayce is quite ill at his home in East Farmington. Mr. Barney Pelty is the recepient [sic] of a splendid portrait of Weyman Cayce who is "over there."[52] Mr. Cayce is one of our home boys who is making good…Mr. Booker T. Baker returned

to Crystal City Sunday."

30 August 1918, pg. 6, col. 4.
"Miss Bertha Staten and Master Sumner Swink visited St. Louis this week…
Mr. and Mrs. George Tullick [sic] [,] Misses Lucile and Maud Cosely [sic] and
Miss Arizona Armstrong of Ironton were the guests of Mrs. Henry Amonette
Sunday…Mrs. Velma Reed and children who have been visiting relatives here
returned to their home in St. Louis Friday. Mrs. Eliza Overton accompanied
them as far as Festus. Mrs. Ed. Harris and daughter, Edna and Mrs. Jerry
Bridges returned from Potosi Sunday where they had been the guests of Mrs.
O. Vaughn…Miss Hilda Kennedy arrived Sunday from a vacation spent at
Festus, Mo…A miscellaneous shower was given for the bride-to-be at the
residence of Mrs. John Franks, Tuesday evening. Miss Mae Baker[,] the recepient [sic], is a young lady who is much esteemed in the community and her
absence will be regretted. She is quite popular in social circles and we hope
she will be equally so in her home when the words have been said and she is
safely "anchored" in her Arkansas home…Mrs. Nancy Buford and daughter
Laura, Lethia Taylor, Wm. Taylor and Mrs. Etta Cayce visited at Potosi Saturday…Mr. Henry Amonette enjoyed Sunday at Saint [sic] Genevieve…The
social given at the home of Mrs. W.I. Roberts Friday evening was an enjoyable fete…If The Argus is worth the borrowing, then why not subscribe for it
and save yourself the weekly war[?]…Misses Edith Cayce, Estacada Baker and
Nadine Baker arrived home Thursday from a visit at Potosi."

06 September 1918, pg. 7, col. 3.
"Mrs. Dora Maul and children of Bonne Terre visited here Sunday…Mr. and
Mrs. Fred Chappelle and children have returned to Coffman…Mrs. Joseph
Carson of Potosi accompanied Nadine Baker home from Potosi where the
latter has been a guest of the Carson family for two months or more…Miss
Maude Burke will be pleased to have her friends call during these days of ill-
ness…Miss Costella Shaw of St. Louis is the guest of Mrs. W.I. Roberts…
Miss Mary Poston of St. Louis returned home Monday after a week's visit with
Mr. and Mrs. Felix Poston…Misses Pearl Baker, Alice Occamore and Master
Wm. Taylor of Madison, Ill., are the guests of Mr. Richard Occamore…News
reached us here that Mr. Harry Cayce has been recently called to the service
of Uncle Sam and is in camp…Mrs. Eliza Overton was bitten severely by a
dog last week. The wound is healing nicely…Messrs. Booker Baker and L.
Murphy returned to Crystal City Sunday…Miss Cora Meyers has returned
from a two weeks' visit at Crystal City…Mr. Augustus Cayce is yet quite ill…
Miss Estacada Baker has been elected to the school at Mineral Point. School
will open there September 9…Mrs. Charlotte Franks and sister, Miss Mattie

Valle, came up from Coffman, Sunday. The latter will remain indefinitely...
Mr. Thos. Cayce was a visitor here Saturday...Mr. Elmer Amonette chaperoned a party of young people to Ironton Sunday...Mr. Frank Singleton of St. Louis was the guest of Miss Myrtle Thornton the first of the week...
Mrs. Chas. Douthit and son Fielding were up from Coffman in their new car Sunday...Douglass school will open Monday, Sept. 9. Miss Edith O. Cayce is the assistant teacher and a resident of this place. Miss Cayce has taught several terms at Mineral Point."

13 September 1918, pg. 7, col. 3.
"IRONTON, MO. Mrs. H.C. Green has gone to Jefferson City where she has charge of the dining room department for the ensuing year...Miss Katherine Fletcher has opened school with good attendance...Mrs. Edgar Brown and son Robert have returned from a visit in the city...Mrs. Freeman Martin is visiting friends in St. Louis...Mr. Archie Blanks visited friends in DeSoto... Mrs. John Anthony made a short visit to St. Louis Saturday...Mr. Will and Charley Bullner visited their brother Mr. Anthony and Abe Bullner of Arkansas...Rev. William Slatter is contemplating selling his home and residing with his daughter at Springfield, Ill., who recently lost her husband... Mr. John Anthony is convalescent...Mr. Jim Johnson has been visiting home folks for the past week...Mr. Clifford Boyd left last week for Hannibal where he will spend the winter...Rev. Jonas preached an excellent sermon at the M.E. Church."

20 September 1918, pg. 5, col. 5.
"Mr. George Tulleck [sic] and a party of friends from Ironton visited here Sunday...Mrs. Mahalia Madison was a visitor at Festus, Mo., last week...Miss Sophia Mudd has gone to Crystal City for an indefinite period of time...Mr. and Mrs. Onan Poston, of Kirkwood, Mo., were guests at Douglass School Monday. Mrs. Poston addressed the school with much interest to all concerned...Mr. Booker Baker is with home folks for the week...One Sept. 4 Miss Mae Baker a popular young lady of our community was married to Mr. W.H. Powers, of Pocahontas, Ark. The wedding and reception took place at Poplar Bluff. Rev. S.B. Anderson officiated. Her mother, Mrs. Katie Bridges accompanied her to Poplar Bluff. They will reside at Pocahontas...On Sept. 7 Miss Corinne Wilkins, a well known [sic] teache[r] of our city, was married to Mr. Weyman Chappelle, of Coffman, Mo., a prosperous farmer. Rev. J.H. McCallister officiated. Mr. Berd J. Wilkins, of St. Louis, was present... The Fortnightly Club presented Douglass School with articles of necessity for the medicine chest. This club has for a long time supplied such needs... Mr. James Ford, of Salt Lake City, was the guest of Mr. John Franks the

first of the week...Mr. Thomas Cayce spent a few days with home folks this week...Mr. Augustus Cayce has resumed his work...Mr. Robert Simpson, of Crystal City, enjoyed Sunday here...Rev. A. Poston conducted Quarterly Meeting services at St. Paul M.E. Church Sunday. He delivered two very able sermons. Rev. F.P. Greenlee delivered a message of truth at the afternoon services...Russel [sic] McCallister left Sunday to resume his course at George R. Smith College Sedalia...Miss Mildred Chappelle of Coffman, visited friends here Sunday...Messrs. Clarence Bridges[,] Russell McCallister and Prof. W.I. Johns were visitors at Douglass School last week."

27 September 1918, pg. 3, col. 4.
"Miss Estacada Baker is teaching school at Mineral Point...Rev. Chas. Wilkins and wife, of Flint, Mich., are the guests of Mrs. Susie Wilkins... Mr. Finis Blackwell visited relatives here last week...Mrs. Felix Poston, Mrs. Chas. Baker, Miss Florence Hunt, and Mr. Henry Wilburn are among the sick this week...Mrs. M.E. Goins, G.M.A.M., of Jefferson City, was the guest of Queen of Honor Court...Miss Mamie Burke has accepted employment in Crystal City...Mrs. Antoine Murphy is shaking hands with home folks again...The many friends of Miss Minnie Thornton were surprised to hear of her marriage to Mr. Chas. Pryor, of St. Louis, which occurred Saturday[53]... Mrs. James Cayce is visiting relatives in Festus...The reporter is the recipient of a letter from Sergt. Roy B. Casey (game) over there stating that he is doing well and has had a chat with Mr. Freeman Bridges...Rev. Greenlee and congregation are preparing for the annual conference which convenes in St. Louis, Mo.
Daisy F. Baker, reporter."

04 October 1918, pg. 2, col. 4.
"Rev. J.H. McCallister and wife have received the message that their son LeRoy has landed safely "over there."...We are sorry to know that scarlet fever has invaded our midst. Miss Florence Taylor has the misfortune to have it... Rev. Chas. Wilkins preached two very interesting sermons Sunday at St. Paul in the absence of Rev. McCallister who was assisting Rev. James at Fredericktown...Rev. Wilkins and wife left Monday for their home at Flint, Mich... Mrs. J.C. Staten is indisposed...Mr. Geo. Meyers of Crystal City is visiting his daughter, Miss Cora Meyers, this week...Mrs. Gabriel Cayce visited Mrs. Ellen Carson of Potosi, Sunday...Mr. Weyman Chappelle was up Monday to meet the official board of the War Department...Mr. and Mrs. Fred Chappele [sic] attended to business last week...Mrs. Alice PoPwers [sic] and baby Jeanette of 1011 N. Newstad [sic], St. Louis, and Mrs. Mamie Foulk of Champaigne, Ill., are the guests of Mrs. Peter Swink, their mother...Mrs.

Maggie Thornton received the message this week that her daughter Miss Myrtle Thornton of this place, had married Mr. Frank Singleton of Oklahoma City, Okla[54]...Mrs. Rebecca Bridges is visiting her son Elmer Bridges of St. Louis[55]...Mrs. Jerusha Poston accompanied her son Halfred as far as St. Louis as he was en route to Fulton to school...A letter from Mr. Samuel Burke in camp at Fort Riley states that they are anxious to go "over there" and get real busy...Mrs. Fannie Baker is improving...Rev. Greenlee will end his conference year work Sunday. Rev. McCallister and congregation will worship with him and his members Sunday night."

11 October 1918, pg. 2, col. 4.
"Miss Pearl Baker of Madison, Ill., who has been the guest of relatives for five weeks returned home Saturday, accompanied by her aunt, the reporter... Messrs. Earl Wright, Henry and Artie Fulton of Bonneterre [sic] were visitors here last week...Mrs. Eliza Overton of Crystal City is the guest of Mrs. Emma Boddie...Mr. Elmer Amonette chaperoned a party to Ironton Sunday...Mr. Rossie Madison and his aunt, Mrs. Jane Mitchell, are the guests of Mrs. Mahalia Madison this week...Miss Estacada Baker is at home on the account of the illness of her mother. Mrs. Baker is slowly improving...Rev. Greenlee left Tuesday for conference, taking with him an excellent report for the conference year. His congregation and the community would welcome his return for another year. His work has been worthy of much praise...Miss Hortense Kennedy underwent a minor operation Tuesday and is convalescing...Mr. Edgar Kennedy and I.P. Boddie have resumed their work at Crystal City...Mrs. Ada Murphy and son, Euguene, were visitors at Douglass School Tuesday...Mr. ClarSence [sic] Bridges and sister [sic] Christibell, accompanied their mother home from St. Louis Sunday...Mr. Augustus Cayce has recovered...Mrs. J.C. Staten is suffering from an attack somewhat akin to rheumatism...Mr. Lewis Murphy returned to Crystal City Sunday...Mr. P. Boddie is visiting in St. Louis."

25 October 1918, pg. 2, col. 4.
"School has been closed for two weeks on account of the flu. As yet no cases have developed in our immediate city...Misses Lorene and Imogene Staten and Mrs. Mazie Lyons enjoyed Sunday with home folks at Coffman...Mr. Ed Harris was severely wounded last Monday morning when a mule kicked him. The bones of his limbs were not broken, but very badly bruised. He has been unable to work at his usual vocation since...Miss Leslie Poston was [two words and one entire line illegible] at the residence of Mrs. E.J. Harris... Mrs. Katie Cayce and family have moved to St. Louis, their former home...

Edgar Kennedy passed the examination like a land slide and is quite anxious to get busy in military service...Mrs. Lewis Kennedy is suffering from a severe attack of rheumatism...Rev. F.P. Greenlee has been returned as pastor of St. Luke's Chapel...Prof. J.C. Staten is at home for a sojourn with the family. Mrs. Staten is much improved...Mr. Henry Wilburn is critically ill at his home in West Farmington...Mrs. Fred Chappelle was here the first of the week for treatment for an abscess of the head...Messes Weyman, Fred and Wilson Chappelle attended to business here this week...Miss Maud Burke is able to be out again...Little Villetta Wilburn was seriously burned Monday while playing near a fire in the yard. Before help could be obtained she was burned quite badly about her limbs."

01 November 1918, pg. 2, col. 4.
"IRONTON, MO. Zetta Bonds[.] Mr. and Mrs. Charles Bulliner of Poplar Bluff, have been the guests of Mr. and Mrs. John Anthony...Mr. William Lax of St. Louis has been visiting his sister for a few days before going to camp... Mr. John Fletcher has returned from St. Louis and is on the sick list...The community is greatly shocked by the death of Mr. Jim Coleman, who died of pneumonia last Thursday. He was a member of the Pythians...Mrs. Jim Coleman and little daughter left last Sunday for DeSoto."

08 November 1918, pg. 2, col. 4-5.
"Mr. Mose Bridges is nursing a wounded hand which is the result of an accident of last week...Mrs. Chas. Baker is improving each day...Mr. and Mrs. Robert Simpson are very proud of Little Miss Robertine Annette, who arrived Tuesday, October 22...Mr. Lewis Murphy and Mrs. Simpson returned to Crystal City Sunday...Mr. Clarence Bridges has accepted work in St. Louis and is now employed...Mr. Edgar Coyce [sic] of St. Louis had a pleasant visit with home folks the first of the week...Mr. Henry Amonette and family enjoyed Sunday amid the "Ozarks" at Ironton...Mrs. Wesley Douthit has been quite ill for several days...Mr. Edward Harris is able to be out...Mrs. Ada Cayce made a business trip to Festus Saturday...Since the ban is still on, many persons have roamed the wods [sic] on Sunday and enjoyed the beauties and delicacies of nature. The home fires are burning with much expectancy of an early declaration of peace. Farmington has quite a number of boys overseas. They write interesting letters and say "It will soon be over... Mrs. Lewis Kennedy and family of Greenville were the guests of Mrs. Jerry Bridges Sunday...Misses Lorene and Imogene Staten and Mrs. Mazie Lyons have returned from a trip to Coffman, their home...Mr. J.E. Bridges of St. Louis enjoyed the week's end with relatives...[one line illegible] Minnie Wilbury [sic], is yet quite ill from burns received a couple of weeks ago...Mr.

Henry Wilburn, a well-known and respected citizen, passed away Oct. 24, after an illness of many months. He was a man of marked industry and his passing away is the passing of a much beloved gentleman and friend of this community."

06 December 1918, pg. 2, col. 4-5.
"Mr. Weyman Chappelle returned to Coffman Saturday. Mr. and Mrs. John Franks entertained Mr. and Mrs. Howard Smith and son, Mr. and Mrs. Boddie and family and Mrs. Elizabeth Overton Thanksgiving evening with a spread of good things. Miss Cora Meyers has gone to Crystal City to reside. Mrs.Berdia Marshall and son, Alphonso, of Festus, were the guests of Mr. and Mrs. Scott Cole Saturday. Mr. Booker T. Baker is at home for an indefinite period. Miss Zelma Swink was a hostess at a Thanksgiving social at her home where the evening was greatly enjoyed by a jolly bunch of friends. Mesdames Mayme Foluk [sic], Felix Poston, Estella Roberts, John Franks and the reporter attended the funeral of Mrs. Frankie Arnold at Bonne Terre Wednesday. Her many friends will no doubt remember her as Mrs. Frankie Baker Maul. Mrs. Ada Cayce returned to Festus Sunday after a day's visit here. She was accompanied by her son, Robert. You know you want the Argus, and why don't you just take it right away? There is danger in delay. It is impossible for you to keep up with the great things that are happening among our people unless you read the leading publications, of which the Argus is one. Buy it; read it; and then pass it along."

13 December 1918, pg. 2, col. 4.
"Death claimed the three-year-old son of Mr. and Mrs. Mose Bridges last Thursday. The many friends of little Harry Lee will miss him as well as the devoted parents and sisters...Mr. Richard Occamore is a recent subscriber to The Argus...Mr. Phillip Bridges of St. Louis has returned to the city after a visit with parents, Mr. and Mrs. Jerry Bridges...Miss Sophia Mudd and Master Jessamine Madison of Crystal City were the guests of Mrs. M. Madison this week...Mr. Robert Clay is at home from Camp Funston honorably discharged and full to the brim with information concerning camp life... Mr.B.J. Wilkins of St. Louis, while visiting his mother, Mrs. Susie Wilkins, became ill and has been confined to his room for a week...Mrs. Julia Burke of St. Louis was the guest of Mrs. Charlotte Clay last week."

28 February 1919, pg. 3, col. 5.
"Mr. and Mrs. Lee Roden of St. Louis, were the Sunday guests of Mr. and Mrs. Jerry Bridges...The infant Charles Elwood, son of Mr. and Mrs. Artie Reed, passed away Saturday evening. The funeral services were held at the

A.M.E. Church, Monday afternoon...Mr. Booker Baker has returned to St. Louis for employment...Mr. and Mrs. Talbert Burns of Crystal City enjoyed Saturday and Sunday here...Mr. Earl Wright of Bonne Terre, enjoyed Sunday here...Mr. and Mrs. Fred Chappelle returned to their home at Coxman [sic], Monday...Mr. Wm. Wright is touring the eastern states...Mr. and Mrs. Howard Smith of Festus, attended the funeral Monday...Mr. Peter Swink is enjoying the week with home folks."

07 March 1919, pg. 3, col. 4.
"Mr. William Wright of St. Louis is the guest of his mother, Mrs. Louisa Anthony...Miss Hortense Kennedy and Mrs. William Kennedy enjoyed Sunday at St. [sic] Genevieve. They were accompanied home by Mr. Frank Lewis who has just returned from overseas...Mrs. Eliza Overton and Mr. Artie Reed accompanied Mrs. Laura Jordan to Festus Sunday...Rev. W. Spurlock; presiding elder of the Cape Girardeau district, conducted quarterly meetings at St. Luke Chapel Sunday. Rev. J.H. McAllister delivered an able sermon in the afternoon...Messrs[.] Jerry and Phillip Bridges attended to business at Weingarten Sunday...Mrs. Laverna Smith of St. Louis had a visit of a few days here this week...Mr. James Mills of Kansas City is the guest of Miss Mamie Burke...Mr. Paul Alexander of Bonneterre [sic], a recent arrival from overseas, enjoyed a f[ew] hours here Sunday. He, with Rev. Greenlee and Spurlock were entertained at the residence of Mr. and Mrs. J. Fransk[.]"

14 March 1919, pg. 3, col. 4.
"Mr. and Mrs. P.M. Cayce entertained at their residence Thursday evening in honor of their mother, Mrs. Annie Bridges, who was enjoying the sixty-third milestone...Rev. Rivere, district superintendent of St. Louis District conducted quarterly meeting services at St. Paul Chapel Sunday. Rev. Greenlee preached the sermon at the communion period. Rev. J.H. McCallister conducted love feast Sunday evening...The reporter is the recipient of an interesting letter from Mr. Philip Thornton, mailed at Verdun, France. He is enjoying a series of football games. He hopes to be home in time to enjoy the commencement exercises of Douglass School...Mrs. Eliza Douthit, Mrs. Chas. Baker, Miss Florence Taylor, Mrs. Louisa Anthony, and Mrs. Charlotte Clay are among the ill of the week...The famous Six Hundred will entertain the public on the 28th inst...Mr. Rossie Madison and family have returned to Farmington to live...Mr. and Mrs. J.P. Evans are rejoicing over the advent of a brand new bady [sic] boy...The choirs of St. Paul and St. Luke are rehearsing for the rendition of a musicale which will be March 21...Miss Hortense Kennedy is visiting friends in St. Louis...Mrs. John Franks and Rev. Spurlock were visitors at Douglass School last Friday. Mrs. P.M. Cayce delivered an

able address at the M.E. Church Friday [illegible] on the subject: "The parent and the Child."

28 March 1919, pg. 6, col. 4.
"Rossie Madison is recovering from the flu...The Knights of Pythias and Calanthes rendered a program at the A.M.E. Church last Sunday afternoon. The speakers were Revs. Greenlee and McAllistr [sic], Sirs Chas. Baker and P.M. Cayce...Miss Mamie Burke and Mr. James Mills were united in holy matrimony Sunday, Rev. Martin, officiating, at the home of the bride's sister, Mrs. R. Occamore...The musicale rendered by the choirs was largely attended and was a financial success. Those present from out of town were Mr. Robert Simpson of Crystal City; Mr. Artie Fulton, Earl Wright and Frank Baker of Bonneterre [sic]...Mrs. Charlotte Clay has recovered from an injury of the knee, which caused her disability for several weeks...Miss H[.] Kennedy returned home from a visit to Saint Louis, Missouri...Mr. Dewey Staten, Reuben Staten, Mr. and Mrs. Chas. Douthit of Coffman visited here last week...Mrs. Janie Hunt is recovering from a recent illness...Mr. Peter Hill and family of Herculaneum have moved here...Mrs. Malinda Murphy returned from St. Louis a few days ago where she was given the care of an infant which she brought home with her...Rev. J.H. McAllister is putting forth his best efforts to make Sunday the crowing day of the conference year. Rev. Greenlee and congregation will worship with his people Sunday evening... Mrs. Ben Chappelle was the guest of her sister Mrs. Eliza Douthit last week. The latter has been quite ill for several months...Mrs. Tillman Cayce and Mr. Walter Matthias returned from over seas Monday night. They were very much fatigued but rather glad to be at home. We are preparing to give the boys a joyous home-coming when more have arrived.—Dayse F. Baker."

04 April 1919, pg. 3, col. 5.
"Rev. J.H. McAllister left Thursday afternoon enrute [sic] to Springfield, Mo., the seat of the annual conference...The concert rendered by the Twelve Hundred of [t]he A.M.E. church at the Masonic hall was very largely attended and was quite a financial success...Mr. Tillman Cayce recently from overseas, delivered an address to the pupils of Douglass School, Friday afternoon... Mr. Henry Renfroe another of the recent returned boys from overseas, has been in our midst for several days...Mrs. W.I. Roberts and son Addison, visited relatives in St. Louis last week...Mrs. Gorgia [sic] Harris and daughter Francis of Crystal City were the guest of Mrs. Emily Boddie this week... Mesdames mamie Foulke, Mazie Lyons, Misses Lorine State, Imogene Staten and Thelma Swink, attended the exercises of the Coffman School, Saturday night...Messrs. Lewis Murphy and Artie Reed of Crystal City visited here last

week…Mrs[.] Annie Yeager and Mr. Henry Amonette attended to business in St. Louis last week…Mrs. Eliza Douthit, Mrs. Chas. Baker and Miss Florence Taylor are among the ill of the week…Douglass School is nearing its close. Will you not put your name on the visiting list? This is cleanup week. Who'll win the prize?"

25 April 1919, pg. 3, col. 1-3.
"FARMINGTON, MO. A Brigher Dawn. Mrs. Fannie D. Baker, wife of Chas. Baker, of Farmington, Mo., passed into the great beyond early Saturday morning, April 12, after an illness of more than a year. Had she lived until the dawn of another day she would have reached the forty-third milestone of her life, but her Master summoned her to a brighter dawn[.] Mr. and Mrs. Baker were united in holy matrimony September 28, 1895, and to this union six children were added, all of whom survive her; also a husband, mother, brother, one sister and many other relatives. The funeral services were conducted Monday afternoon at St. Paul M.E. Church with her pastor, Rev. J.H. McCallister, officiating. Queen of Honor Court No. 38, Order of Eastern Star, and Masoleat Court Order of Calanthe of which she held the offices of Matron, Royal Matron and Worthy Counselor, respectively, paid honorable tribute to the deceased. The Bank of Farmington, in whose employ Mr. Baker has been for more than 30 years, closed Monday and the entire staff of officers attended the funeral. The deceased was a woman of noble character such as is needed to mother a home. She had been a Christian since her childhood, and for weeks beforce [sic] the end came, she planned her business matters so that when the end came she would be ready to wholly surrender. She was well aware that the end of her pilgrimage was near. She expressed herself as being happy to know that she would soon inherit the promised reward for the faithful. Death, to her, was only a sleep. A FRIEND."

09 May 1919, pg. 6, col. 2.
"Mr. Nelson Hunt of Topeka, Kan., is enjoying a visit here with his brother, Mr. Moses Hunt and other relatives…Mr. Philip Thornton writes us from France that he will soon turn his eyes towards the dear old home of the U.S.A…Nothing has perhaps shocked us more than the sudden passing away of Mr. [sic] James Cunningham last Tuesday morning. She had spent the evening at the home of her friend, Mrs. Ellen Busch, and had attired herself the next morn, started home, but feeling somewhat ill she turned to re-enter the house. She fell and ere a physician could administer to her she had passed away. The funeral of this much beloved Christian woman was held Wednesday afternoon at the M.E. Church with Rev. J.H. McCallister and Rev. Greenlee officiating. Mrs. Cunningham will long be missed. A husband

and brother survive her…Mr. Scott Cole has been among the ill of the work [sic]…The many friends of Mrs. Wesley Douthit regret that she does not seem to imrove…Mrs. David Buford, who underwent a serious operation last Thursday is slowly improving…Mr. Lewis Smith is still indoors from the results of a fractured foot…Edgar Kennedy and Robert Baker enjoyed Sunday at Coffman…Douglas [sic] school will close May 30. The members of the graduating class are Samuel Carl Blackwell, Charles Kossuth Baker, Patrick Henry Cayce, Florence Bertha Hut, Ruth Valeria Boddie, Beatrice Stella Swink, Hilda Mae Kennedy, Leslie Ophelia Poston, Vivian Valeria Staten, Clara Virginia Kennedy, Virginia Flora Matthews, and Edna Costella Harris. The Civil Club of this city presented the school with a small purse as a result of thrift on cleanup day…The fourth and sixth year students entertained the eighth grade Thursday afternoon at the school with bountiful refreshments. The afternoon [illegible] was of much enjoyment."

16 May 1919, pg. 6, col. 2.
"Mrs. Louise Lee, one of the oldest residents of this community, was stricken with paralysis Friday afternoon…Miss Pet Tucker delivered an interesting talk at Douglas [sic] School Monday at which time all pupils were assembled and rendered several musical selections…Fielding Douthit and Robert Franks of Coffman were the guests of J.P. Boddie Sunday…Chas. Baker and Lewis Hill attended to business in Bonne Terre Sunday…Mr. Mert Hunt arrived in Farmington Sunday from overseas, feeling fine and happy…Miss Selma Swink visited in Bonne Terre Sunday…Mrs. Mamiee [sic] Foulke returned from Champagne, Ill., Sunday night…Principal Wilfred E. Wise delivered an able address at the Masonic Hall Friday night. The eighth grade rendered several patriotic selections…Rossie Madison played on the Bonne Terre team at a ball game at Festus Sunday when Festus was victorious…Mr. Scott Cole has recovered sufficiently to resume his work…Mrs. Cora J. Turner of St. Louis is nursing Mrs. Eliza Douthit, who is seriously ill…Mrs. Ada Murphy, accompanied her daughter, Mrs. Simpson, to Crystal City Saturday…Mrs. Mahalio [sic] Madison has recuperated…School will close May 30…Watch these columns for further announcements."

23 May 1919, pg. 7, col. 4.
"Mr. A.A. Simons of St. Louis attended to business here Monday…Mr. Geo. Sutherland of St. Louis attended to business here Monday…Mr. and Mrs. Talbert Burns have come back home to live…Mrs. Ada Cayce and sons were the guests of Mrs. Wm. McCallister Sunday. She returned to Festus in the afternoon, taking her brother, Harvey, for a visit…Mr. Wm. Hunt of Champaign, Ill., was a guest of home folks last week. He was accompanied to St.

Louis by his brother, Mert, who has been "over there."...G.W.C. Mrs. Bertha T. Buckner addressed Masoleat Court Sunday afternoon and found the members quite happy to have her with them. The address was timely and grand. Mrs. Buckner always enjoys her trip to Southeast Missouri, because of the hearty co-operation of the courts...Mr. Roy Cooley, Filding [sic] Burr and Lewis Fletcher of Ironton enjoyed the evening here Sunday...Quite a number of friends of Mrs. [sic] James Robinson were entertained at his residence Thursday in honor of another milestone in his life. The out-of-town guests were Mr. Nelson Hunt of Topeka, Kans., Mr. Wm. Hunt, Mr. Mert Hunt, and Mrs. Cora J. Turner of St. Louis...Douglass primary program will be rendered May 31. The graduating exercises will be held June 2. Rev. A. Poston will preach the bacculaureate [sic] sermon June 1."

20 June 1919, pg. 7, col. 3.
"With the passing away of the two noble characters of our community, Mrs. Eliza Douthit and Mrs. Emma Harris, sorrow prevails with quite a number. Both of these women were women of strong character and great influence. In the fraternal organizations, their usefulness will be missed and the church, St. Paul, of which they were both members feel deeply the loss. The bereaved families have a host of friends who are striving to bring hope and cheer to them in these their saddest of hours. Mrs. Donthit [sic] had been a sufferer for more than ten years while Mrs. Harris' illness never confined her to her bed... Miss Vergia Simms was called home Sunday to be with her sister, Miss Leslie Poston who is quite ill...Mr. and Mrs. J.L. Murphy of Indianapolis, Ind., are the guests of Mrs. Lewis Murphy...Mr. Thomas Cayce spent the first of the week with home folks...Burleigh Lodge No. 29 had one more "scrumpshus" time Saturday night when a feast was spread for fifty persons and at the time nine persons were led into the mystic way of Pythianism. These nine were of Farmington and St. Mary's. Visitors were here from Minnith, Coffman, Avon, Potosi and Bonne Terre. This increases the membership to 75...More than forty persons from here attended the graduating exercises of the Bonne Terre school Friday evening at which time among other interesting renditions, Pres. Clement Richardson of Lincoln Institute delivered a splendid address. The members of the class were Carrie Madison and Ruth Harris...Mrs. Laura Jordan of Charleston passed through this city, Saturday...Miss Laurine Boddie accompanied Mrs. Howard Smith to Festus Sunday."

27 June 1919, pg. 7, col. 3.
"The home of Miss Dayse F. Baker was a scene of great cheer Monday evening when twenty-five persons were assembled in splendid attire to be entertained in honor of Mr. and Mrs. Q.L. Murphy of Indianapolis, Ind., Mr. A. Simms,

the honored musician of St. Louis and Miss L. Laurena Mitchell the book-keeper and efficient secretary of the Argus Publishing Co. The evening was one continuous round of gayety: Misses Edith Cayce, Thelma Swink and Estacada Baker furnished the music for the occasion. Vocal music was an attractive means of entertainment. Short talks were made by Messrs. A. Simms, A. Reed, Chas. Baker, Q.L. Murphy, Felix Poston, James Robinson and Miss Mitchell. Others present who assisted in making the evening worth while [sic] were: Misses Mattie Valle, Imogene Staten, Hortense Kennedy, Mr. and Mrs. John Franks, Mr. and Mrs. P.M. Cayce, Mr. Lewis Smith; Mesdames Clara Poston, Ada Murphy, Mayme Foulke, Susie Robinson and Ora M. Williams. Very early in the morning they went to their several abodes. Mr. and Mrs. Murphy will remain for a few weeks. The other guests have returned to their respective homes...At the M.E. Church Sunday evening there was rendered a program by "home comers." The chief numbers wer[e] the adress [sic] by Mr. Q.L. Murphy on the subject of the great Centenary Movement and the timely address by Mr. A. Simms on the subject of "duty."...Miss Zella Baker and Rev. Greenlee attended the S.S. convention at DeSoto last week and report a splendid session...Mr. and Mrs. Scott Cale [sic] and grandson Master Kossuth enjoyed Sunday at Festus, visiting relatives...A number of our boys are sailing and a rousing good time is expected when they reach their dear old "home."...Miss Virgia Merriman returned to St. Louis Monday after spending a week with home folks...Queen of Honor Court expects to increase her number this week...It had grown so hot for the last few weeks that the goat was sent out on pasture. He'll return however for his official duties."

04 July 1919, pg. 3, col. 5-6.
"Mesdames Ora M. Williams, Misses Edna Harris, Beatrice Swink, Clara Kennedy, Estacada Baker of this place and Mrs. Eliza Carson of Potosi were given the degrees of H. of J. Saturday night...Mrs. Joe Carson of Potosi attended the initiation also. She was accompanied home by Little Nadine and Glendora Baker Sunday...Mr. Freeman Bridges has returned from France, looking fine and healthy. His description of the country, etc., is quite entertaining...The many friends of Rev. W.H.H. Brown, who died at DeSoto, sympathize deeply with his wife...Mrs. Melissa Anthony is the guest of Mrs. Hattie Matthews...Miss Leslie Poston is convalescing...Mrs. Lillian Chappelle and daughter attended to business here one day last week...Mr. Richard Occamore, a prosperous farmers, was busily engaged in his wheat harvest last week...Miss Odessa Cayce is spending the summer with her parents in St. Louis...Mrs. Lee Roden of St. Louis is the guest of her mother, Mrs. Jerry Bridges, who is among the ill of our community...Mr. Felix Poston is visiting relatives in St. Louis...Mrs. Melview Evans was hostess to a number of

friends from home, Festus, Bonne Terre, Ste. Genevieve and Coffman, Monday night...Mr. Lewis Murphy, Mr. and Mrs. Robert Simpson and children of Crystal City are the guests of home folks...It's up to you to read the Argus and you'll know more of the current news. Subscribe now while you may sit in the shade and enjoy it."

11 July 1919, pg. 2, col. 3.
"Mrs. Lee Roden has returned to her home in St. Louis, leaving her mother, Mrs. Jerry Bridges much improved...Mr. Cornelius Cole, of St. Louis enjoyed a day or two of this week with his brother, Mr. Scott Cole...Miss Edith Cayce and Master Elbert Baker returned from Potosi Monday, accompanied by Little Miss Glendora Baker...Mrs. Mamie Foulke and Miss Edith Cayce were chaperones at the "On to Blomeyer," an outing given on the Fourth of July in honor of Mr. and Mrs. Q.L. Murphy of Indianapolis, Ind., and Mr. B.J. Wilkins of St. Louis. A spread of luncheon consisted of almost everything in season. Croqueting, boating, frogging, wading, swimming and foot racing were the chief amusements. The number consisting of 21 was sorry when the hour of departing homeward came. The guests left for their homes Sunday morning...Mr. Elmer Amonette gave a river party to a bunch of jolly boys and girls Friday at which time Mrs. Lulu Kennedy and Miss Lorene Staten chaperoned the crowd...Elbert Baker badly mangled one of his fingers while celebrating Friday...Mr. Henry Renfroe and wife of St. Louis were the guests of Mr. and Mrs. John Franks a portion of last week...Mr. Percy Swink and Mr. John Baker are back from France...Miss Florence Hunt is visiting in St. Louis...Mr. Peter Hill is reported quite ill...Mrs. Mattie Occamore of Route No. 2, was a Farmington visitor Saturday...Mrs. Cora Brown, of Iowa, was the guest of her parents, Mr. and Mrs. Peter Hill the latter part of last week."

18 July 1919, pg. 7, col. 4.
"Damon Hill has arrived from overseas and brought great cheer to his parents, Mr. and Mrs. Peter Hill...Mr. and Mrs. Percy Swink are visiting in Coffman...Quite a number of friends of Fredericktown were up to visit Mrs. Jane Hunt Sunday...Mr. Mert Hunt was called home on the account of the illness of his mother, Mrs. Jane Hunt, who is now improving. He will return to St. Louis soon...While hunting one day last week Alonzo, the little son of Mr. and Mrs. Lewis Kennedy, was shot by a white man, inflicting a terrible wound in his hand. The lad had shot a squirrel. This villain commanded him to let it lay. The boy reached to pick it up when the man fired. The man, a stranger to the boy, escaped in an automobile...Mrs. Ada McCormick and daughters, Miss Leonora and Little Miss Rosa, also Master Ernest, of Chenault, Kans., are the guests of Mrs. Lewis Murphy. Mrs. McCormick is

a niece of Mrs. Murphy. She resided here in her youth. Her father, Mr. John Horn, a former well to do farmer of this vicinity, passed away more than a year ago...Mrs. Louisa Anthony, Mrs. Moses Hunt and Mrs. Sallie Valle visited at Fredericktown last week...Mrs. Pyrtle Evans is the manager of an up-to-date ice cream parlor, where refreshments of the season may be had... Rev. J.H. McCallister and wife are rejoicing over the safe arrival of their son, Leroy McCallister, who has arrived safe from overseas...Mrs. Jane Farris of St. Louis is the guest of her niece, Mrs. Gabriel Cayce...Mrs. [sic] Thos. Cayce has been given a route on the main line of the Missouri Pacific...Mr. Talbert Burns is among the ill of the week...Mr. Philip Thornton and Mr. J.E. Wilkins are the only boys that have not arrived from overseas. When they all get home we are going to have one of Old Aunt Dolly's times. There'll be eating and drinking and more, too."

25 July 1919, pg. 7, col. 4-5.
"Mrs. Jane Hunt remains quite ill...Master A.B. Harris returned Friday from a visit with relatives at Charleston, Mo...Mr. and Mrs. Artville Chappelle visited Mrs. S.O. Wilkins the latter part of the week...Masoleat Court No. 127, O.O.C. had an initiation of the following persons Saturday night: Mrs. Minnie Cayce, Mrs. Ethel Madison, Mrs. Ella Staten, Mrs. Melview Evans, Miss Sophia Mudd, Miss Alcesta Douthit and Miss Laura Wilburn. The Luncheon was a feast in reality...Mrs. Ada McCormick and children of Chenault, Kans., were accompanied to Crystal City Monday on their homeward way by Mrs. Robert Simpson and children and Mrs. Lewis Murphy. They passed through St. Louis Monday en route to their home...A lawn social on the parsonage lawn Friday night was enjoyed by Rev. McCallister and congregation...Messrs. John Franks, Moses Hunt, Charles Baker and the reporter attended the Grand Session of the K. of P. and O.G.C. in St. Louis this week... Miss Imogene Staten visited at Coffman last week...Mrs. Lucy Bridges is the guest of her daughter, Mrs. Lee Roden of St. Louis...Mr. Damon Hill is the guest of relatives at Herculaneum, Mo...Masters Alonzo Kennedy and Elbert Baker are getting along nicely with their wounded hands...Miss Hortense Kennedy is enjoying her usual vacation at the Greenville home...Little Miss Cornelia Franks entertained Wednesday afternoon in honor of Little Miss Rosa McCormick of Chenault, Kans...The ice cream parlor managed by Mrs. J.P. Evans is quite a place for social inspiration...The S.S. Convention of the St. Louis District will not convene at DeSoto until September, having been postponed on account of the Business League."

01 August 1919, pg. 7, col. 4-5.
"The many friends of Anna Robinson, of Bonne Terre, are sorry to hear of

the death of her brother which occurred at Cincinnati, Ohio…Mr. and Mrs. Percy Swink are attending to business in St. Louis…Mr. and Mrs. Arvilla Wilkins, B.J. Wilkins and Ernest Wilkins who has just returned from "overseas," were the guests of Mrs. Susie Wilkins this week. The latter is able to tell many interesting things about his experience…Miss Hortense Kennedy was hostess Tuesday evening at a reception given at the Masonic Hall in honor of these visitors. The evening was much enjoyed by all who attended. Music was a feature of entertainment…Mr. Moses Hunt is employed in St. Louis…Mr. and Mrs. James Robinson entertained Thursday evening in honor of Mr. and Mrs. Arvilla Wilkins of St. Louis…"On to Festus" is the slogan for Aug. 4. where Simmons' band will furnish music for the picnic…Leo, the family pet dog of the reporter, barely escaped death from a vicious dog Thursday night. Medical attention may render it unnecessary to kill him…Miss Hadassah Bridges and niece, Miss Nadine Cherry of Champaign, Ill., are expected here soon…Miss Florence Hunt has returned from a visit with relatives at St. Louis…LeRoy Baker is the guest of his grandfather, Mr. Richard Occamore, of route No. 2. Mr. Occamore has been dealing in real estate…Mrs. Jane Hunt is able to sit about in her room and is thought to be convalescing…Mr. Peter Hill, and family, have moved to their recently purchased home…Mr. Leroy McCallister has returned to his home at Springfield, Mo…Little Miss Mary Drew is the guest of her grandmother, Mrs. Eliza Blackwell…Mr. McKinley Fulton of Bonne Terre, chaperoned an auto party here Sunday night…Mr. Evert Wilkins of St. Louis, was the guest of Mr. and Mrs. Antoine Murphy last week…When Mr. Philip Thorton [sic] reaches home, then we'll write "Finis" on the home coming from "overseas."…Mrs. Dave Buford was called to Coffman on account of the illness of her daughter, Mrs. Fred Chappelle."

08 August 1919, pg. 7, col. 3.
"Mrs. Delia Payne, of Madison, [Madison Co.,] Ill., visited her sister, Mrs. Jane Hunt, last week. She was accompanied here by Miss Vee Occamore… Mrs. Virginia Phillips, of Charleston, Mo., is the guest of her father, Mr. George Blackwell…Mr. Charles Douthit cut his leg severely while farming a few days ago…Miss Edith Cayce, Miss Estacada Baker and Mr. Booker Baker visited in Bonne Terre Sunday…Mrs. Jane Mitchell accompanied her daughter, Mrs. Lucinda Matthews, to St. Louis Sunday…Mrs. Julia Burke, of St. Louis, was the guest of her mother, Mrs. Charlotte Clay, last week… Mrs. Gabriel Cayce attended to business at Mineral Point last week…There were many, many persons who enjoyed the fourth inst. at Festus, Mo., and quite a few remained over for a short visit…Mrs. Louisa Anthony is making good as an agent for toilet necessities…Mr. Fred D. Bridges, of St. Louis, is enjoying a few days with home folks…Mr. and Mrs. A. Reed and daughter,

Lonie [sic], have return [sic] to St. Louis…Subscribe for The Argus and read the happenings of the people of your race and you will then be able to discuss with intelligence the vital issues of the day."

15 August 1919, pg. 7, col. 4.
"Little Miss Pearl Baker and Master Eugene Simpson returned from Crystal City Saturday…Mrs. Frances Craig and family of Herculaneum are the guests of Mr. and Mrs. P. Hill…Mrs. Gertrude Oliver and daughter Clementine, of St. Louis are sojourning with Mrs. Antoine Murphy, while her husband is attending the State Fair…Miss Sarah Occamore of Madison, Ill., was the guest of her father Sunday. Mr. Richard Occamore expects to move to our city soon, where he has purchased a cozy little cottage in East Farmington… Miss Zelma Swink is enjoying a visit with her sister, Mrs. Alice Powers, of St. Louis…Mr. Philip Thornton has arrived and we can now rejoice that every boy who left has returned. The grand banquet is now in order. ["]Wardrobes and chifforobes [sic], fly wide your doors."…After a pleasant visit with home folks, Mr. Ernest Wilkins left Thursday for St. Louis and other points…Mrs. Jerry Bridges has returned from a visit with her daughter, Mrs. Lee Roden of St. Louis…Miss Mattie Valle is enjoying the week at Coffman…Mrs. J.C. Staten is having serious trouble with an affected foot…Miss Leslie Poston has gone to St. Louis for the rest of the summer…Mrs. Sarah Kimball and son of Coffman were visitors of Mrs. Carrie Burns the first of the week…Mrs. Jane Hunt recovered sufficiently to go to St. Louis for treatment…Mrs. Virginia Phillips of Charleston had a pleasant visit of a week with her father, Mr. Geo. Blackwell, and was accompanied home by little Miss Lelia Franks and one of Mrs. Craig's little ones…Mr. and Mrs. Moses Hunt and son, Scott, expect to spend the winter in St. Louis…Miss Laura Wilburn is visiting at Coffman… Mrs. Ann Yeager accompanied Mrs. Jane Thornton to St. Louis last week… Mr. Charles Baker is in the number to go to Atlantic City to the Supreme Session…Threshing at Greenville was an interesting attraction this week. Mrs. Kennedy found herself hostess to quite a brigade…We're awful, awful sorry that we left you out this week, but no one told the reporter of your being away. Now come on. Don't get mad this time."

05 September 1919, pg. 6, col. 3.
"Mrs. Dave Buford barely escaped what might have been a fearful accident, when a team of mules ran away, last Monday morning. The injuries were not serious…Miss Estacada Baker has been confined to her room for several days…Miss Margaret Robinson of Bonne Terre and Miss Florence Johnson of St. Louis were visitors in this city a few days ago…Quite a number of people attended the Circus at Fredericktown, Monday…Mrs. J.C. Staten and family

left for St. Louis, Sunday, where they expect to make their future home... Mrs. Minnie Wilburn and family are making their home in St. Louis...Mrs. Lewis Murphy accompanied Mr. and Mrs. Chas. Douthitt [sic] to Coffman, Monday. The latter was here for medical attention...Mrs. Joseph Carson accompanied Nadine Baker home from Potosi, Friday. Little Miss Nadine was hostess to a number of little friends at her birthday party, Saturday...We regret that Mrs. Ellen Carson is still ill...Mr. Edgar Cayce of St. Louis, visited home folks, Sunday...Miss Maude Burke and Mrs. Georgia Harris, attended a picnic at Festus, Labor Day...Mrs. Jane Hunt is convalescing...Mr. Benjamin Ranson [sic] was here Sunday for optical treatment. While here he was entertained at the residence of Mr. Scott Cole...Mr. Lewis Murphy returned to Crystal City Sunday...Mrs. Martha Villars and Mrs. Dorthy [sic] Abernathy attended to business in St. Louis, last week...Mesdames Rebecca and Annie Bridges were the guests of relatives in St. Louis, this week...Quarterly meeting services will be held at the M.E. Church, Sunday...Mr. Wm. Baker is ill at this writing...Mesdames Louisa Anthony, Mable Harris and Miss Corinne Wilkins enjoyed their visit to Fredericktown."

12 September 1919, pg. 6, col. 3.
"Mr. Clayton Alexander accompanied his grandmother, Mrs. Annie Bridges home from St. Louis Tuesday...Mrs. Rebecca Bridges returned from St. Louis Friday, where she had been the guest of her sister, Mrs. Rosa Parker, and her son, Clarence Bridges...Mrs. Lou Dupee and daughter Cora and Mrs. Lulu Turner of Little Rock, Arkansas, were the guests of Mrs. Emma Jones, Mr. P.M. Coyce [sic] and Mrs. Vergia Baker the first of the week. The latter entertained with a dinner Sunday...Miss Hilda Kennedy and sister Ina left here Sunday en route to Bowling Green. Mrs. Kennedy, Floyd and Opal joined them Tuesday at Festus. A social was given in their honor by a number of young people at the residence of Mrs. Emma Boddie Thursday night...At the school opening Monday there were twenty-four visitors. Rev. J.H. McCallister delivered a very timely address. Mr. Scott Cole made a short talk. Appropriate music was enjoyed. At ten o'clock class legislation was taken up and the entire day's work was full of enthusiasm. City Supt. W.L. Johns was present at the afternoon session...Rev. F.P. Greenlee assisted Rev. J.H. McCallister in quarterly meeting services Sunday. Rev. Pitcher of Bonne Terre was a visitor at the A.M.E. church Sunday evening. Rev. King of Bonne Terre visited here Thursday...Mrs. Minnie Cayce and Mrs. Annie Bridges are the possessors of bone felons...Mrs. Geneva Walker of St. Joseph, Mo., a former resident of this place, is visiting in Farmington and vicinity...Mrs. Dave Buford had returned from Coffman much improved...Mr. and Mrs. James Robinson, Miss Hortense Kennedy and Mr. Philip Thornton attended an entertainment

at St. Mary's Saturday night…Miss Ottawa Cayce of Cape Girardeau was the guest of Mr. and Mrs. Augustus Cayce the first of the week…At the Grand Musicale given at the Masonic Hall Friday night Miss Florence Johnson of 4442 Maffit avenue presided at the piano. The participants were Misses Edna Harris, Florence Hunt[,] Hilda Kennedy, Daisy McCallister, Edgar Kennedy, Rossie Madison, Booker Baker and Elmer Amonette. Miss Johnson played to relieve Miss Estacada Baker, who was ill. Miss Margaret Robinson and Mr. McKinley Fulton of Bonne Terre were visitors…Mrs. Maggie Kennedy visited at Crystal City last week…The A.M.E. church is preparing to have a fair. They will be assisted by the members of the M.E. church."

19 September 1919, pg. 7, col. 4-5.
"Rev. F.P. Greenlee and a number of persons from Farmington attended the Quarterly meeting at Bonneterre [sic], Sunday…Mr. Irvan Thompson of Crystal City was the guest of Miss Maud Burke Sunday. * Henry Amonette underwent a successful operation Thursday. * Miss Hortense Kennedy was hostess to about twenty-five persons, Monday night. The happy number went to her beautiful country home on an "old-time hay frame." The refreshments served were quite delicious. The visitors on board were Mrs. Geneva Walker of St. Joseph and Mr. H.J. Wilkins of St. Louis. * Mrs. J.H. McAllister left for points in Mississippi last Tuesday. * Rev. J.H. McAllister attended the District Conference at DeSoto last week. * Damon Hill has returned for an indefinite period. * Mrs. Katie Bridges and John Baker attended the funeral of Mr. Frank Baker at Bonneterre [sic] Friday. * Mrs. James Cayce entertained Mr. and Mrs. John Franks and daughters, Cornelia and Lelia at dinner Sunday. * Mr. Arville Chappelle of Coffman, was a Sunday visitor. * Two cars of persons from Ironton, chaperoned by Messrs[.] Boyd and Blanks were Sunday visitors. * After a few days visit with her sister, Mrs. Louisa Gunnell at 2627 Bernard street, St. Louis, Mrs. Geneva Walker will return to her home. Mrs. Walker made a splendid address at the M.E. Church Sunday Evening * Miss Leila Baker is suffering from the effects of blood a poisoned hand [sic]. * Mrs. Eliza Overton is visiting relatives at Coffman. * Mr. Wm. Baker has recovered sufficiently to resume his work as fireman at the ice plant. * Mrs. Antoine Murphy is visiting relatives in St. Louis * Mr. Richard Occamore sold his farm, north of town and has purchased a cottage in east Farmington to which he has already moved and is comfortably situated. * Mrs. Felix Poston, Mrs. Maggie Burke and Mrs. Lewis Kennedy are numbered with the ill."

26 September 1919, pg. 7, col. 4.
"Rossie Madison played ball at Festus Sunday…Mr. Scott Cole received the news Sunday announcing the serious illness of his brother, Mr. Cornelius

Cole, at Barnes Hospital, St. Louis...Mr. William Cayce and daughter, Mrs. Edith Mellon, of Cape Girardeau, were the guests of Mr. Augustus Cayce the first of the week...Mrs. Ada Murphy, Mrs. Leora Simpson and children enjoyed Sunday at Crystal City...Mrs. Melview Evans was hostess Tuesday evening to a number of guests from Ste. Genevieve and Fredericktown, Mo... Mrs. Jennie Thornton and family have gone to St. Louis to reside...Mrs. Maggie Thornton and grandson, Sam Blackwell, are visiting in St. Louis this week...Rev. F.P. Greenlee and congregation are preparing for a church fair to be held Oct. 3 at the Masonic Hall...Mrs. Georgia Harris and family will leave for Crystal City Sunday, where they will reside...Douglass School has had twenty-eight visitors and last week the percentage of attendance was 100 per cent in each room. Friday afternoon a social was given at the building for the period of an hour in honor of Daisy McCallister, Laura Milburn, and Elbert Baker, who are each members of the seventh grade. Misses Ruth Boddie, Nellie Bridges an[d] Florence Hunt were visitors at school Thursday."

03 October 1919, pg. 7, col. 5.
"The Farmington baseball boys went to Festus last Sunday for a game, but the rain caused the game to be called off...Mr. Scott Cole returned from St. Louis reporting his brother, Mr. Cornelius Cole, much improved...Mr. Thomas Cayce is remodeling his residence in East Farmington...Glenard Cayce and Robert Cayce visited their grandmother, Mrs. William McCallister, the first of the week...Mr. Lindsey Clay of St. Louis, visited his mother, Mrs. Charlotte Clay, Sunday...Miss Zelma Swink visited at Bonneterre [sic] Sunday... Messrs. Artie Fulton and Rolla Johnson of Festus, enjoyed Sunday evening here[56]...Miss Maude Cooley and Mr. Tullock of Ironton, were the guests of Mrs. Henry Amonette Sunday...Miss Maude Burke enjoyed Sunday at Festus...Miss Mary McCallister of St. Louis is the guest of her mother, Mrs. William McCallister...Mrs. Mazie Lyons is enjoying a month's vacation at Coffman...Mr. H.F. Boyd of Ironton will be in our midst Saturday mosiacting [sic]. He will be pleased to see folks from 2 years to 50...Mr. and Mrs. Fred Chappelle and family, visited Mr. and Mr. J. Buford Monday."

10 October 1919, pg. 3, col. 5.
"Mr. Boddie has been making improvements on his home in South Farmington...Messrs. Weyman Boddie and Frank Stubbs of St. Lois were enjoying their annual hunting trip here this week...Mr. H.F. Boyd of Ironton spoke Saturday night at the M.E. Church G.W.I....Mrs. Anna B. Milburn of the O.O. C. was the official guest of Masoleat Court Friday evening. The ritualistic demonstration given by her was splendid. Her visit to this court was in inspiration to the members. A reception was tendered to her at the close

167

of the meeting…Mr. Lewis Murphy returned to Crystal City, Sunday…Mr. Scott Cole and Master Kossuth Baker enjoyed the first of the week in St. Louis…Miss Mayme Burke of Webster Groves visited here Saturday and Sunday…Mr. and Mrs. P.M. Cayce have made their children a gift of a palver piano which they will no doubt enjoy…Miss Nellie Bridges is the guest of her brother Clarence Bridges of St. Louis and her aunt Mrs. Rosa parker…Miss Edith O. Cayce has made the Argus a welcome member of her household… Mrs. Howard Smith and son and brother, J.P. Boddie arrived from Crystal City Saturday…Mrs. Anthony had business in Fredericktown last week… Messrs. Henry Fulton, McKinley Fulton and Mr. and Mrs. Percy Swink were down from Bonne Terre Sunday on a pleasure run…Mrs. Minnie Cayce went to St. Louis Tuesday to enjoy the Veiled Sights…Samuel Blackwell has accepted employment in St. Louis…It is reported that the wedding bells will soon ring in our [illegible]…Mr. Geo. Maul and Mr. Ed Alexander attended the lodge here last Thursday night…Rev. F.P. Greenlee will attend the Annual Conference next week."

17 October 1919, pg. 3, col. 4.
"Mrs. Katie Hunt and son Scott returned to St. Louis Sunday…News reached us early Monday morning announcing the death of Miss Lethia Taylor, a young lady of our town who had recently moved to St. Louis. She was the eldest daughter of Mrs. Minnie Wilburn…Mrs. Leora Simpson and children have gone back to their home at Crystal City, accompanied by Mrs. Lewis Murphy…Miss Hadassah Bridges of Champagne, Ill., is the guest of relatives. Miss Bridges is a young lady of charming habits and was a former resident of this place…Mrs. Scott Cole and Mrs. Rebecca Bridges spent a few days of last week visiting Mr. Cornelius Coe, who has been quite ill…Miss Clara Kennedy was a visitor at Douglass School Monday…Miss Mattie Valley has gone to Bonne Terre for an indefinite period…Mrs. Louisa Anthony, Miss Corinne Wilkins and Rev. F.P. Greenlee are attending the Annual Conference at St. Louis…The board of directors surprised the student body very agreeably by installing at telephone at Douglass School this week…Miss Nellie Bridges returned from St. Louis Monday. She had a pleasant week's stay…Messrs. Weyman Boddie and Frank Stubbs had many happy hours on their hunting expedition and returned to St. Louis Thursday by motorcycle speed…Mrs. James Cayce and Miss Maud Burke attended the funeral of Miss Lethia Taylor of St. Louis…Mrs. Howard Smith and son have returned to Festus…Mrs. J.H. McCallister has returned from points in Mississippi where she visited relatives. She reports a splendid time."

24 October 1919, pg. 8, col. 5.

"Mrs. Maggie Burke is among the ill of the week...Rev. J.H. McCallister has rallied from a severe attack of pleurisy...Mrs. J.P. Evans will have the closing feature of her ice cream parlor October 31. Bills are out announcing the affair...Mrs. James Cayce and Miss Maude Burke have returned from St. Louis...Miss Ruth B. Davis, of Springfield, Ill., was a visitor at the Annual Conference at St. Louis last week...Miss Imogene Staten is enjoying the week with home folks at Coffman...Mr. Philip Thornton and Mr. and Mrs. Talbert Burns spent Sunday there...Mr. and Mrs. Buford and family enjoyed Sunday the guests of Mr. and Mrs. Fred Chappelle, of Coffman...Mrs. Eliza Overton has arrived from an extended visit with relatives at Coffman...Messrs. Chas. Baker and Booker Baker were guests at a dinner Sunday at the residence of Mr. and Mrs. Jerry Bridges given in honor of Mr. and Mrs. Lee Roden of St. Louis...Mr. Wilburn Smith, Mr. and Mrs. J.P. Evans, Miss Edna Harris and Miss Estacada Baker attended the Simms' concert at Festus, Wednesday evening. They report a splendid time...Mrs. Louisa Anthony and Miss Corine [sic] Wilkins returned from St. Louis Monday...Misses Estacada Baker and Edna Harris were visitors at Douglass School Monday...Mr. Bartley Smith chaperoned a party from Fredericktown here Sunday...Mrs. Antoine Murphy and son, Edward, have returned from an extended visit to St. Louis... Mrs. Anna Yeager has made the Argus a welcome guest in her home."

07 November 1919, pg. 6, col. 4.

"As a community we are painfully shocked to hear of the death of Prof. Cobb at Cape Girardeau. He was one of the oldest and ablest teachers of the state. He was a man of great worth and character[57]...Mrs. James Cayce attended to business in St. Louis last week...Mr. Irvin Thompson of Festus visited here last week...Mrs. Evans was hostess to quite a number of friend[s] on Hallowe'en evening at the Masonic Hall...Mrs. Macie [sic] Lyons has returned from a pleasant visit at Coffman...Mr. Robert Simpson and son Eugene were the guests of Mrs. Ada Murphy Saturday. Mrs. Murphy accompanied them to their home in Crystal City on their return trip...Mr. Thomas Cayce visited home folks this week...Miss Luette Cooley, of Bonne Terre, was the guest of Mrs. Henry Amonette last week...After a pleasant week's visit with Miss Estacada Baker, Miss Lora Robinson returned to Bonne Terre Tuesday...Miss Hadassah Bridges returned to her home in Champaign Friday after a pleasant fortnight with relatives. She was highly entertained at the residence of Mr. and Mrs. James Robinson by quite a number of old friends the evening preceding her departure...Rev. W.H. Spurlock preached at the A.M.E. Church Sunday evening...Mrs. Ellen Carson, of Potosi, is the guest of Mrs. Dave Buford... Robbers or plunderers entered the home of Mr. George Burns and completely searched it through…Mr. and Mrs. Burns are away for the winter…Mrs. Mabel Harris enjoyed a few days of last week visiting relatives in St. Louis… Miss Maude Burke visited friends in Crystal City this week…Mrs. Mannie [sic] Mills, of Webster Groves was the guest of her mother, Mrs. Maggie Burke, last week…Miss Maude Townsend, Messrs. Harry Aubochonn [sic], and Samuel Townsend of Bonne Terre and Alfred Ellis and Farris Franks, of Festus, were present here at the Hallowe'en festivities…Miss Imogene Staten has returned from a visit to Coffman…Friday ended two months of work at Douglass School. The per cent of attendance for the school was 99.94. The students are doing splendid work and attending well."

14 November 1919, pg. 11, col. 3.
"Miss Maude Burke and Mr. Irvin Thompson were united in holy matrimony, Wednesday evening Nov. 5, at the residence of the former's sister, Mrs. Richard Occamore. The ceremony was performed by Rev. J.H. McAllister. The happy couple are now at home to friends at Crystal City. * Mr. Scott Cole visited his brother Mr. Cornelius Cole at Barnes Hospital last week and found him much improved. Mrs. Richard Philipps and family were the guests of Mr. George Blackwell and family the first of the week. * Mr. [sic] J.W. Baker, wife of Rev. Baker, arrived last week for a short visit. * The marriage of Mr. Henry Fulton and Miss Good of St. Louis, brings hope and happiness from their many friends. * Mr.. [sic] Wesley Douthit of St. Louis is the guest of home folks. * Mr. Thomas Cayce was at home last week assisting in remodeling of the home. * Mr. and Mrs. Perce [sic] Swink of Bonnetrre [sic], attended to business here last Saturday. * The faculty of Douglass School attended the State Teachers' Association at St. Louis last week. * A period of sorrow was held at Douglass School last Monday afternoon, through respect to Miss Vera Brooks, an ex-pupil of this school who so fatally met with death. Her career here as a pupil was worthy of emulation. As a community, we regret that in our race there exists such a character as the villain who committed the crime."[58]

21 November 1919, pg. 7, col. 4-5.
"Mrs. Ellen Carson, who is visiting Mrs. Minnie Cayce, came down from Potosi, hoping to recuperate…Miss Mattie Valle of Bonneterre [sic] was the guest of Miss Imogene Staten Sunday…Mr. James Robinson chaperoned a number of young people who went to Bonneterre Saturday night to cheer the newlyweds, Mr. and Mrs. Henry Fulton…Mrs. Richard Phillips and family left for Booneville Saturday to join Rev. Phillips in the beginning of a new conference year…Mr. Moses Hunt of St. Louis, is reported quite ill…Master Leroy Bridges received slight injuries Saturday while playing near an auto

truck...Mrs. Melissa McCallister was among the ill of last week...Mrs. Comfort Staten of Coffman was the guest of her daughter, Miss Lorene Staten Saturday...Mrs. Mayme Foulkes [sic] was the hostess to a few friends at her home Thursday evening...The many friends of Mr. Edcar [sic] Cayce of St. Louis, are sorry to learn of his recent accident...The slogan of our little town is: "Sugar Wanted." We've been forced to go to the old custom of "molasses in coffee" and "molasses in tea." It beats "nuthin" and it takes like the same... School was dismissed for a half day last Tuesday for Armistice celebration... Mrs. Anna Yeager and Mrs. Vergia Pugh have made the Argus their home guest. Now why not subscribe for it and quit reading your neighbors. You owe it to your family to have it in your home...Next Thursday is Thanksgiving Day. The churches are preparing to observe it...Mrs. Charlotte Clay, one of the oldest citizens of our community was stricken with paralysis Monday and at this writing she is very ill. We know of no one in our community who is more deserving that this woman. Her many friends wish her a speedy recovery."

28 November 1919, pg. 6, col. 4.
"Mrs. Charlotte Clay is quite ill. Her daughter, Mrss. [sic] Julia Burke, of St. Louis, and her sister, Mrs. Ben Chapple [sic] of Coffman, have been with her the past week. Her son, Mr. Robert Clay, who is yet in Government service is expected soon. Mr. Fred Chappelle and family of Coffman, visited here Friday. * Master Kossuth Baker was thrown from a wagon last week and received slight injuries about the head. * Messrs. Harry Alexander and Harry Fulton of Bonne Terre were here Saturday. * Mr. and Mrs. Lewis Kennedy entertained quite a number of young people at their "Greenville Home," last Tuesday evening, with a surprise party, given for their son-in-law, J.P. Evans. The young people always enjoy going to their wintry home. Good eats are always in store, and a good time as well. * We are glad to see Uncle George Blackwell able to be out again and at his ussual [sic] vocation. * St. Paul Sunday School is being held in the afternoon instead of morning and it bids fair to be the means of an increase in attendance. * The ice cream parlor managed by Mrs. J.P. Evans has been closed on account of the sugar famine. * Mrs. Maggie Burke is yet among the ill. * Mrs. Dave Buford has been forced to walk on crutches as a result of rheumatism. * Mr. Booker Baker is doing well as an apprentice tailor with a reliable firm here. * Both churches are anticipating a splendid Thanksgiving Day. * Superintendent W.L. Johns and Mr. Tucker, the county attendance officer, were visitors at Douglass School last week. The latter addressed the faculty and student body. * Misses Zelia and Cornelia Franks were at home to quite a number of their friends Tuesday evening, at a social given in honor of Cleophulus, Prudence and Blanche

Phillips...Delicious reffreshments [sic] were served and enjoyed. * Mr. Chris Edwards a former Bonneterre [sic] residence, was seen shaking glad hands with old friends. * While playing football at school, Quenton Hill received a very badly bruised leg which rendered him unable to be present the first of the week. * By calling four five three each morning you may get your order in for a copy of The Argus at 5 cents per copy. It will be delivered each week right at your door, and will not have to read your neighbor's."

02 December 1919, pg. 8, col. 4.
"Mrs. Leora Simpson, Mrs. Ada Murphy and Eugene and Robertine Simpson were Douglass School visitors last week. *** Mr. Robert Poston has enjoyed a few days in S. Louis recently. * Mrs. Belle Mayfield has been numbered with the ill. *** Miss Edith Cayce came down from Herculaneum Friday and remained until Sunday afternoon. She was accompanied as far as Bonne Terre by Mr. and Mrs. B.T. Baker and daughter. *** Mrs. Irene Carter and Mr. Chauncey Bell of Chicago are here with their Grandmother, Mrs. Celia Cunningham. Mr. Tom Cunningham left Sunday for St. Louis having spent a week with her. *** Mrs. Macie Lyons and class had a successful pumpkin pie social Friday night. *** Rev. R. Woods and congregation will conduct a rally at their church Sunday. *** Mrs. Eliza Blackwell cut her hand Thanksgiving Day. The wound is bad one. *** Mrs. Emma Franks was captain of the club that raised twenty dollars Thanksgiving Day for St. Luke. *** Mrs. Robert Woods is president of the Imperial Music Company, recently organized. *** Patronize Mr. Herman Cayce. He has opened a toy shop. The toy automobile recent constructed is worth a patent. *** Rev. Woods was a pleasant visitor at Douglass School one day of last week. *** Mr. and Mrs. J. Herrington of Bonne Terre, chaperoned a number of young people who autoed here Sunday. *** Mrs. Elizabeth Cole is numbered with the ill. *** Mrs. M.J. Bartholomew of Fredericktown, spent the past week with her sister, Mrs. Peter Swink. *** Miss Vergia Merriman and Mr. Wm. Jones were married at Washington, D.C., Nov. 16. Miss Merriman is a former resident of our city, had many friends here who wish the couple a prosperous life. They are comfortably located at Washington, for the present. *** Think of how yon [sic] may be a good fellow Christmas week and do not give all your gifts within your own home. Help to cheer a cripple, a sufferer or a broken heart."

05 December 1919, pg. 8, col. 4.
"Mrs. Charlotte Clay departed this life Wednesday morning, November 26, after an illness of short duration. Having reached her three score years and ten, it seemed that she was aware of the fact that she soon should go and had e'en before she took ill talked with her daughter, Mrs. Martha Villars, and

arranged for her burial, etc. The funeral was conducted Thursday afternoon from the M.E. Church. The son, Mr. Lindsey Clay, and wife, from St. Louis, arrived Wednesday night, the grandsons, James Hill and John Villars arrived Thursday. Mr. and Mrs. Ben Chappelle of Coffman, were in attendance also at the funeral. Mrs. Chappelle is a sister of the deceased...Mrs. Rosa Parker, of St. Louis, was the Thanksgiving guest of her sister, Mrs. P.M. Cayce... Mr. Tillman Cayce of St. Louis was the guest of his sister, Mrs. Emma Jones Thursday of last week...Mrs. Elvira McGee and granddaughter, Miss Marie Anderson of St. Louis, were the guests of Mrs. Martha Villars the first of the week...Mrs. Rebecca Bridges is confined with a severe attack of inflammatory rheumatism. Her son, Mr. Clarence Bridges, of St. Louis, spent a few days of this week with her...Fielding Douthit, son of Mr. and Mrs. Charles Douthit, was found dead in the woods near their home at Coffman Tuesday. He had gone out hunting and in examining some traps that he had previously set, his gun fired and shot him in the head. Just how long he lay there is unknown. He did not come back as early as usual and a search was made which resulted in the finding of his body with one hand as if ready to grasp the trap and other evidence that the shooting was accidental. He was a young man of marked industry, and the news of it to this community was indeed, horrifying. The remains were laid to rest Wednesday. Quite a number from here attended the funeral[59]...Quite a number of people were entertained at the residence of Mrs. Moses Bridges Monday evening in honor of their guests from Pocahontas, Ark. The evening was very pleasantly spent. Delicious refreshments were served. Mr. Pittman returned to his home Tuesday, having enjoyed his stay in our city...Tela-Argus and it will be told to the world."

12 December 1919, pg. 6, col. 4.
"Mrs. Mae Powers of Pocahontas, Ark. left Tuesday after having spent two week here as the guest of her mother, Mrs. Katie Bridges and grandmmother [sic], Mrs. Eliza Blackwell. She has made the Argus her guest for a year. * Rev. W.H. Spurlock conducted quarterly meeting services at St. Luke Chapel Sunday. * Rev. J.H. McAllister preached Sunday afternoon at which time, Rev. Rivers, Supt. of the St. Louis District, will be present. * The Misses Zelma and Beatrice Swink, and Mrs. Mayme Foulke entertained Thursday evening in honor of their uncle, Mr. Kossuth Robinson of St. Louis. The guests from Bonne Terre were, Mr. and Mrs. Perce [sic] Swink, Miss Mattie Valle and Mr. Harry Alexander. * Mr. John Franks is a sufferer from rheumatism. * Mr. Cornelius Cole returned to St. Louis Saturday feeling much improved. * Mr. and Mrs. Irvine Thompson of Crystal City, visited Mr. and Mrs. Richard Occamore last week. * Mrs. Jane Mitchell has returned from an extended trip to St. Louis. * Mrs. Rebecca Bridges is slowly recovering. * Mrs. Rossie Madison

and Mrs. James Cayce were royally entertained while visiting in Crystal City. * Mr. and Mrs. Howard Smith and son of Festus are visiting Mrs. Emily Boddie. * Mrs. Farris Franks of Festus was seen on our streets last week. * Mrs. Moses Bridges and Mrs. Mae Powers were visitors at Douglass School Monday. * It's been proven that Mr. Eric Mathews has a charm on "hares and possums." Few escape him. * Mr. Wilson Chappelle of Coffman attended to his business here Saturday. * Mr. Peter Hill is having success as a carpenter at Champaign, Ill. His family has remained here. * The Douglass boys put the "F" in football. They are playing well and hard. * Mrs. Scott Cole had Santa Claus bring her a "brand new" victrola. He delivered it before Christmas for fear of bad weather."

19 December 1919, pg. 6, col. 4-5.
"Mr. James Cunningham has returned from a visit to relatives in St. Louis... Mrs. Mary McCallister and Mrs. Nellie Cayce enjoyed a trip to the country last week where they were entertained at dinner at the residence of Mr. and Mrs. Jerry Bridges...Rev. Rivere, Dist. Supt. of St. Louis District, conducted quarterly meeting services at St. Paul Sunday. Rev. J.W. Baker preached a splendid sermon at 2:30. The superintendent preached two spiritual sermons during the day...Mr. Charle[s] Baker has been quite a sufferer from an injured leg for more than a week. He has been unable to be at his usual vocation...Mrs. Louisa Anthony was called to Festus Sunday to see a sick relative...Mrs. Henry Amonette and little niece, Melvina Johnson, visited Mrs. Julia Cook at Bonne Terre last week. Mrs. Cook is quite ill...Mrs. Rebecca Bridges is improving very slowly...Messrs. Peter Hill and Damon Hill returned from Champaigne [sic] last week to enjoy the holidays with home folks...Mr. and Mrs. Fred Chappelle and daughters, of Coffman, visited Mrs. Nancy Buford the first of the week...Mr. John Baker is the guest of Mrs. Mae Powers, of Pocahontas, Ark...The S.S. of the M.E. Church is preparing to entertain the public Christmas night. May features of amusement are being prepared...Mrs. Anna Yeager has returned from a business trip to St. Louis... The many friends of Mrs. Julia Cook, of Bonne Terre, regret to learn of her serious illness...Mr. Geo. Tulleck, Mr. Leroy Cooley and Miss Lucile Cooley, of Ironton were the guests of Mrs. Henry Amonette last week...Miss Mattie Valle, of Bonne Terre, visited friends here this week...Mr. and Mrs. Howard Smith and son, Charles, returned to Festus, Sunday...Leave your order for the Argus with Little Miss Pearl Baker or call 435."

26 December 1919, pg. 6, col. 5.
"Mr. and Mrs. Henry Amonette and the Misses Maud and Lucile Cooly [sic] attended the funeral of Mrs. Julia Cook at Bonneterre [sic] Monday. *

Mrs. Minnie Cayce accompanied her sister Mrs. Ellen Carson to St. Louis for medical care. * Mrs. Rebecca Bridges is yet improving. * Mrs. Melissa Anthony has returned to her home at Festus after a pleasant visit with Mrs. Louisa Anthony. * Mrs. Robert Simpson had children, Robertine Annette and Eugene Hartman are the guests of Mrs. Ada Murphy. * Mr. Thomas Cayce of St. Louis and daughter, Mrs. Joseph Carson of Potosi, are the guests of Mrs. Cayce. * Mrs. [sic] Talbert Burns has been a recent sufferer of foot trouble. He has been unable to work for several weeks. * Miss Leslie Poston of St. Louis is the guest of her mother, Mrs. Jerushia Poston. * Mr. Elmer Amonette was a visitor at Douglass School Monday. * Mrs. Louisa Anthony attended the funeral of her brother-in-law, Mr. Lewis Bolduke of Festus one day of last week. * Mrs. Moses Bridges is able to be about in her home after a recent illness. * As a trapper, Master Alonzo Kennedy is famous. He is trapping for the Chicago market. * Mr. Wm. Baker has accepted employment as engineer at the Farmington Rolling Mill. * Master Patrick Cayce presented himself with a graphaphone [sic] last week. The sweat of his own brow. * The wedding bells are supposed to ring ere the dawn of leap year. After Jan 1, [t]he old maids and young widows will have a job of three hundred and sixty-six days. During these [illegible] times it is lovely to know that [illegible] a job that will last. * The Farmington Argus' patrons desire to wish for the entire Argus staff many happy hours during the Yuletide."

02 January 1920, pg. 7, col. 5.
"Little Everett Wilkins is quite ill. * Miss Leslie Poston is having a deal of trouble with her eyes. She hopes to be able to return to St. Louis again. * Mr. Chas. Douthit and family of Coffman, Mo., were in our city Friday. * Mr. John Franks is confined to his room with a very severe attack of rheumatism. * Mr. and Mrs. James Cayce and Mrs. Eliza Overton were the guests of Mr. and Mrs. J. Jordan of Charleston last week. * The reporter entertained last Sunday in honor of Rev. A.L. Reynolds, Kinloch, Mo., Mrs. Dora Dorsey[,] Potosi, Mo., and Miss Ruth B. Davis, Springfield, Ill. * Mrs. Rebecca Bridges seems much improved[.[* Mr. Lewis Murphy and Mr. Robert Simpson of Crystal City visited here last week. * Rev. A.L. Reynolds preached two eloquent sermons at the M.E. Church Sunday[.] He was greeted by large crowds at each service. * Little Miss Mary Drew accompanied Miss Bertha Staten to St. Louis Sunday. * Mr. and Mrs. Lee Roden of St. Louis were the guests of Mr. and Mrs. Jerry Bridges the latter part of the week. * Mrs. J.H. McAllister, Mrs. P.M. Cayce and Rev. A.L. Reynolds were their Christmas day guests. * Mrs. Mahalia Madison entertained Saturday night in honor of her niece, Miss Sophia Mudd of Festus, Mo. Mrs. J.C. Galvin was also a guest of the evening. * Mr. Oliver of Sparta, Ill., was the guest of Mr. H.B. Keatts this week. *

Each church had a Christmas tree and the exercises were largely attended[.] The members and friends of the A.M.E. Church also quite a number of the M.E. Congregation helped in the presentation of a large basket of gifts, the value of which is inestimable. * The Misses Zelma and Beatrice Swink, Mrs. Mamie Foulke and Mrs. Ora Williams are enjoying the week in St. Louis. * Rev. J.W. Baker spent the holidays at Webster Groves[.] * School will open Jan 5, Douglass students are anticipating a joyous opening for the year 1920."

09 January 1920, pg. 7, col. 4-5.
"Mrs. Rebecca Bridges and Mr. John Franks are still numbered with the ill... Mrs. Leora Simpson and children have returned to Crystal City...Miss Mattie Valle and Mrs. M. McGuire, of Bonne Terre, were here the first of the week. Miss Valle was the guest of Mrs. Felix Poston and Mrs. McGuire was the guest of Mrs. Eliza Blackwell...Mrs. Belle Matkins, a very aged lady of our community was found dead in her home Wednesday, December 31. She lived alone and neighbors, missing her usual passing in and out, caused an investigation[.] The same resulted in finding her dead. She had lain there no doubt since the evening of the 30th. Her sons, Mr. Geo. Meyers and Sam Ross, came down from Crystal City and took charge of the remains[60]...Mr. Henry Amonette enjoyed a few days of last week in St. Louis...Mr. Wilson Chappelle, of Coffman, was a visitor in our town last week...Mr. and Mrs. Fred Chappelle have returned to their home at Coffman...Mrs. Nancy Buford is still quite ill at her home in West Farmington...Mr. and Mrs. P.M. Cayce entertained Monday, December 29, in honor of Rev. A.L. Reynolds. Their home was beautifully decorated the refreshments were delicious. Rev. Reynolds returned to Kinloch, Tuesday having spent a joyous time among old friends and acquaintances...Miss Cora Hill of Herculaneum is the guest of her mother, Mrs. Masolet Hill...A party of thirteen attended the Christmas entertainment at Ste. Genevieve December 31...Mr. John Harris and family of Herculaneum were the guests of Mrs. Phylis [sic] McCallister Christmas Day...Mrs. Louise Anthony and Mrs. Sarah Valle returned from Fredericktown, Sunday...Master Raymon [sic] Brown, of Ridgeville, Ohio, is the guest of his grandmother, Mrs. Peter Hill...Laura Wilburn is absent from school on the account of illness...Many resolutions were made just before the passing of the old year, 1919, and the coming of the new year, 1920. Evidence for good were shown in both churches, Sunday. The congregations were larger and the collections were better."

16 January 1920, pg. 7, col. 3-4.
"Masoleat Court No. 127 deeply mourns the loss of Mrs. Ellen Carson of Potosi, Mo. Mrs. Carson had been ill a number of months. * The faculty and

pupils of Douglass School enjoyed a hot lunch Friday, which added much to the inward feeling of all who engaged in the feast. * Mrs. Julia Burke of St. Louis, was the guest of Mrs. Martha Villars this week. * Mrs. Clarence Bridges of St. Louis came down Sunday to be with her mother, who is quite ill. * Mesdames Mary Cayce, Masolent [sic] Hill, Ada Murphy, Minnie Cayce and Mr. and Mrs. Henry Amonette and niece, Miss Melvina Jones, attended the funeral of Mrs. Carso[n] at Potosi, last week. * Master Jessamine Madison is recovering from a recent illness. * Mr. Rossie Madison was the guest of his aunt, Mrs. Geo. Maul Tuesday of last week. * Mrs. Irvine Thompson of Festus, visited her mother Mrs. Maggie Burke last week. * Miss Beatrice Swink has been indoors for quite a few days with an infection on the face caused from a decayed tooth. * The panther delusion which caused a few people to lie awake at night was a farce. It proved to be [a] two-legged panther prowling nightly. * Mrs. Laura Jordan of Charleston, sent Mr. and Mrs. James Cayce and [sic] eight pound fish for their Sunday dinner. This is some of the kind her husband angles. * If you can't keep cool these days the price of coal is not the blame. * Little Dorothy Villars was among the ill of last week. * Mr. and Mrs. Fred Chappelle were called to Farmington last week on the account of the illness of Mrs. Buford's daughter, Miss Laura. * Rev. J.W. Baker attended the funeral of Mrs. Pat Swink at Coffman last week. * Mr. Peter Swink has returned from a pleasure trip to his old stamping [sic] grounds at Coffman. * Mr. James Robinson, Sr., has returned from a visit with relatives in St. Louis. * Mr. H.B. Keatts has returned from a business trip at Bonneterre [sic], Mo. * J.P. Boddie has accepted a position at Festus. * Edgar Kennedy and Damon Hill left Monday enroute [sic] for Festus and other points. * Mr. Wilburn Smith is employed at Fredericktown, Mo. * Mrs. Cora Brown has returned to her home at Ridgeville, Ohio. * Master Everette Wilkins is in the grip of old "Mr. Whooping Cough." * Mrs. Louisa Anthony has been employed as a cook at the Farmington High School to prepare hot lunches for the student body. * Miss Leslie Poston is able to be out. Her sight is very much improved. * Rev. J.H. McAllister preached a splendid sermon on Meditation. We are glad to report an increase in attendance. * Mr. and Mrs. William Baker are rejoicing over the arrival of a "brand new boy." He heads our list for the New Year's boys. * Nearly every family in Farmington is reading The St. Louis Argus. We realize the fact that in order to keep up with the leading issues of the day we must read the most reliable publications—The Argus is one of these kind."

23 January 1920, pg. 3, col. 4.
"The curfew whistle blows at 8:30 p.m. This means that little, unchaperoned boys, must scamper or be caught by the "billet man." * Mrs. Maggie Burke

and daughter, Edna, have moved to Festus, Mo. * Master Izell Taylor of St. Louis is the guest of his grandfather, Mr. Richard Occamore. * Mr. Edward Harris has completed a plastering job at the A.M.E. Church. * Mr. Lewis Smith is having considerable trouble with his foot, that was injured many months ago. * Mrs. Nancy Buford and Miss Laura Wilburn are convalescing. * Mr. Fred Chappelle and daughter have returned to their home at Coffman. * Misses Lavada and Mary Jane Chappelle were visitors at Douglass School Tuesday. * Mrs. Rebecca Bridges is improving very slowly from a severe attack of muscular rheumatism. * News has reached us of the illness of Mrs. J.C. Staten of 4346 N. Market Street, St. Louis. We wish her a speedy recovery. * Under the management of Mrs. Jane Hunt as superintendent, the A.M.E. Sunday school is having an awakening revival of attendance. Miss Zelma Swink, the assistant superintendent, is quite busy increasing the enrollment. * Rev. J.H. McAllister received a message last week announcing the death of Rev. Richard Davis of Kansas City. The Methodist Episcopal Church has lost one of its ablest men.[61] * Mr. John Franks is back at his usual vocation after a serious attack of rheumatism. * Now don't censure the reporter for all of the "crooked news." Sometime it is misquoted to her, and too, oftentimes it is a typographical error. Our aim is to please you.—Dayse F. Baker."

30 January 1920, pg. 3, col. 5.
"The young people of the M.E. Church are preparing to render the play "Popping the Question" Feb 12 at the Masonic Hall. Remember the date. * Mr. Rossie Madison visited friends in Bonne Terre last week. * Mr. and Mrs. Wm. Kennedy of Bowling Green[,] [Pike Co.,] Mo., is the guest of her sisters, Mrs. Wm. McAllister, and Mrs. Talber [sic] Burns. * Master Arville Kennedy is absent from school with an injured limb. * Miss Lucy Mooten, Mrs. Lewis Murphy, Mrs. Dave Buford and Miss Laura Wilburn are numbered with the ill. * Mr. Damon Hill has returned from a trip to Herculaneum. * Masoleat Court is planning a good night Feb. 7. Miss Edith Mason of Herculaneum is one of the number who will be led into the mysteries of Calantheanism. Mr. Peter Hill is quite busy drawing candidates for the Court. * How many of the men of our community will see to it that we get a way constructed so as to reach the school room without taking a mud bath? How many? Who'll start the movement? * Rev. J.W. Baker spent Sunday with the congregation at St. Luke's Chapel. He divides his time with Coffman circuit. * Mr. and Mrs. James Robinson served the annual Fortnightly Social at the Club room Friday afternoon. * Rev. J. H. McCallister and congregation are planning a Tacky Leap Year Social for Feb. 27. Children, grown ups [sic] visitors and friends are requested to take a part. The costumes will be odd[.] Ladies are expected to bring gentlemen and pay his entrance fee. Don't fail to take a part as it is

an entertainment that will be long remembered. This will be the last drive for this conference year."

06 February 1920, pg. 3, col. 1.
"Mr. George Evans is convalescing. * Mr. Thomas Cayce enjoyed a few days with home folks this week. * Mrs. Jerry Bridge[s] received a message announcing the illness of her son-in-law, Mr. Lee Roden who is confined with pneumonia in St. Louis. * Mr. and Mrs. Charles Douthit of Coffman visited relatives here Sunday. * Mrs. Ada Cayce and son Robert returned to Festus Sunday. She left her son Glenord [sic] here to attend school. * Mr. Robert Simpson of Crystal City enjoyed Sunday with relatives here. * Rev. J.H. McAllister led a period of sorrow Sunday night at the M[.]E. Church in memory of Rev. Richard Davis who recently passed to the great beyond. * Mrs. Rebecca Bridges has not been so well for several days. She is yet unable to walk. We bowed our heads in sorrow when we were informed of the death of Mr. Ben Ransom, which occurred at Festus last week.[62] * There are not enough physicians here to handle the influenza epidemic. The number of colored victims are few. We hope that they will soon recover. * M[rs.] Anna Yeager had a business trip to St. Louis last week. * Mrs. Lulu Kennedy and son Floyd have returned to Bowling Green, Mo. * Mrs. Mable Harris has moved to the residence formerly occupied by the widow Burke. * Mrs. Elmer Amonette is having considerable trouble with a growth on the neck. * Mrs. Eliza Overton is improving. * A wave of undaunted prosperity is passing over St. Luke A.M.E. Sunday School. Many persons are attending who have not attended before since the days of early childhood. Much good will be delivered from this religious movement. * A movement is on to construct a walk to Douglass School."

13 February 1920, pg. 3, col. 4.
"While playing with some other youths at the turn table on the Houck Line in the eastern part of the city Sunday afternoon, Leroy Baker, had his right heel almost severed from the rest of his foot. He is the oldest son of Mr. Wm. Baker...Mr. John Douthit met with a painful accident Saturday afternoon. While moving a piano in company with other men, his third finger on the right hand was caught in some way and was badly lacerated. The physicians are trying to save the finger. It was thought at first that it would be necessary to amputate it...Mr. and Mrs. Jno. Franks received a message Friday announcing the death of Mrs. Henry Renfroe [sic], which occurred Wednesday, Feb. 4, at St. Louis. The remains were taken to Jackson, Mo., her home[63]... Mrs. Lena Evans Brown of Cleveland, Ohio, arrived Saturday to visit relatives. She is being entertained in the home of her niece, Miss Edna Harris

and brother-in-law, Mr. Ed. Harris…Mrs. [sic] and Mrs. Jno. Franks had as their house guests Saturday, Mr. and Mrs. Roscoe Davis, of Fredericktown. Mr. Davis was here consulting Dr. O.A. Smith, the eye specialist, who says he will not lose the sight of either eye from his recent accident[64]…There are too many ill with the flu to publish their names, however, those who are ill seem to have it only in a mild form…Mrs. Comfort Staten of Coffman has been here quite a week attending at the bedside of her daughter, Miss Lorinne [sic] Staten who has been quite ill…The home of Mr. and Mrs. Dave Buford burned completely Monday night between seven and eight o'clock. The fire started in the kitchen and when it was discovered it was too late to save anything of consequence from the building. The firemen and other men fought the fire hard and constantly and saved the residence of James Coyce [sic] which was only fifteen or twenty feet away…The "Flu Ban" is on most public gatherings. School has been recessed…Gossip and flu seem to be king. Let us carefully consider Psalm 39:1."

20 February 1920, pg. 7, col. 4-5.
"M[iss] Edith Cayce underwent a successful operation last week[.] A growth was removed from her nose[.] Dr. O.A. Smith was the attending physician. * Mrs. Hildred Overton and son, Melvin of Kansas City, are the guests of Mrs. Pleas Boddie. Mrs. Overton's visit to Farmington is always a panacea to her many friends. * Mr. Geo. Burns arrived from St. Louis a few days ago to recuperate from an attack of Flu. * Mrs. Mamie Cayce has recovered from a recent illness, but is now suffering the result of being salivated. * Mr. Chas. Douthit of Coffman has made the Argus a welcome member of his home for a year. * Rev. J.W. Baker conducted services at Coffman Sunday. * Mr. James Cayce is planning to accept a position at Detroit[,] Mich. Mrs. Cayce will remain here indefinitely. * Mr. Dave Buford and family have begun housekeeping in the residence of their sister, Mrs. Mamie Cayce. The house is five or six doors from their former home. * Mr. Henry Amonette is having great success with his Buckeye incubator. He is much interested in poultry raising. * The list of sick persons is yet too great to publish. * Schools reopened Wednesday with a decline in percentage of attendance, owing to illness. * M[r.] John Douthit is suffering a deal with his injured hand tho [sic] the wound is healing nicely. * Mr. Elmer Amonette got his finger dislocated Monday while at work. * Popping the Question will be presented to the public Feb. 27. * Mrs. Jerushia Poston has returned from a visit to St. Louis. She reports her daughter Miss Leslie's eyes very improved. * It's so nice to have the Argus come to your home especially when you have the Flu and don't feel like talking. Try it once—not the Flu but the Argus. Call 435 and it will be delivered at your door by the little paper girl, Miss Pearl Baker."

27 February 1920, pg. 3, col. 3.

"Mrs. Ada Murphy was called to Crystal City Tuesday to be at the bedside of her daughter, Mrs. R. Simpson. * Master Lewis Villars was slightly injured about the head Saturday while at play. * Mrs. Lee Roden and Mr. Philip Bridges of St. Louis arrived the first of the week to be with their mother Mrs. Jerry Bridges, who has been quite ill. * Mrs. Edith Cayce was able to resume her work Monday. * Mrs. Edna Kemp of Fredericktown was here Sunday at the bedside of her aunt, Mrs. Lucy Mooten. * Mrs. Floyd Kennedy has accepted employment at Kansas City, Mo. * Master Leroy Baker is around on crutches. * Mrs. Dora Carson of Potosi was the guest of her mother, Mrs. Mary Cayce Saturday and Sunday. * Mr. and Mrs. Otis Vaughn of Potosi visited relatives here Sunday. * Mr. James Cayce is at Detroit, Mich., where he expects to remain for a while. * Mrs. Rebecca Bridges is convalescing also Master Arville Kennedy. * Mr. and Mrs. Perce [sic] Swink of Bonne Terre, Mo., were the guests of Mrs. Peter Swink Sunday. * Mrs. Moses Bridges had a message announcing the illness of her son-in-law Mr. W.H. Powers of Pocahontas, Ark. * Masoleat Court will initiate four candidate[s] Feb. 28. They all hail from Herculaneum, Mo. * Church services were well attended Sunday. Quite a number of persons have not as yet awakened to the realization of the fact that it is their duty to sit in some church at least once each Sabbath day."

06 March 1920, pg. 3, col. 2.

"News has reached us of the death of Little Cosetta Wilburn, daughter of Mrs. Minnie Wilburn of St. Louis, Mo.[65] * The participants of the play rendered at Masonic hall last Friday night, did much credit to themselves. It was well attended. Miss Mattie Valle, Mr. Harry Alexander were in attendance. * Miss Edith Nelson, Mrs. Ada Staten, Mrs. Nellie Coinne [sic] and Mrs. Lillie Nelson of Herculaneum were acquainted with the mystries [sic] of Calantheism Saturday night. Mrs. Jennie Nelson was a visitor at the great Feast. * The family of Mr. Charles Baker completely and favorable surprised him on his birthday, Feb. 29. The following were the guests: Messrs. Lewis Hill, John Douthit, James Robinson, John Franks[,] Lewis Smith, Ed. Harris, Eritch [sic] Matthews and Felix Poston gathered early in the afternoon. When the refreshments were brought in, then Mr. Baker realized that he was in the mdst [sic] of [an] "honest to goodness" stag party. * Miss Daisy McCallister is spending the week at Crystal City assisting in carrying for the family of her brother, Mr. Robert Simpson. * Mr. Tine Murphy has about completed the walk leading to the Douglas [sic] School. It is a splendid improvement. Mr. Charles Baker donated two loads of cinders. They way has been prepared, patrons and friends and if you have not registered on the visiting roll you have only fifty-five more days, as we have only eleven more weeks of school.

* Mrs. James Cayce returned from Crystal City Sunday leaving Mrs. Georgia Harris and family convalescing. * M[rs.] Dorris Abernathy of St. Louis accompanied her niece, little Helen Villars, home Sunday[.] Mrs. Abernathy returned Monday. * Mrs. Anna Whitener and son, Rudolph and Mrs. Viola Scott of Crystal City, and Mrs. Edna Kemp of Fredericktown, were here the first of the week to be with their aunt, Mrs. Lucy Mooten, who is quite ill. * Mr. Henry Amonette is delighted at the success of the Buckeye Incubator. He is now the owner of a nice brood of chickens. * Quarterly meeting services will be held at the A.M.E. Church Sunday. Rev. J.H. McCallister and congregation will attend the afternoon services. * Mr. Richard Occamore is quite ill at his home in East Farmington."

12 March 1920, pg. 3, col. 3.
"The funeral of Mrs. Lucy Mooten was held at the M.E. Church Saturday afternoon. This noble character gave up life's conquest Friday at the age of 67 years. She had been a loyal member of this church for more than 30 years and had been a burning light. Her life in the community was an exemplary one, and to her many friends he made it known that her death would only be a welcome sleep as she had suffered long and hard. * Revs. J.W. Baker and J.H. McCallister conducted quarterly meeting services at St. Luke Chapel Sunday. * Mrs. George Maul is the guest of Miss Ruth B. Davis of Springfield, Ill. * Mrs. Antione [sic] Murphy entertained Mrs. Reed, a missionary, at her home Saturday and Sunday. Mrs. Edna Kemp returned to her home at Fredericktown, Monday. * Mrs. Viola Scott returned to her home at Crystal City, Saturday. * Mrs. Jerry Bridges is recovering slowly. * The many friends of Mr. Richard Occamore are sorry to know of his continued serious illness. * Misses Laurine Boddie and Zella Baker received the ordinances of baptism last Sunday at the A.M.E. Church. They are promising young ladies and will prove quite helpful in the work. * Mrs. J.W. Baker enjoys frequent visits to Farmington, the guest of her husband, Rev. Baker. * Mrs. D. Buford and daughter, Laura, are visiting at Coffman, Mo. * Remember the concert that is to be given March 27, by the elderly ladies and gentlemen. * The Pythian anniversary will be observed Monday, March 28. * Quarterly meeting at the M.E. Church, March 21. * Remember that there remains only a few more weeks of school and we desire to enroll you on the visitation list. * Every now and then, you visit the place where your chickens stay and see if it is alright. Why not visit the place where your children stay and see if they are comfortable and see if they are being treated properly? This is food for thought."

19 March 1920, pg. 3, col. 2-3.
"Mr. Elmer Amonette has been confined to his bed with a serious attack of

tonsillitis. Mr. Wm. Hill received the said intelligence of the death of Mrs. Mary Harris Ward, which occurred at Hackensack, N.J. Mrs. Sallie Taylor, Mrs. Mable Harris, Miss Edith Cayce and the reporter enjoyed Sunday afternoon out in the country at the residence of Mr. and Mrs. Jerry Bridges. Miss Mattie Walle [sic], of Bonneterre [sic], enjoyed Sunday evening as the house guest of Miss Edith Cayce. Rev. J.W. Baker conducted services at Coffman on Sunday. Rev. W.H. Spurlock filed [sic] the pulpit here at St. Luke. The funeral services of Mr. Richard Occamore were conducted at the A.M.E. Church Saturday morning. The daughters, Misses Sarah, Lena, and Lula Occamore, Mrs. Ada Taylor, and the granddaughters, Alice and Vee, were in attendance from Madison, Ill. Mrs. Maggie Burke and Mrs. Maud Thompson were present from Crystal City. The deceased left a wife, fifteen grand children [sic], two great grand children [sic] and four daughters. Mr. Occamore had farmed successfully on his property north of this town until about eight months ago, when his health failed him. He then exchanged for a cottage home in East Farmington, where he resided until the end came. Mr. Harvey McCallister had the misfortune to thrust his head against a nail and inflicted a wound which has caused him great pain. Miss Daisy McCallister has returned from Crystal City and has resumed her school duties. St. Paul Sunday School has been favored the past two Sundays with addresses from Mesdames Dorothy Overton and Emma Franks. Misses Virginia Matthews and Katheryn Drew accompanied Miss Zella Baker as far as Flat River on her way to Crystal City Sunday. Rev. J.W. Baker is visiting his wife at Webster Groves this week. Miss Alcesta Douthit and Miss Clara Kennedy are visiting relatives at Coffman this week. The entertainment of the M.E. Church has been changed to March 26."

26 March 1920, pg. 3, col. 2.
"News reached here this week that Mrs. F.P. Greenlee, formerly Mrs. Estelle Roberts of this place, is critically ill at Poplar Bluff, Mo...Mrs. Ada Murphy, of Crystal City, was the guest of the reporter Sunday and Monday... Mesdames W. Wise, Maggie Townsend, Nancie Daggs and Nevada Harris, of Bonne Terre, attended the quarterly meeting at St. Paul Sunday...Rev. G. Glasky and wife and Mr. Bartley Smith and wife accompanied Rev. Rivere to Farmington from Fredericktown Sunday afternoon. Rev. Glasby [sic] preached a very interesting sermon...Mrs. James Cayce expects to join her husband at Detroit, Mich., the latter part of this week...James Baker, Robert Baker, Izell Taylor and Willie Taylor left Sunday for Madison, Ill...Mrs. Felix Poston was indisposed a few days of last week, also Mrs. P. Boddie...Queen of Honor Court will observe Palm Sunday at the Castle Hall by rendering a program at 2 o'clock...Pythians and Calanthians will observe their anniversary at

3 o'clock at the M.E. Church…Mr. John Douthit has recovered sufficiently to be at work…Mr. Elmer Amonete [sic] has recovered…Rev. Rivere, district superintendent, conducted quarterly conference Monday evening and departed Tuesday for other points of the district."

09 April 1920, pg. 3, col. 1-2.
"Mr. James Robinson was the host to a large crowd of people from Bonne Terre, Festus, Crystal City, Fredericktown, Coffman, St. Louis and St. [sic] Genevieve and our own little city, at a ball at the Masonic Hall, Monday night. * Rev. Hildred Overton preached at the M.E. Church Sunday morning and at the M.E. Church Sunday evening. * Rev. J.H. McAllister has just finished a three-year pastorate at St. Paul and as he leaves for conference he leaves a splendid record in he [sic] social as well as in the spiritual field. * News has reached us announcing the death of Mrs. F.P. Greenlee at Popular [sic] Bluff, Mo. The deceased was a resident of this place until a few months ago. While here she was the [sic] an earnest church worker. * Mr. Nelson Turner of St. Louis was the guest of Mrs. Anna Yeager, Sunday. * Mrs. Laura House of St. Louis was the guest of Mrs. Minnie Cayce, her sister.[66] * Mrs. James Robinson and daughter, Miss Alberta Lea of Detroit, Mich., are visiting relatives here. * Mr. and Mrs. T.H. Powers and daughter Janet of St. Louis, enjoyed Easter with their parents, Mr. and Mrs. Peter Swink. * Miss Beatrice Swink enjoyed a visit from Irene Franks of Festus, Sunday. * Messers[.] Edcar [sic] Cayce and Tillman Cayce of St. Louis were here the first of the week. * Mrs. Simpson and children and Mrs. Lewis Murphy returned from Crystal city Friday. Mr. Simpson enjoyed a couple of days here this week. * Mrs. Elizabeth Cole[,] Miss Glendora Baker and Master Kossuth Baker are the guests of Mrs. M. Curtaindoll at 2941 Pine street. * The Juveniles were entertained at the home of Miss Estacada Baker, Sunday afternoon. The Seniors enjoyed a splendid hour at the residence of the Misses Swink. * Prof. Koschman of the Lutheran Parish, Miss Traunericht and Miss Rickus reviewed the work at Douglahs [sic] School Monday. * Rev. H. Overton addressed the school Tuesday afternoon. * Register at Douglass within the next thirty days or you will have made us think you are not mindful of us."

16 April 1920, pg. 6, col. 4.
"Mrs. Susie O. Wilkins, the Douglass faculty and little Miss Nadine Baker, attended the conference in St. [L]ouis. * Mr. Lindsey Clay is reported quite ill. * Ere this issue of The Argus, Miss Hortense Kennedy will be the bride of Mr. Lewis Smith. The wedding date was the 15th. * The many friends of Prof. A. Simms desire to congratulate him on being elected delegate to the A.F.M. Convention. Yes, he helped to put the "F" in Farmington, too. He has our

hearty cheers. * Mr. Lewis Murphy returned to Crystal City Sunday. * The funeral of Mrs. F.P. Greenlee was held at St. Luke's Chapel Wednesday of last week. Rev. Spurlock conducted the services. Mrs. Greenlee leaves to mourn their loss a husband, son, four sisters and six brothers, all of whom were present except a brother who lives in Canada. There were two neices [sic] present also, Mrs. Dollean Alexander, the youngest sister, took the little son, Addison to St. Louis to live with her. * Mrs. John Franks and Mrs. W.H. Spurlock were visitors at school last Thursday. * Mr. and Mrs. Dave Buford, Miss Laura Wilburn and Miss Daisy McAllister visited at Coffman Sunday. * Mr. Hiram Green, formerly of Bonneterre [sic] was buried in St. Louis Sunday.[67] * Mrs. Martha Villars received a message the first of the week announcing the death of Mrs. Elvira McGee of St. Louis.[68] * Mrs. Leslie Poston has regained her usual eyesight and is at home for a few weeks after having spent a number of weeks in St. Louis under optical care. * This is a busy year for the ladies. It is a political leap year. It is a specially prepared one for old maids and widows. Others may take a part. * Rev. Thomas of East St. Louis has been appointed as pastor of the M.E. Church. * Rev. J.H. McAllister will go to Macon City, [Marshall Co.,] Iowa. Rev. McAllister and wife are leaving a host of friends who regret to see them go, but we welcome the coming minister and family. * Mr. Frank Staten of Fredericktown, has accepted a position here at the St. Francois Hotel."

30 April 1920, pg. 6, col. 5.
"Rev. C.W. Thompson, wife and little Clyde Wesley arrived here from East St. Louis, Saturday. * Master Harvey Villars is among the ill. * Mr. and Mrs. Frank Kinder of Fredericktown visited Mrs. Minnie Cayce, Sunday. * Miss Mattie Valle has returned from St. Louis. * Little Mary Drew of St. Louis is the guest of her cousin, Flossie Bridges. * Mrs. Annie Robinson of Bonne Terre was here last week soliciting members for the Mosaics. * Mrs. Jane Hunt made a business trip to Fredericktown last week. * The married ladies and ex-pupils of Douglass School played the Seventh grade girls baseball last Friday. Score 10 to 5 in favor of the girls. Next game Friday, May 7. * Miss Willa Jones was hostess at a social given at her home Sunday for a few friends."

14 May 1920, pg. 3, col. 3.
"Mr. Turner of St. Louis was the guest of Mrs. Annie Yeager Sunday. * Miss Estacoda [sic] Baker is indisposed. * Mrs. George Maul of Bonne terre [sic] was in attendance at the Installation of Queen of Honor Court Friday evening. She was entertained at the residence of Mrs. M. Madison. * At the ball game Friday, betwen [sic] the 7th grade and the In Towns, the Douglas [sic] team won out in a nifty little score. The In Towns are determined that they

will win yet. * Miss Alcesta Douthit and Mrs. Rossie Madison returned from Festus Sunday. * Mrs. P. Boddie is enjoying a visit at Festus with Mr. and Mrs. Howard Smith, who are rejoicing over the new comer, little Miss Cosetta Nadine. * Mr. Lewis Hill is in St. Louis under an optician's care. * Rev. C.W. Thompson spends the first of each week in East St. Louis, looking after business interests. * Mrs. Louisa Anthony visited in Festus last week. * Mrs. Mahalia Madison is attending the General Conference. * Mr. Henry Renfro of Webster Groves is the guest of Mr. and Mrs. Tillman. * Mr. M. Turner of St. Louis and Mrs. Annie Yeager of this place were married Monday afternoon. * Miss Mary McCallister of St. Louis is visiting relatives here. * Miss Willa Jones, J.P. Boddie, Freeman Bridges and Herman Cayce, spent Sunday at Crystal City. * Mr. Edgar Kennedy of Crystal City was the guest of home folks last week."

21 May 1920, pg. 3, col. 3.
"The faculty and pupils of Douglas [sic] School enjoyed a musical treat Tuesday afternoon. The music was furnished by Mrs. O.W. Bleeck. * Dr. Parks and Mrs. G.W. Patton conducted a clinic the same afternoon. * Mrs. Martha Villars has returned from attending the funeral of her brother, Mr. Lindsey Clay, who died a few days ago in St. Louis. * Mr. Lewis Hill, underwent an operation of the eyes Thursday in St. Louis. * Rev. C.W. Thompson and family, left Monday to visit relatives in the vicinity of Chicago. Rev. Thompson will arrive to fill his place Sunday. Mr. Henry Renfro has returned to Webster Groves. * Miss Mary McCallister returned to St. Louis Tuesday. * Mrs. Mayme Foulke is visiting in St. Louis. * Quarterly meeting services will be held at the M.E. Church June 26-27. * Miss Estacada Baker is improving. * Mrs. Emily Boddie is under medical treatment in St. Louis. * Mr. P.M. Cayce spent the day Tuesday at Festus. * Mrs. Jane Mitchell is in St. Louis. * Rev. G.W. Baker is attending the general conference this week. * Douglass Batters won another victory Friday, over the InTowns [sic] * Vacation is here. Employ your young boys['] and girls' hands, as well as minds. The big question is how."

28 May 1920, pg. 2, col. 1.
"[two lines illegible] Rev. G.W. Baker and congregation [four words illegible] excellent sermon [Sunday?]. * Mrs. M[ahalia?] Madison has returned from St. Louis. * Mr. and Mrs. [two words illegible] and Miss Melvina Jones Ironton Sunday afternoon. There were [accompanied?] home by Mr. Burrell Tullock. * Master Carl Staten came home with Mr. Abe Cayce from Herculaneum Saturday. They will be here indefinitely. * Messrs. Carl Robinson, Irving Yeargin, Lathan [sic] Robinson and J. Marvin Fulton of Bonnterre spent a few hours

here Sunday. * The A.M.E. Quarterly meeting will be held June 29. The M.E. Quarterly meeting, June 27. * While in our city on business, Dr. Porter of St. Louis had headquarters at Mr. Scott Cole's residence. * Mr. Joseph Carson and brother, Ed., of Potosi, were here the first of the week. * Mr. and Mrs. Price [sic] Swink returned to Bonneterre [sic] Monday."

04 June 1920, pg. 7, col. 5-6.
"Mrs. Flora Vaughn, Mrs. Dora Carson, Glendora Baker, Nadine Baker and Elizabeth Matthews went to Potosi Monday. * Little Miss Odessa Cayce is enjoying her vacation at Festus, Mo. * Miss Edith O. Cayce enjoyed the week's end at Potosi. * Mrs. Chas. Douthit, Mr. Roy Douthit, Miss Christine Douthit and Mrs. Lillian Chappelle and daughters visited relatives here Sunday. * Rev. C.W. Thompson enjoyed tea at the residence of Mr. and Mrs. Talbert Burns Sunday. * Mrs. Virginia Pugh and daughter Anna are spending the week at Cape Girardeau[.] * Mr. Samuel Burke who has been in military service for the past two years is enjoying a visit with home folks. * Dean R.S. Cobb of Dalton, Ill, was entertained at the home of Mr. and Mrs. John Franks last week. He is touring the country in the interest of Bartlett Agricultural School. * Mr. Burrell Tulleck of Pilot Knob is the guest of his sister, Mrs. Henry Amonette. * Mrs. Minnie Pryor of St. Louis visited her mother Mrs. Maggie Thornton Sunday. * Mr. Lewis Hill has returned from St. Louis much improved. * Mr. B.J. Wilkins of St. Louis is enjoying his vacation with his mother Mrs. Susie Wilkins. * Mr. and Mrs. Lewis Smith entertained quite a number of friends in honor of Mrs. Mayme Foulke, Friday[.] * Mr. William Baker is yet quite ill. * Miss Estacada Baker is improving. * Mr. Phillip Bridges of St. Louis enjoyed a few days last week with his parents, Mr. and Mrs. Jerry Bridges. * Mrs. Rebecca Bridges who has been ill for a number of months is now able to walk in and about the home."

11 June 1920, pg. 5, col. 4-5.
"A social was tendered Miss Ruth Boddie Tuesday. She will leave for St. Louis Sunday. * Rev. C.W. Thompson is visiting relatives in Chicago. * Master Patrick Cayce has accepted employment in St. Louis. He will reside with his aunt, Mrs. Rosie Parker. * Mr. George Blackwell is on the sick list. * Mrs. Jane Hunt and Mrs. Jennie Swink have returned from St. Louis. * Mrs. Anna Yeager, Mrs. Katie Bridges, Mrs. Mattie Occmore and Miss Edna Burke attended the annual sermon of the Mosaics at Bonneterre [sic]. * Mr. Samuel Burke is visiting in St. Louis. * Little Miss Audelle Cayce and Mrs. Lewis Murphy visited in Crystal City Sunday. * Mrs. Lewis Smith is convalescent. * The Misses Swink entertained a few friends in their home Tuesday evening. * Mr. Ellis Taylor received the sad intelligence of the death [o]f his wife, which

occurred at Madison, Ill., a few days ago. * Rev. C.W. Thompson and Mr. Wesley Douthit were entertained at dinner at the home of Mrs. S.O. Wilkins Sunday. * Miss Virginia Mermon and Mrs. Onan Poston of Kirkwood are the guests of their mother, Mrs. Jerushia Poston. * Children's Day will be observed at both churches Sunday."

18 June 1920, pg. 6, col. 4.
"Mrs. Henry Amonette entertained an auto party from Ironton Sunday. * Messrs. Harry Alexander and Mack Fulton motored from Bonneterre [sic] Sunday afternoon and enjoyed a short visit. * Mrs. Mary Cayce is numbered with the sick. * Miss Edna Burke spent a few days of last week at Crystal City. * Mrs. Nellie Bridges is visiting in St. Louis. * Mrs. Dave Buford is quite indisposed with muscular rheumatism. * Mrs. Lucy Bridges is expecting a visit from her sister, Mrs. Allie Magness of Oklahoma City. * Mrs. Emily Boddie who is under a physician's care at St. Louis is convalescing. * Rev. C.W. Thompson and wife and son, C.W., Jr., arrived from Chicago last Saturday. * The entire community was sadly alarmed when the news was given early Wednesday morning that Mr. Wesley Douthit, Sr., was stricken by paralysis. He died Thursday afternoon, June 10. The funeral was held Saturday afternoon at the M.E. Church under the direction of Burleigh lodge of which he was a senior member. On March 4, the deceased passed his seventy-third milestone. The loss of Mr. Douthit to the community, church and lodge is inexpressable [sic]. He lived an exemplary life; was a constant church attendant and will be sadly missed. The nearest relatives surviving are Wesley Douthit, Jr., of St. Louis, Mrs. J.C. Gayton of Curryville [Pike Co., Mo.], Mrs. S.O. Wilkins of this place, who are sisters of Mr. Chas. Douthit of Coffman; all of whom were present. Quite a number of other relatives and friends were present from nearby places."

25 June 1920, pg. 6, col. 3-4.
"Mr. Gus Cayce and son Hermon [sic] visited in St. Louis the first of the week. * Mrs. Lillian Chappelle and daughter were the guests of Mr. and Mrs. Dave Buford Sunday. They returned to Coffman Monday. * Mrs. Lewis Murphy is the guest of Mrs. Douthitt [sic] at Coffman this week. * Rev. Morrison of Wellston was the guest of Rev. J.W. Baker Sunday. He and Rev. C.W. Thompson assisted in the quarterly meeting services. The latter preached the Sacramental sermon at 3 o'clock[.] * Douglass School had their annual outing last Friday at St. Francis River. * Miss Clara Taylor of Madison, Ill., is visiting her father, Mr. Ellis Taylor. * Mr. and Mrs. Abe Cayce, Mrs. Annie Turner, Mrs. Mabel Harris, Misses Laura Wilburn, Clara Taylor and Carl Staten motored to Caledonia Sunday. * The many friends of Master Addison Roberts of

St. Louis, are deeply grieved to hear of his being injured by an automobile.[69] * Mrs. Onan Poston has returned to her home at Kirkwood after a pleasant visit with her mother-in-law, Mrs. Ruth Poston. * Sunday will be Quarterly meeting day at the M.E. church. Rev. Rivere, district superintendent, will be present. * Mrs. Emily Boddie has returned from St. Louis much improved. * Mr. and Mrs. Lee Roden, Mrs. LeRoy Pitcher, Mrs. Allie Magness and Mr. Phillip Bridges of St. Louis, were guests of Mr. and Mrs. Jerry Bridges Saturday. All returned Sunday except Mrs. Magness who will be here until the latter part of the week. * Rev. R.H. Phillips of Booneville was the guest of Mr. and Mrs. Geo. Blackwell Monday. * Mrs. Jno. Franks conducted a very successful entertainment at St. Luke A.M.E. Church Friday. * Mrs. Lewis Smith is convalescing. * Mrs. Eliza Blackwell had a pleasant visit at Bonneterre [sic] Sunday."

09 July 1920, pg. 6, col. 2.
"Mrs. Annie Bridges and grandson Clayton Alexander enjoyed Sunday in Fredericktown. * Mesrs[.] Fred Bridges and Hermon [sic] Cayce of St. Louis were the guests of Mr. Gus Cayce and Mr. Frank Cayce the first of the week. Rev. C.W. Thompson and family were entertained at the residence of Mr. and Mrs. Abe Cayce Thursday. * Master Edward McCallister is feeling the effects from having stuck a nail in his foot. * Mr. and Mrs. Lewis Murphy were entertained Monday at the residence of Mr. and Mrs. Jerry Bridges on route 2. * Mr. Elmer Amonette[,] Wilfred Thompson, Misses Willa Jones[,] Clara Kennedy and Alcesta Douthit motored to St. Francois Monday. * Mrs. Mattie Occamore went to Crystal City Monday afternoon. * Mrs. Rossie Madison and son Jessamine are visiting in St. Louis. * Mrs. Rossie Madison played on the Bonneterre [sic] baseball team when Crystal City put it over them on July 4. * Miss Laurine Boddie is the guest of her sister, Mrs. Howard Smith of Festus. * Miss Corinne Wilkins accompanied Miss Hattie Matthews to Festus a few days ago. * Mrs. Rebecca Bridges is able to be out after an illness of many months. * Mr. James Robinson was chaperone for the number who went on the fishing trip down on the Saline Monday."

16 July 1920, pg. 6, col. 5-6.
"Everybody most will be at the Masonic Hall July 30...Mr. Chas. Sutherland of St. Louis visited his mother, Mrs. Elizabeth Cole the first of the week. * Mrs. Ell Murrill and daughter, Nadine of Detroit, Mich., is the guest of home folks. * Mrs. Oats of Kirkwood, was the guest of Mrs. Jane Hunt Tuesday. She was here on her usual Missionary tour. * Mrs. Lewis Smith and Miss Estacada Baker are convalescing. * Mrs. Eliza Overton was accompanied by little Miss Odessa Cayce to Charleston, Saturday. * Mrs. Emily Boddie has returned to

St. Louis for an indefinite period. * At the M.E. Church Sunday at the blue and white division rally, a great interest was manifested on the part of the members and friends of both churches as well as by the two captains, Misses Daisy McCallister aud [sic] Ethelean Cayce. The latter won the contest. Miss McCallister raised &86.46 and Miss Cayce $105.50. On Monday evening a reception was tendered the successful workers. * A program was rendered.* Rev. C.W. Thompson is a wide awake pastor and is having marked success. The first prize was a watch bracelet and the second a gold coin. * Mr. and Mrs. Lewis Murphy left the week for Indianapolis, Chicago and other points. * Mr. Roy Douthit of Coffman brought quite a few persons to our city for a Sunday visit. * Mrs. Robert Simpson and children, Eugene Hartmann and Robertine Annette, are here for a few week's visit. * Mr. Thomas Cayce is the guest of home folks this week. * Mrs. Julia Burke of St. Louis, is enjoying the week with her sister, Mrs. Martha Villars. * Mrs. Celia Cunningham and daughter, Mrs. Irene Carter of Chicago, are enjoying a few days at Crysal City. * Mr. Talbert Burns had recovered. * Master Clayton Alexander entertained quite a number of his little friends, Sunday afternoon. * Mrs. Nancy Buford is improving slowly. * Rev. J.W. Baker is in St. Louis this week. * Messrs. Harry and Paul Alexander of Bonne Terre were here Sunday...Mrs. Ada Cayce of Crystal City was the guest of her mother, Mrs. Wm. McCallister Sunday. * Mrs. Minnie Pryor of St. Louis is the guest of her mother, Mrs. Maggie Thornton. * Mrs. Mahalia Madison entertained Tuesday evening in honor of Mrs. Jennie Walker of St. Louis and Mrs. Irene Carter of Chicago. Both are former Farmingtonians."

13 August 1920, pg. 6, col. 4-5.
"Miss Ruth B. Davis of Springfield, Ill., who was a guest of the reporter, has returned home...Mr. and Mrs. Henry Amonette entertained relatives from Ironton, Sunday...Mrs. Jno. Franks and daughters, Lelia and Cornelia, are visiting Mrs. Howard Smith of Festus...Mr. Abe Cayce has accepted employment in St. Louis...Mr. and Mrs. Pryor of St. Louis, who were guests of Mrs. Maggie Thornton, have returned...Mrs. Mahalia Madison is visiting relatives in St. Louis...Miss Corinne Wilkins accompanied her mother, Mrs. Katie Hunt, to St. Louis, Monday...Miss Odessa Cayce has returned from a visit at Charleston...Miss Laurine Boddie has returned from a visit at Festus...Miss Ruth Boddie was hostess to a few friends at a social Monday evening...Mrs. S.O. Wilkins has gone to Flint, Mich., for an extended visit with her daughter, Mrs. Weyman Chappelle...Mrs. Lewis Murphy is visiting in Kansas City... Mrs. Mert Hunt of St. Louis is the guest of Mrs. Jane Hunt this week. She expects her husband to join her at the week's end...Miss Mary Drew is spending her vacation at Coffman...Mrs. Masoleat Hill will spend her vacation at

Indianapolis, Ind. She will be the guest of her daughter, Mrs. Frances Craig...
Mr. Tillman Cayce of St. Louis shook glad hands with friends and relatives
here the first of the week...Miss Lorene Staten has returned from a pleasant
visit at home...Miss Luetta Matthews passed through our city enroute [sic]
to Coffman, her former home...The M.E. church is getting dressed up in
the interior. The congregation and pastor are preparing for a week's camp
meeting next month...Mr. Moses Cayce of St. Louis is enjoying the vacation
with his brothers, Messrs. Gus and Frank Cayce...The reporter is the guest
of Mrs. Marshall Curtaindoll, 2941 Pine St., St. Louis. Mrs. Leora Simpson
will report while she is away. Phone your items of interest to 459...Mrs. Eric
Matthews visited in St. Louis the latter part of last week...A few more days
and the vacation will be past history."

20 August 1920, pg. 6, col. 4-5.
"Mrs. Lora Simpson. Rev. C.W. Thompson has returned from attending the
District Conference at Peoria, Ill. Quite a number of persons attended the
picnic at Festus, Saturday. Miss Ora Hunt, entertained, Friday evening in
honor of Mr. and Mrs. Myrtle Hunt, of St. Louis. Misses Hilda and Ina
Kennedy of Bowling Green, are visiting relatives and friends in Farmington.
Messrs. Orvelle and ilson Chappelle of Coffman, passed through Farming-
ton, Saturday, enroute [sic] to Festus picnc [sic]. Miss Edna Harris was the
guest of her Aunt, Mrs. Ottis Vaughn of Potose [sic], Saturday and Sunday.
Mr. Harry Alexander of Bonne Terre, Mo. was a Farmington visitor Sunday.
A crowd of young men motored from Coffman to Farmington, Sunday eve-
ning. Mrs. Melview Evans and Mrs. Hattie Mathews [sic], spent the day at
Greenville, Tuesday, with Mrs. Lewis Kennedy. Mr. Ed. Harris and Mrs. Jerushia Poston, were quietly married at the parsonage, Friday evening by Rev.
C.W. Thompson. Mr. and Mrs. Myrtle Hunt, were entertained at the home
of Miss Zelma Swinks [sic], Sunday. Mr. Clarence Bridges and Patrick Cayce,
visited home folks last week. Both have employment in St. Louis. Mr. Booker
Baker spent Saturday and Sunday in Potosi with his sister, little Nadine. Mrs.
Elizabeth Myers died at her home in Crystal City, Monday, at 1:15 a.m. After
an illness of several days, Mrs. Meyers [sic] was a former resident of Farmington. The funeral services will be held at St. John M.E. Church at Festus,
Mo., Wednesday. Queen of Honor Court No. 38, Farmington, Mo. will have
charge of the services, we extend sympathy to the sorrowing relatives."

27 August 1920, pg. 6, col. 4.
"Mr. Rueben Staton [sic] of Coffman was a Farmington visitor, Tuesday. *
Misses Lottie Simms and Adele Ward of St. Louis, spent the week end [sic]
with the reporter. * Misses Edith Cayce and Glendora Baker left for Potosi,

Saturday for a week's stay with Mr. and Mrs. Joseph Carson. * Miss Virginia Matthews and Mr. Everett Cunningham of St. Louis spent the week end [sic] with Mr. and Mrs. Eric Matthews. * Mrs. Emma Swinks [sic] and daughter Frances of Caffman [sic], Mo., returned home Friday after spending several days with Mrs. Swink's father, Mr. Geo. Blackwell. * Mr. Mose Cayce returned to St. Louis after a visit with his sister and brothers. * Mr. Carl Robinson and Lawrence Fulton of Bonne Terre, were Farmington visitors Thursday evening. * Mr. Ed Harris of Bonne Terre, visited Farmington Sunday. * Mr[.] and Mrs. James Robinson entertained five couples on last Friday evening. An elaborate supper was served. * Those who attended the funeral of Mrs. Elizabeth Meyers at Festus, were Messrs. Scott Cole and Harvey McAllister, Mesdames Clara Poston, Emma Body, Hortense Smith, Carrie Burns, Phylis [sic] McAlister, and Miss Lorene Staten. * Rev. C.W. Thompson has secured a number of prominent preachers for the Church Camp which will begin on the 6th of September. Get yourselves in readiness, let's make it a success. It is a Century move, do your part. * Mr. Charles Douthit and family of Caffman [sic], spent the day in Farmington, Sunday. * Mrs. Annie Turner returned home Monday, after spending several days in St. Louis. * Mr. Abe Cayce, who has employment in St. Louis, spent the week end [sic] with his wife."

10 September 1920, pg. 6, col. 3-4.
"Miss Beatrice Swink left last Tuesday for St. Louis to visit her sister, Mrs. George Powers. * Mrs. Lewis Murphy returned Thursday night from Chanute, Kan. * Mrs. Ora Williams and Miss Zelma Swink left Monday for St. Louis to visit relatives and friends. * Mrs. Abram Cayce returned from St. Louis Monday. She expects to move to St. Louis this fall. * Mrs. Mary Blackwell of St. Louis is the guest of her mother, Mrs. William McAllister. * Mrs. Lewis Murphy was the guest of home folk Sunday. * Mr. and Mrs. Mrs. [sic] James Robinson left Sunday for several days' visit in St. Louis. * Mr. Felix Poston returned from St. Louis Sunday. * Mr. Edgar Cayce of St. Louis is spending a few days with his parents Mr. and Mrs. Gus Cayce. * Master Elbert Baker returned from St. Louis Sunday. * Mr. H.B. Keatts returned from Crystal City Monday night. * Quite a number of Farmingtonians attended the dance at Bonne Terre Saturday night. * Mrs. Moses Bridges and daughter Flossie, returned from Pocahontas, Ark., last Monday. * Mesdames Louisa Anthony and Emma Franks left for Herculaneum Saturday to attend the funeral of Aunt Melissa McAllister. * Master Patrick Cayce spent Saturday night with homefolks. * Miss Dayse F. Baker returned Monday from St. Louis, where she had been the house guest of Mrs. Marshall Curtaindoll. Miss Baker received quite a few social courtesies during her stay in St. Louis. * Mrs. Cora Ivy and grandson, Vincent Clark, left for their home in St. Louis

Sunday. * Mr. Felix Poston left Tuesday for DeSota [sic] to visit Mrs. Alice Murphy. * Rev. King of Bonne Terre preached a very able sermon Monday night. Rev. Reynolds of Kinloch Park will fill the pulpit Tuesday night. Other visiting ministers will be present during the week. Let us make the meeting a success in every way. * Mr. A.A. Simms of St. Louis will take his band to St. Mary's Sept. 25. Mr. Simms has a band worth hearing. * Messrs[.] McKinley Fulton, Harry Alexander and Carl Robinson of Bonne Terre were Farmington visitors Sunday. * A crowd of young men motored from St. Genevieve to Farmington Monday night. * Rev[.] and Mrs. J.G. Walker of St. Joseph, Mo., are visiting in Coffman, Mo. Rev. Walker is expected to return this week to assist in the meeting."

17 September 1920, pg. 6, col. 3.
"Miss Augustine Swink of Minneth [sic] spent the weekend with Mrs. John Franks. * Mr. Henry Renfro of St. Louis is visiting friends in this city. * Mr. George Meyers of Crystal City attended the quarterly meeting here Sunday. * Mr. Fred Chappelle and children of Coffman, Mo., are the guest[s] of Mrs. Chappelle's mother this week. * Master Patrick Cayce of St. Louis came home ill Monday night. We are glad to report him as getting along alright. * Mesdames Dora Carson, Eliza Carson, Anna Gill, Flora Vaughn of Potosi and Miss Cosetta Carter of Indiana attended the church camp last week. * Miss Cora Meyers and daughter, Louise are the guest[s] of Mrs. Henry Amonette. * Mrs. Walter Franks and mother, Mrs. Laura Valley of Coffman attended the church camp last week. * Mrs. Jerry Bridges left Sunday for St. Louis where she expects to spend the winter. * Master Halfred Poston left Sunday for Boonville, Mo. to take up his studies in school. * Rev. C.W. Thompson and congregation are rejoicing over the success of the camp meeting. It was as a spiritual as well as a financial success. The visiting ministers were Rev. A. Reynolds of Knloch [sic][,] J.W. Baker of St. Luke Chapel of this city, Rev. J.B. Walker of St. Joseph, Mo., and Rev. J.C. Jackson of Festus, Mo. who served as district superintendent at the quarterly meeting Sunday. Seven persons received the ordinances of baptism Sunday evening. An old time Love Feast was enjoyed at the same time. Rev. Thompson and his faithful committee were pleased to report $112 net procds [sic] for the week."

24 September 1920, pg. 6, col. 2-3.
"Off to St. Mary's with the Simms' Band is the slogan for Saturday. * Mrs. Sophia Galvin and Master Charles Smith of Crystal City were the guests of Mrs. Mahalia Madison, Sunday and Monday. * Mrs. Emma Franklin entertained Mrs. Laura Jordan of Charleston and Rev. Baker and Thompson Saturday evening at her home in South Farmington. * Mrs. C.W. Thompson

is convalescent. * Mrs. Susie Wilkins has returned from an extended visit at Flint, Mich., Chicago and other points. * Mr. and Mrs. Lewis Smith entertained Mrs. Laura Jordan and Miss Dayse Baker Sunday with a dinner. * Mr. and Mrs. Abe Cayce moved to St. Louis Wednesday. * Mr. Harvey Mosby of Festus was the guest of Miss Ruth Boddie this week. * Rev. Baker was assisted at Quarterly meeting services Sunday by Rev. Thompson and congregation[.] Rev. Baker has one more Sunday during this conference year. * Mr. Wesley Douthit of St. Louis and Mr. John Douthit were entertained Sunday at the residence of Mrs. S.O. Wilkins. * Mrs. Beatrice Swink and Kossouth [sic] Baker are enrolled at Sumner High, St. Louis. * Mr. [sic] a few of their friends Sunday. * Messrs[.] Carl Robinson and Harry Alexander of Bonne Terre were Farming [sic] and Mrs. Jas. Robinson entertained [sic] ton's [sic] visitors Sunday. * Mr. and Ms. [sic] Henry Amonette and Melvina Jones went to St. Louis Saturday for several days visit with relatives and friends."

08 October 1920, pg. 6, col. 4-5.
"Rev. J.W. Baker is attending the annual conference this week. * Mrs. Leora Simpson and children have returned to Crystal City. * The wedding bells will soon ring in Farmington. * Among those who are attending the foll [sic] festivities at St. Louis this week are Mrs. Louisa Anthony and grandson, Scott Hunt, Mrs. Mary Cayce, Miss Edith Cayce, Miss Glendora Baker, Mrs[.] Annie Turner and Mrs. Emma Jones and son Leroy. * Freeman Frankle [sic] of Crystal City is a Farmington visitor this week.[70] * Madame Buckley came down from St. Louis Saturday, made an address on parental influence at the M.E. Church Sunday morning and spoke to a large audience Sunday night on mission; organized a W.H.M.S. and then delivered an address at the A.M.E. Church. Her visit to this community brought inspiration to all who desire to live for God. * Mrs. Susie O. Wilkins is enjoying a few days in St. Louis. * Mr. Frank Staten visited friends at Coffman last week. While there he bagged an opossum. It isn't the "possum" that took him there. * Mr. Elmer Ammonette [sic] has accepted work in St. Louis. He was accompanied to St. Louis Sunday by his father, Mr. Henry Ammonette [sic]. Mrs. Lillian Cappelle [sic], Miss Pearl Mayfield and Mrs. Mary Jackson were the guests of Mrs. Nancy Buford Saturday. * Mr. Dave Buford, Mr. Burrill Tulleck, Mrs. Buford and Miss Laura Wilburn enjoyed Sunday at Coffman. * Mr. Thomas Neuson has returned to St. Louis. * Messrs[.] Stubbs and Boddie returned to St. Louis Sunday having captured fish, oppossums [sic] and frogs enough to spare. * Mr. and Mrs. Lewis Smith entertained in honor of them with an old time farm party. Misses Zelma Swink an[d] Ora Hunt were dressed in country maid style. The gentlemen wore coarse home-spun. Of the menu the soup, beans were the best. Ask Mr. James Robinson how many pints it takes

194

to make a meal. He is an authority. Mr. John Franks was host to a few friends in honor of Messrs[.] Stubbs and Boddie Friday night."

15 October 1920, pg. 6, col. 3.
"Mr. Booker T. Baker enjoyed a pleasant trip to St. Louis the first of the week. * Miss Edith O. Cayce and Miss Glendora Baker visited Potosi Sunday. * Mr. Burrell Tullck [sic] returned from Ironton Sunday. * Master Eugene Simpson had a slight operation of the right arm from which he is improving rapidly. * Mr. Rollo Johnson and Master Robert Cayce of Crystal City were down the first of the week. The former was a visit to Mr. and Mrs. Lewis Kennedy; the latter to Master Edward McCallister. * Master Clayton Alexander has recovered sufficiently to be back in school. * Rev. Randolph of Louisiana has been appointed pastor of St. Luke's Chapel and has arrived. * Mrs. Lewis Smith is numbered with the sick. * The Junior choir of which Miss Edna Harris is organist, entertained the public with an interesting program Sunday night. * Mrs. Leora Simpson entertained Misses Edith O. Cayce[,] Dayse Baker and Mrs. Ella Murrill at a hot roll contest luncheon Tuesday evening at which time her mother, Mrs. Ada Murphy proved to be the winning consumer. * Mrs. Susie Smith is reported ill at 15 S. Compton. Members of Masoleat Court, O.O.C., are repuested [sic] to go and see her. * It pays to take The Argus for it keeps you well posted now as to how, when and where to cast your November ballot."

22 October 1920, pg. 6, col. 2.
"Mr. Rollo Johnson who has been the guest of Mr. and Mrs. Lewis Kennedy of Greenville has returned to Festus, having gained five pounds. He admits that a diet of fowls, milk, butter and eggs is not so bad after all. * Rev. J.A. Randolph and Mrs. John Franks were visitors at Douglass School Monday. Each one addressed the school. * Mrs. Ada Murphy has returned from Festus. * Mrs. Louisa Anthony and Miss Virginia Matthews returned from St. Louis Monday. * Mr. Rossie Madison attended to business at Bonneterre [sic] Monday. * Mr. and Mrs. Jerry Bridges have moved to East Farmington. Mr. Scott Cole is an authority on pumpkin cultivation. * Mrs. Hattie Matthews was hostess to a number of young people Monday evening at which time these youngsters stacked a large amount of wood. The last thing on program was the eats. * Mrs. Anna Turner and Mrs. Moses Bridge attended the funeral of Mrs. Minnie Robinson at Bonneterre [sic] Thursday.[71] * The members of St. Luke had a parsonage shower Monday night in order to replenish the house furnishing. Mrs. Lewis Smith is yet ill. * Rev. J.W. Sebastion [sic] of Memphis, Tenn., has been assigned as pastor of St. Paul M.E. Church. * Master Leroy Baker will deliver The Argus at your door each Saturday for the small

sum of 5 cents."

05 November 1920, pg. 6, col. 2.
"Mr. Rossie Madison enjoyed a few hours in Bonneterre [sic] Saturday. * Mr. Bartley Smith of Fredericktown was a visitor here Sunday. * Mr. Macie L[sic] Lyons is visiting at Festus. * Mrs. Sara [sic] McMinn ha[s] returned to Festus after a pleasant visit as a guest of Mrs. Scott Cole. * Mrs. Minnie Cayce of 120 Gratiot Street, St. Louis attended to business here last week. * Mr. Phillip Thornton is visiting relatives in St. Louis. He expects to visit in Detroit Michigan also. * While hunting one day of last week, Mr. Rossie Madison accidentally shot and killed his faithful dog, Dude. The dog had been with the family many years. * Rev. J. Pitcher and Mrs. B.F. Lindsay of St. Louis were in our city last week on a political mission. They were entertained in the home of Mr. and Mrs. John Franks. * Messrs. Fred Fulton, Artie Fulton, Ivan Yeager and Carl Robinson enjoyed Sunday here as visitors from Bonneterre [sic]. * Rev. J.H. Randolph conducted services at Coffman Sunday. * Mrs. Jane Hunt chaperoned a numebr [sic] of young people on a "persimmon hunt" Sunday afternoon. A splendid afternoon was reported. * Mrs. Lillian Chapelle [sic] and children have returned to Coffman after a ten days' visit with Mrs. Dave Buford. * Mr. and Mrs. Herman Cayce, the newly weds [sic] are cozily quartered in their home in South Farmington and will be glad to receive their friends. * Mr. and Mrs. Jerry Bridges have moved in from the country and are located in East Farmington. * Mr. and Mrs. Mayfield are contemplating wintering here. * Mr. H.B. Keatts has had a visit to Bonneterre [sic], Festus and St. Louis. Mrs. Maggie Kennedy of Greenville is indisposed. * Farmington Colored people voted 100 per cent [sic] Republican in the regular election. We desired to do more."

Endnotes
[1] Costella Shaw, daughter of Ferdinand "Fred" Shaw and Louisa Poston, was born 26 January 1907 in St. Francois Co., Mo. When this data about Costella was written in the St. Louis Argus, she was only seven years old—just a few weeks away from turning eight. The trip to Farmington with her maternal aunt may have been a special trip in light of Costella's upcoming birthday.

In 1920, the thirteen-year-old Costella, who was incorrectly enumerated as a male, was living in St. Louis City with her parents and siblings Katherine (b. ca. 1905 in Mo.) and Ferdinand (b. ca. 1910 in Mo.). During this time period, her father Fred was supporting the family by working as a porter for a tobacco company. By the age of eighteen, Costella had herself found employment in St. Louis working as an elevator girl. She died on 21 July 1925 in St. Louis City, Mo. after she was accidentally struck by an elevator which fractured her skull, causing her brain to hemorrhage. Costella was buried on 25 July 1925 in Greenwood Cemetery, St. Louis, Mo.

Almost eight years later, Costella's father, Fred, died prematurely from chronic myocarditis on 12 March 1933 in St. Louis City, Mo. Fred was buried in the same cemetery as his daughter—in Greenwood Cemetery—on 15 March 1933.

See Costella Shaw, death cert. no. 22557 (1925), Mo. Dept. of Health, Jefferson City; Ferd Shaw household, 1920 U.S. census, St. Louis City, Mo., pop. sch., Ward 19, ED 375, SD 10, sh. 13A [printed], dw. 220, fl. 287; NA microfilm T625, roll 956; Fred Shaw, death cert. no. 11414 (1933), Mo. Dept. of Health, Jefferson City.

[2] "Grandma Evans" was Malissia Evans. Malissia was born about 1824 in Mo., and died 20 February 1915 in Farmington, St. Francois Co., Mo. She was buried on 21 February 1915 in the Colored Masonic Cemetery, Farmington, St. Francois Co., Mo. In 1910, she was enumerated as the eighty-five year-old widowed "Elissa Evans." In that census, she reported giving birth to only a single child.

See Malissia Evans, death cert. no. 05932 (1915), Mo. Dept. of Health, Jefferson City; Elissa Evans household, 1910 U.S. census, St. Francois Co., Mo., pop. sch., Farmington, ED 96, SD 11, sh. 8A, dw. 57, fl. 65; NA microfilm T624, roll 808.

[3] Mrs. Meyers was Elizabeth E. "Bettie" (Reynolds) Meyers. Bettie, the daughter of Wash Reynolds and Jane Coffman, was born 6 March 1865 in Ste. Genevieve Co., Mo., died 16 August 1920 in Jefferson Co., Mo. Elizabeth was buried on 22 August 1920 in Mt. Zion Cemetery, Festus, Jefferson Co., Mo. She married on 12 November 1887 in St. Francois Co., Mo., George Meyers. George was born August 1866 in Mo.

From 1900 until 1910, the family was living in Farmington. By 1920, George, Elizabeth, and several members of their immediate family had moved to Jefferson County where George had found employment as a glass worker.

George and Elizabeth had several children, including: Julia E. (b. Jan. 1882 in Mo.), Charles W. (b. Jul. 1883 in Mo.), Eugene (b. Aug 1889 in Mo.), Wilson (b. Aug 1890 in Mo.), Cora (b. Jul. 1892 in Mo.), Mable (b. Sep 1895 in Mo.), and Clarence (b. Nov. 1898 in Mo.).

Cora Meyers, daughter of George Myers [sic] and Betty Townsend [sic], was born 29 July 1895 in Farmington, St. Francois Co., Mo., died 20 July 1954 in St. Louis City, Mo., and was buried on 21 July 1954 in Oak Dale Cemetery, St. Louis Co., Mo. She married on 18 May 1921 in Jefferson

Co., Mo., Albert Schaffer, son of Aaron Shaffer [sic] and Cynthia Boyce. Albert was born 21 March 1882 in Mo., died 4 March 1933 in St. Louis City, Mo. He was buried on 11 March 1933 in Festus, Jefferson Co., Mo.

Mable married on 29 November 1916 in St. Francois Co., Mo., Samuel W. Burks. In the 1920 census, Mable and two of her children—three year-old George and eleven month-old Margaret—were enumerated with her parents. Margaret Helen Burks, daughter of Sam Burks and Mabel Myers, was born 13 December 1918 in Crystal City, Jefferson Co., Mo., died 5 December 1920 in Crystal City, Jefferson Co., Mo. She was buried on 5 December 1920 in Mt. Zion Cemetery, Festus, Jefferson Co., Mo.

Clarence married on 21 May 1923 in Jefferson Co., Mo., Luella Casey.

See Elizabeth Meyers, death cert. no. 27280 (1920), Mo. Dept. of Health, Jefferson City; George Meyers household, 1900 U.S. census, St. Francois Co., Mo., pop. sch., Farmington, ED 98, SD 10, sh. 9B, dw. 183, fl. 189; NA microfilm T623, roll 887; George Meyer [sic] household, 1910 U.S. census, St. Francois Co., Mo., pop. sch., Farmington, ED 96, SD 11, sh. 25B, dw. 84, fl. 90; NA microfilm T624, roll 808; George Meyers household, 1920 U.S. census, Jefferson Co., Mo., pop. sch., Crystal City, ED 34, SD 11, sh. 20B, dw. 392, fl. 419; NA microfilm T625, roll 930; Cora Schaffer, death cert. no. 25187 (1954), Mo. Dept. of Health, Jefferson City; Albert Schaffer, death cert. no. 11241 (1933), Mo. Dept. of Health, Jefferson City; Margaret Helen Burks, death cert. no. 37230 (1920), Mo. Dept. of Health, Jefferson City.

[4] Sarah Green, daughter of Dolly Green, was born 4 June 1846 in Washington Co., Mo. She married on 15 November 1865 in Washington Co., Mo., Henry Amonett[e]. Sarah died on 15 April 1918 in Farmington, St. Francois Co., Mo., and was buried on 17 April 1918 in the Caledonia Cemetery, Caledonia, Washington Co., Mo.

Annie Amonette was born in February 1879-1880 in Mo. She married on 8 February 1896 in St. Francois Co., Mo., Frank Yeargain [sic]. Frank was born January 1875 in Mo.

Kenneth Yeager, son of Frank Yeager (b. Farmington, St. Francois Co., Mo.) and Annie Amonett [sic] (b. Caledonia, Washington Co., Mo.), was born 29 April 1897 in Farmington, St. Francois Co., Mo., and died 21 April 1932 in St. Louis City, Mo. He was buried on 24 April 1932, probably in the Colored Masonic Cemetery, Farmington, St. Francois Co., Mo. He married Cornelia (____).

See Sarah Amonett [sic], death cert. no. 14451 (1918), Mo. Dept. of Health, Jefferson City; Kenneth Yeager, death cert. no. 14582 (1932), Mo.

Dept. of Health, Jefferson City; Frank Yeager household, 1900 U.S. census, St. Francois Co., Mo., pop. sch., Farmington, ED 98, SD 10, sh. 182A [stamped], dw. 195, fl. 201; NA microfilm T623, roll 887.

[5] Peter "Pete" Taylor, son of John Taylor, was born 16 December 1861 in Mo., died 29 January 1915 in Koch, St. Louis Co., Mo. He was buried on 2 February 1915 in Greenwood Cemetery, St. Louis, Mo. He was married at the time of his death.

See Pete Taylor, death cert. no. 2360 (1915), Mo. Dept. of Health, Jefferson City.

[6] The Rev. A.L. Woolfolk is probably Arthur Woolfolk, son of James Woolfolk (b. Troy, Lincoln Co., Mo.) and Clara Perkins (b. Robertson, St. Louis Co., Mo.), who, according to his death certificate, was a minister. Arthur was born 26 December 1882 in St. Louis Co., Mo., died 9 December 1948 in Clayton, St. Louis Co., Mo. He was buried on 14 December 1948 in Washington Park Cemetery, St. Louis Co., Mo. He married 1) Georgia Glover, and after their divorce, 2) Mabel E. Hopkins.

In 1900, Arthur was living with his widowed mother Clara and two of his seven surviving siblings—Moss, born January 1888, and Elwood, born February 1890. Clara (Perkins) Woolfolk had given birth to twelve children, but by 1900, only eight of those children remained alive, including Arthur. Clara was raising her youngest children in Bridgeton, St. Louis Co., Mo., and it was there that she owned her own home, though it was mortgaged. Clara was born in April 1849 (according to the census) or 14 April 1850, according to her death certificate. She died on 24 March 1932 in Overland, St. Louis Co., Mo., and was buried on 27 March 1932. Although Arthur's death certificate stated that his mother's maiden name was Perkins, her own death certificate provided her father's surname as Ritner.

See Arthur Woolfolk, death cert. no. 41998 (1948), Mo. Dept. of Health, Jefferson City; Clara Woolfolk household, 1900 U.S. census, St. Louis Co., Mo., pop. sch., Bridgeton, ED 127, SD 10, sh. 22A [printed], dw. 368, fl. 379; NA microfilm T623, roll 888; Clara Woolfolk, death cert. no. 9918 (1932), Mo. Dept. of Health, Jefferson City.

[7] Mary Hannah (____) Allen, wife of William C. Allen, was, according to her death certificate, born 25 December 1829 in Madison Co., Mo. However, the 1920 census enumerated her as being born about 1855. She died 29 November 1942 in St. Louis City, Mo. She was buried on 30 November 1942 in Fredericktown, Madison Co., Mo. She married William Allen. He was born about 1860 in Ky.

"Mrs. Eric Matthias" is Hattie (Anthony) Matthews, the wife of Charles Erich "Eric" Matthews, Sr. and daughter of Charles Anthony and Louisa Smith. Hattie was born 30 March 1880 in Libertyville, St. Francois Co., Mo., died 21 February 1958 in Farmington, St. Francois Co., Mo. She was buried on 25 February 1958 in the Colored Masonic Cemetery, Farmington, St. Francois Co., Mo. She married on 20 August 1902 in St. Francois Co., Mo., Charles Erich "Eric" Matthews, Sr., son of Alfred Matthews (b. Miss.) and Catherine (____). He was born 4 August 1881 in Mississippi, and died 3 July 1937 in St. Louis City, Mo. He was buried in the Colored Masonic Cemetery in Farmington, St. Francois Co., Mo., on 6 July 1937.

See Hannah Allen, death cert. no. 35130 (1942), Mo. Dept. of Health, Jefferson City; William C. Allen household, 1920 U.S. census, Madison Co., Mo., pop. sch., St. Michael twp., ED 57, SD 11, sh. 13B, dw. 246, fl. 249; NA microfilm T625, roll 920; Charles Erich Matthews, Sr., death cert. no. 25293 (1937), Mo. Dept. of Health, Jefferson City; Hattie Matthews, death cert. no. 6908 (1958), Mo. Dept. of Health, Jefferson City.

[8] Phillip Mac Thornton, son of Godfrey Thornton and Maggie Cayce, was born 26 February 1894 in Knob Lick, Mo., died 14 February 1950 in Farmington, St. Francois Co., Mo. She was buried on 20 February 1950 in New Calvary Cemetery, Farmington, St. Francois Co., Mo. He married Imogene.

See Phillip Mac Thornton, death cert. no. 5888 (1950), Mo. Dept. of Health, Jefferson City.

[9] Aldrew A. Evans was the son of George J.O. Evans and Nellie Murphy. Aldrew was born 4 November 1899 in Farmington, St. Francois Co., Mo., and died 7 March 1915 in Farmington, St. Francois Co., Mo. He was buried on 8 March 1915 in the Colored Masonic Cemetery, Farmington, St. Francois Co., Mo.

See Aldrew A. Evans, death cert. no. 9922 (1915), Mo. Dept. of Health, Jefferson City.

[10] Amie Busch was the daughter of Beff Busch and Ellen Taylor. She was born 12 March 1895 in Farmington, St. Francois Co., Mo. Shortly before her twentieth birthday, Amie became pregnant. At this point in her life, she was unmarried and the social milieu of the era not only stigmatized African American women, but also unmarried women who gave birth to children out of wedlock. Apparently anxious to end the pregnancy and cognizant that she could not legally obtain an abortion, she attempted to abort using mercury which, during this time period, was often used by women in an effort to end unwanted pregnancies.

After taking the mercury, Amie was sick for approximately ten days prior to her death. According to her death certificate, mercurial poisoning caused "...Ptyalism & Gangrene of Mouth & throat & Abortion." In order to understand Amie's experience of intense suffering, it is necessary to understand what Pytalism is. Amie's death certificate does not indicate whether she ingested the mercury orally or inserted it vaginally. However, once it entered her bloodstream, Ptyalism began to appear in its three successive stages: First, the victim's gums and teeth become extremely tender and the victim begins to salivate. Second, this tenderness develops into the inflammation and ulceration of the gums, the teeth become loosened, and the mouth salivates constantly. During this stage, the victim's face and particularly the lips become swollen and their throat becomes very sore. This second stage develops into the third phase, gangrene. In this phase, the victim's breath bears a stench that is the result of their skin literally rotting away. Their face swells and becomes very hard and the gums often "...slough away and leave the alveolar processes of the jaw completely bare..." (Oke 1856: 953). In this case, both Amie's mouth and her throat were gangrenous, so if she would have been lucky enough to survive the poisoning and the onslaught of pain that accompanied it, she would have probably died of starvation later.

During this time, Amie's twentieth birthday—on 12 March—passed. However, it is likely that at this point, she neither cared nor noticed. Amie suffered in this manner for nearly ten days before finally succumbing to the effects of mercury poisoning on 14 March 1915 in Farmington, St. Francois Co., Mo., being consoled by her sister, Mrs. Lucas, at the time of her death. Amie was buried on 15 March 1915 in the County Cemetery, probably the Masonic Colored Cemetery in Farmington. She was only twenty years and two days at the time of her death. The man who impregnated her was possibly a matter of local knowledge at the time of Amie's death, but in our modern era, it remains a mystery to this day.

See Amie Busch, death cert. no. 9924 (1915), Mo. Dept. of Health, Jefferson City; Angus McLaren, "Women's Work and Regulation of Family Size: The Question of Abortion in the Nineteenth Century," History Workshop 4 (Autumn 1977): 73; David A. Grimes, et al., "Unsafe Abortion: The Preventable Pandemic," The Lancet (October 2006); Russell S. Fisher "Criminal Abortion" Journal of Criminal Law and Criminology 42 (Summer 1951): 245; W.S. Oke, "Mercurial Pytalism and Erethism," Association Medical Journal 4 (November 1856): 952-954.

[11] Odessa Casey (also spelled Cayce) was the illegitimate daughter of Robt. Murphy and Bulah [sic] Body. She was born 19 May 1909 in Farmington, St. Francois Co., Mo., and died 29 October 1933 in Farmington, St. Francois

Co., Mo. Odessa was buried on 31 October 1933 in the Masonic Colored Cemetery, Farmington, St. Francois Co., Mo. She was single at the time of her death. However, Beulah married Harry Edward Cayce two years after Odessa was born⊠on 25 July 1911 in St. Francois Co., Mo.⊠and Odessa took her step-father's surname.

    See Odessa Casey, death cert. no. 34231 (1933), Mo. Dept. of Health, Jefferson City; St. Francois Co., Mo., Marriage Book X: XXC; County Clerk's Office, Farmington.

[12] No child with the name Leonard Bridges was found in Missouri death certificates. However, a child who died on that date with the name Elwood B. Baker-Bridges does appear—they are probably the same child. Elwood was the son of Moses Bridges and Ellen Baker. He was born 6 July 1912 in Farmington, St. Francois Co., Mo., died 5 June 1915 in Farmington, St. Francois Co., Mo. He was buried on 5 June 1915 in the County Cemetery, probably the Masonic Colored Cemetery, Farmington, St. Francois Co., Mo.

    See Elwood B. Baker-Bridges, death cert. no. 19875 (1915), Mo. Dept. of Health, Jefferson City.

[13] According to his death certificate Abraham Thomas "A.T." Lewis was the son of Abraham Lewis. Abraham was born February 1845, 31 October 1847, or 1855 in Mo. or Miss., and died 15 June 1915 in DeSoto, Jefferson Co., Mo. He was buried on 17 June 1915 in the City Cemetery at DeSoto, Jefferson Co., Mo. He married on 7 September 1874 in Cape Girardeau Co., Mo., Ellen Ann or Helen "Ella" Thomas aka Lane, daughter of Elijah Thomas and Matilda Miller. Ella was born January 1860 or 22 February 1861 in Cape Girardeau Co., Mo., died 13 August 1935 in DeSoto, Jefferson Co., Mo. She was buried on 16 August 1935 in the City Cemetery, DeSoto, Jefferson Co., Mo.

    A twenty-four year-old named Abraham Lewis Jr., born in Mo. ca. 1845, was found in the 1870 household of Abraham Lewis (b. ca. 1820 in Mo.) along with a female Lovica Lewis (b. ca. 1810 in Mo.) a younger male named John Lewis (b. ca. 1854 in La.) and a farm laborer named John Daniel in Rapides Parish., La. It is possible that prior to the Civil War, Abraham and his father Abraham, if they were slaves, were sold south. However, additional research should be conducted in order to determine whether or not this individual is our Abraham of interest. What we do know is that by 1874, Abraham was in Cape Girardeau Co., Mo. where he married Ellen. Abraham was a school teacher who, since at least 1880, had been engaged in educating African Americans in Missouri. Shortly after his marriage, Abraham found employment in Scott Co., Mo., and it was there that he was found in 1880 as a married teacher who was boarding in the household of Payton Ross. By 1900, he and his family had moved to Jefferson County. By 1910, the couple was enumerated as "Henry E. Lewis" and "Hellen" with their children. However, in this census, Albert was enumerated as being a janitor for a post office. They family remained in Jefferson County until Abraham's death.

See Abraham T. Lewis, death cert. no. 19298 (1915), Mo. Dept. of Health, Jefferson City; Ellen Ann Lewis, death cert. no. 26801-4 (1935), Mo. Dept. of Health, Jefferson City; Abraham Lewis household, 1870 U.S. census, Rapides Parish., La., pop. sch., Cotile post office, pg. 37 [printed], dw. 334, fl. 347; NA microfilm M593, roll 528; Payton Ross household, 1880 U.S. census, Scott Co., Mo., pop. sch., Commerce twp., ED 142, SD 2, sh. 23C [printed], dw. 214, fl. 221; NA microfilm T9, roll; Abraham Lewis household, 1900 U.S. census, Jefferson Co., Mo., pop. sch., DeSoto, ED 63, SD 10, sh. 19B, dw. 334, fl. 408; NA microfilm T623, roll 867; Henry E. [sic] Lewis household, 1910 U.S. census, Jefferson Co., Mo., pop. sch., DeSoto, ED 45, SD 11, sh. 310A [stamped], dw. 224, fl. 232; NA microfilm T624, roll 792.

[14] The term "cur" is used to refer to a mixed-breed dog. The word is also defined as a specialty breed of dog, such as hunting dogs (e.g. coon hounds).

[15] William Young, son of William Young, was born in 1888 in Mo., died 8 July 1915 in St. Louis City, Mo. He was buried on 12 July 1915 in St. Peter's Cemetery, St. Louis, Mo.

See William Young, death cert. no. 23146 (1915), Mo. Dept. of Health, Jefferson City.

[16] According to his death certificate, Cornelius Cole was born about 1860 in Farmington, St. Francois Co., Mo. However, the 1870 census enumerates him as a 6 year-old living in Washington Co., Mo. Based upon this age, Cornelius would have been born about 1864. He died 2 June 1942 in Wellston, St. Louis Co., Mo., and was buried on 6 June 1942 in Greenwood Cemetery, St. Louis, Mo. He married 1) on 8 April 1893 in St. Francois Co., Mo., Mary Jane Cunningham, 2) Cutie Hall, daughter of Flan and Elizabeth Hall. Cutie was born about 1871 in Ill., died 27 April 1951 in St. Louis City, Mo. She was buried on 3 April 1951 in Greenwood Cemetery, St. Louis, Mo.

In 1870, the six year-old Cornelius was living in Washington Co., Mo. his brother Scott, other presumed siblings, and his parents, Cyrus and Harriet Cole. Although Harriet's age was listed as 18 in the 1870 census, this was apparently a mistake made by the enumerator, because in 1880 Harriet's age is given as 59. By the time the 1880 census was enumerated, Scott and other siblings had left the household, and the only children that remained was 18 year-old Andrew and 17 year-old Cornelius. On 8 April 1893, Cornelius married Mary Jane Cunningham in St. Francois Co., Mo.

By 1900, Cornelius was enumerated as a single male living in his brother's household. Sometime between the 1900 and 1910 censuses, Cornelius moved to St. Louis where he was enumerated in the household of Mary Poston. In 1920, Cornelius was living as a boarder in the same household of a Farmingtonian—Mary Poston, and others. Cornelius remained in St. Louis, later moving to Wellston in St. Louis County and remaining there until he died.

See Cornelius Cole, death cert. no. 18938 (1942), Mo. Dept. of Health, Jefferson City; Mary Poston household, 1920 U.S. census, St. Louis City, Mo., pop. sch., Ward 19, ED 379, SD 10, sh. 100A [stamped], dw. 197, fl. 289; NA microfilm T625, roll 956; Cutie Cole, death cert. no.17932 (1951), Mo. Dept. of Health, Jefferson City; Cyrus Cole household, 1870 U.S. census, Washington Co., Mo., pop. sch., Osage post office, pg. 11, dw. 84, fl. 84; NA microfilm M593, roll 825; Cyrus Cole household, 1880 U.S. census, Washington Co., Mo., pop. sch., Belgrade twp., ED 172, SD 2, sh. 4D, dw. 29, fl. 32; NA microfilm T9, roll 740; Scott L. Cole household, 1900 U.S. census, St. Francois Co., Mo., pop. sch., Farmington, ED 98, SD 10, sh. 9B, dw. 185, fl. 191; NA microfilm T623, roll 887; Mary Poston household, 1910 U.S. census, St. Louis City, Mo., pop. sch., Ward 19, ED 30, SD 10, sh. 5B-6A, dw. 84, fl. 122; NA microfilm T624, roll 820.

[17] George Talbert, son of David Talbert and Ellen Winsor, was born in 1855 in Johnson Co., Mo., died 18 July 1915 in Wellington, Lafayette Co., Mo. He was buried on 2 [sic] July 1915 in Wellington, Lafayette Co., Mo. The informant for his death certificate—David Talbert—wrote an "X" for his signature. Just five years later, David Talbert also died. According to his death certificate, David was born on 3 April 1864 in Warrensburg, Mo., the son of David Tolbert and Ellen Violet (both b. Johnson Co., Mo.). He died 17 May 1920 in Wellington, Lafayette Co., Mo., and was buried on 18 May 1920 in the Martin Cemetery in Wellington, Lafayette Co., Mo. Prior to his death, David married Myrtle (____).

See George Talbert, death cert. no. 22203 (1915), Mo. Dept. of Health, Jefferson City; David Tolbert, death cert. no. 19820 (1920), Mo. Dept. of Health, Jefferson City.

[18] Helen Smith daughter of Lewis Smith and Lavenia Hill, was born 3 November 1911 in Mo., died 15 July 1915 in St. Louis City, Mo. She was buried on 18 July 1915 in Farmington, St. Francois Co., Mo., probably in the Masonic Colored Cemetery.

See Hellen [sic] Smith, death cert. no. 23292 (1915), Mo. Dept. of Health, Jefferson City.

[19] Albert A. Simms, son of James Simms, was born 8 April 1885 in Farmington, St. Francois Co., Mo., died 19 November 1943 in St. Louis City, Mo. He was buried on 22 November 1943 in Washington Park Cemetery, St. Louis Co., Mo. He married Grace Amelia Woods, daughter of Benjamin Woods and Annie Wyatt. Grace was born 24 September 1909 in Memphis, Tenn., died 30 May 1949 in St. Louis City, Mo. She was buried on 2 June 1949 in Washington Park Cemetery, St. Louis Co., Mo.

See Albert A. Simms, death cert. no. 36988[?], (1943), Mo. Dept. of Health, Jefferson City; Grace Amelia Woods Simms, death cert. no. 21688 (1949), Mo. Dept. of Health, Jefferson City.

[20] Reverend John H. Noland, son of James Noland, was born 1 January 1862 in Tenn., died 12 August 1915 in Central Twp., St. Louis Co., Mo. He was buried on 16 August 1915 in Greenwood Cemetery, St. Louis, Mo.

See John Noland, death cert. no. 25786 (1915), Mo. Dept. of Health, Jefferson City.

[21] Grace Anthony was the daughter of William Charles Anthony and Louise aka Louisa Smith. Grace was born 1 August 1895 in Knob Lick, St. Francois Co., Mo., and died 1 September 1916 in Farmington, St. Francois Co., Mo. She was buried on 3 September 1916 in the Colored Masonic Cemetery in Farmington, St. Francois Co., Mo. The school Grace attended was probably Western University at Quindaro, Wyandotte Co., Kansas, a historically black college which was established in 1865.

See Grace Anthony, death cert. no. 32214 (1916), Mo. Dept. of Health, Jefferson City.

[22] George Hutchinson, son of Robert Hutchenson and Eliza Haynes, was born in 1852 in Montgomery Co., Tenn., died 26 August 1915 in String Town, Montgomery Co., Tenn. He was buried on 27 August 1915 in Piskey.

See George Hutchenson [sic], death cert. no. 346 (1915), Tenn. Dept. of Health, Nashville.

[23] Virgil E. Williams dedicated his entire life to the pursuit of African American education. He was born on 15 June 1877 in Chillicothe, Livingston Co., Mo. to Henry W. Williams (b. Howard Co., Mo.) and Fannie B. Moore (b. Livingston Co., Mo.). With the exception of short periods of time, Virgil spent the vast majority of his life in Chillicothe.

The three year-old Virgil first appears in the 1880 household of his parents in Livingston County. In 1900, Virgil was living with his parents and, at the age of twenty-two, was still "...at school..." In 1910, he was still living with his parents, but now he was working as a school teacher. Sometime prior to 1915, Virgil became the principle of the local African American school, Garrison. On 18 September 1915, Virgil married Ora Mae Hunt, daughter of Henry Hunt and Jane Colwell, in St. Louis City. Virgil was about thirteen years Ora's senior; she was born on 9 September 1890 in Farmington, St. Francois Co., Mo. However, the marriage apparently did not work out. Virgil's death certificate lists that he died as a single man—that he was never married nor divorced. In addition, the 1920 census revealed that Ora—who was enumerated as Ora Williams—was living with her mother Jane M. Hunt in Farmington, St. Francois Co., Mo. In that census, she was also listed as a single woman. The failure of their marriage was possibly a difficult one because during that same year—the 1920 census—Virgil was not found in Livingston County, nor was he enumerated in the teaching profession. Instead, the forty-two year-old was found in nearby Howard County living as a boarder in the household of Elijah Jackman and was employed as a common farm laborer. The couple apparently divorced, because Ora remarried a second time to Charles Baker. Ora and Charles remained married until Ora's untimely death on 5 November 1927 in Farmington, St. Francois Co., Mo. from pulmonary tuberculosis. She was buried on 7 November 1927 in the Colored Masonic Cemetery, Farmington, St. Francois Co., Mo.

Sometime prior to 1930, Virgil returned to Chillicothe and from 1930 to 1940, he was enumerated as the principle for the local "colored school." In 1930, he was living in his mother's household, while in 1940 he was living with his brother Will. He died a year later on 19 February 1941 in Chillicothe, Livingstone Co., Mo., and was buried on 23 February 1941 in Chillicothe, Livingston Co., Mo., continuing to teach up until the time of his death.

See Virgil E. Williams, death cert. no. 7490 (1941), Mo. Dept. of Health, Jefferson City; Jane M. Hunt household, 1920 U.S. census, St. Francois Co., Mo., pop. sch., Farmington, ED 104, SD 11, sh. 4A, dw. 82, fl. 82; NA microfilm T625, roll 945; Ora Baker, death cert. no. 34490 (1927), Mo. Dept. of Health, Jefferson City; Henry Williams household, 1880 U.S. census, Livingston Co., Mo., pop. sch., Chillicothe, ED 164, SD 77, sh. 32D, dw. 307, fl. 345; NA microfilm T9, roll 700; Henry Williams household, 1900 U.S. census, Livingston Co., Mo., pop. sch., Chillicothe, ED 92, SD 2, sh. 5A, dw. 83, fl. 84; NA microfilm T623, roll 872; Henry Williams household, 1910 U.S. census, Livingston Co., Mo., pop. sch., Chillicothe, ED 94, SD 2, sh. 4B, dw. 115, fl. 117; NA microfilm T624, roll 796; Eliga

[sic] Jackman household, 1920 U.S. census, Howard Co., Mo., pop. sch., Moniteau twp., ED 97, SD 7, sh. 8B, dw. 196, fl. 198; NA microfilm T625, roll 917; Fannie B. Williams household, 1930 U.S. census, Livingston Co., Mo., pop. sch., Chillicothe, ED 59-9, SD 3, sh. 7B, dw. 145, fl. 147; NA microfilm T625, roll 1210; Virgil E. Williams household, 1940 U.S. census, Livingston Co., Mo., pop. sch., Chillicothe, ED 59-8, SD 1, sh. 21B, hh. 476; NA microfilm T627, roll 2125.

[24] Rev. William Henderson Spurlock was born 21 September 1861 in Ky., died 25 May 1943 in Festus, Jefferson Co., Mo. He was buried on 29 May 1943 in Mt. Zion Cemetery, Festus, Jefferson Co., Mo. He married 1) about 1890, Pollyanna S. Riley, daughter of Henry Riley, 2) Della (____). Pollyanna was born 23 October 1861 (or 1860 according to the 1900 census) in Hardinsburg, Breckenridge Co., Ky., died 11 April 1932 in Fredericktown, Madison Co., Mo. She was buried on 14 April 1932 in Fredericktown, Madison Co., Mo.

Although William's death certificate does not indicate who his parents were, clues are found in the 1900 and 1910 censuses, as well as the St. Louis Argus. On 23 February 1917, St. Louis Argus reporter Dayse F. Baker reported the William was called to the bedside of his father at Columbus, Ohio. A death record for Benjamin was found. Benjamin Spurlock, son of Frank Spurlock and Elizabeth May (both b. Floyd Co., Ky.), was born on 27 January 1831 in Prestonsburg, Floyd Co., Ky., died 18 February 1917 in Columbus, Franklin Co., Oh. He was buried on 22 February 1917 in Green Lawn Cemetery, Columbus, Franklin Co., Oh. The informant for his death certificate was his widow, Theresa Spurlock.

In 1900, William and Polly were living as boarders in the household of Benj. F. Nelson and Benjamin's wife, Mary Elizabeth (____) in Columbus, Franklin Co., Ohio. In that census, Polly is enumerated as having given birth to one child, and that the child was still alive. However, the child is not found living with them. During that time, the thirty-eight year-old William was supporting himself as a preacher. Sometime before the 1910 census was enumerated, the couple left Ohio and moved to Boonville, Cooper Co., Mo. where William continued to preach the Methodist faith. However, Benjamin and Mary Elizabeth Nelson—the couple whose household that William and Polly were enumerated in 1900—remained in Columbus, Oh. Benjamin's household during that year included himself, his wife, and his father-in-law and mother-in-law—Benjamin and Theresa Spurlock, born about 1831 in Ky., and 1845 in Ky., respectively; they were enumerated as having been married since about 1861.

According to Mary Elizabeth Nelson's death certificate, she was born

Mary Elizabeth Spurlock, the daughter of Benjamin Spurlock and Theresa Ross, on 22 September 1862 in Owensboro, Daviess Co., Ky., died 3 July 1929 in Columbus, Franklin Co., Oh., and was buried on 6 July 1929 in Green Lawn Cemetery, Columbus, Franklin Co., Oh.

Moving back in time, the household of Benjamin and Tresse [sic] Spurlock and several minor children were found in Brown Co., Ohio. Included in that household are William H. Spurlock (b. ca. 1861-1862 in Ky.) and Mary E. Spurlock (b. ca. 1862-1863 in Ky.), Benjamin (b. ca. 1863-1864 in Ky.), Hattie (b. ca. 1868 in Oh.), Anna (b. November 1869 in Oh.), and a fifty-seven year-old woman named Hannah Ross (b. ca. 1813 in Ky.). Although this census does not provide a relationship status between household members to the head of house, under Rose Hannah's occupation is listed the notation, "…Lives with son in Law…" If the enumeration is correct, then Hannah Ross was likely Theresa "Tresse" Ross' mother. Additionally, we can hypothesize that the minor children enumerated in the couple's household was their likely children, and that the family moved from Kentucky to Ohio between 1864 and 1868.

The following census—1880—revealed that the family elected to remain in Brown Co., Oh. and for the first time, the censuses records relationships. In this census, Benjamin is listed as the head of household that included his wife, Theresa; son Henderson, age 18; daughter Elizabeth, age 17; daughter Hettie, age 12; daughter Amie, age 10; daughter Dora, age 8; son Everett, age 7; son Frank, age 5, son Rutherford, age 3; and mother-in-law, Hannah Ross, age 72.

By 1900, William, his wife Polly, his sister Mary Elizabeth, and brother-in-law Benjamin F. Nelson were living together, along with other siblings, in Columbus, Ohio. As stated earlier, Polly had given birth to one child that was living at the time the census was enumerated, but the child could not be found. During that same year, William's parents, Benjamin and Theresa, remained in Brown Co., Oh., and enumerated with them was Theresa's Mother, Hannah Ross, born October 1814 in Ky. Additional searches into the 1900 Brown Co., Oh., revealed a child, Frank Spurlock, born June 1892, who was enumerated in the household of his grandparents, Charles and Amanda Clennie. Additional research is needed to verify whether or not this child was indeed William and Polly's son.

By 1915, they moved to Farmington, St. Francois Co., Mo. for several years. After the couple left William's pastorage at Farmington, they moved to Kirkwood, St. Louis Co., Mo., where William was a preacher for the A.M.E. Church in 1920. By the time the 1930 census was enumerated, they had moved to DeSoto, Jefferson Co., Mo. Sometime between 1930 and 11 April 1932, the couple moved to Fredericktown, Madison Co., Mo. where

Polly died and was buried. On 1 April 1935, William was living, once again, in St. Francois County. Sometime between the 1930 and the 1940 censuses, William married a second time—to Della—and the couple was found living in Festus, Jefferson Co., Mo. in 1940.

The earliest census Polly was found in was the 1870 census for Hardinsburg, Breckinridge Co., Ky. In this census, the seventeen year-old Polly was living in the household of Horace Scott. Included in the household are several people. The only non-white household members are seventeen year-old mulatto Polly and two year-old mulatto Horace Riley. It is not certain whether or not this particular woman was Polly Riley, the future wife of William Spurlock. However, because the household does include a two year-old child, it is a possibility, as Polly was later enumerated as having given birth to one child. Additional research in this area is needed in order to positively identify whether or not this is indeed our Polly of interest.

See Rev. William Spurlock, death cert. no. 21704 (1943), Mo. Dept. of Health, Jefferson City; Polly Ann Spurlock, death cert. no. 13199 (1932), Mo. Dept. of Health, Jefferson City; Horace Scott household, 1870 U.S. census, Breckenridge Co., Ky., pop. sch., Cloverport post office, pg. 4, dw. 25, fl. 25; NA microfilm M593, roll 450; Benj. F. Nelson household, 1900 U.S. census, Franklin Co., Oh., pop. sch.,Columbus, ED 72, SD 11, sh. 2B, dw. 42, fl. 42; NA microfilm T623, roll 1268; William H. Spurlock household, 1910 U.S. census, Cooper Co., Mo., pop. sch., Boonville, ED 62, SD 8, sh. 15B, dw. 347, fl. 366; NA microfilm T624, roll 773; William Spurlock household, 1920 U.S. census, St. Louis Co., Mo., pop. sch., Kirkwood, ED 114, SD 11, sh. 8A, dw. 167, fl. 165; NA microfilm T625, roll 945; William H. Spurlock household, 1930 U.S. census, Jefferson Co., Mo., pop. sch., DeSoto, E 50-22, SD 14, sh. 7A [printed], dw. 140, fl. 148; NA microfilm T627, roll 1206; William Spurlock household, 1940 U.S. census, Jefferson Co., Mo., pop. sch., Festus, ED 50-8, SD 8, sh. 12A, hh. 247; NA microfilm T627, roll 2119; Dayse F. Baker, "Farmington News," St. Louis Argus (St. Louis, Mo.,) 23 February 1917, pg. 2, col. 3-4; Benjamin Spurlock, death cert. no. 10243 (1917), Oh. Dept. of Health, Columbus; Benjamin F. Nelson household, 1910 U.S. census, Franklin Co., Oh., pop. sch., Columbus, ED 60, SD 11, sh. 6B, dw. 130, fl. 132; NA microfilm T624, roll 1180; Mary Elizabeth Nelson, death cert. no. 46283 (1929), Oh. Dept. of Health, Columbus; Benjamin Spurlock household, 1870 U.S. census, Brown Co., Oh., pop. sch., Ripley post office, pg. 71 [printed], dw. 475, fl. 574; NA microfilm M593, roll 1175; Benj. Spurlock household, 1880 U.S. census, Brown Co., Oh., pop. sch., Ripley, ED 16, SD 3, sh. 32D-33A, dw. 301, fl. 358; NA microfilm T9, roll 996; Ben Spurlock household, 1900 U.S. census, Brown Co., Oh., pop. sch., Ripley, ED 24, SD 5, sh. 2A-2B [printed], dw. 36, fl.44; NA microfilm T623, roll 1243; Charles Clennie household, 1900 U.S. census, Brown Co., Oh., pop. sch., Ripley, ED 24, SD 5, sh. 5A [printed], dw. 101, fl. 122; NA microfilm T623, roll 1243.

[25] James Wesley Douthit, son of James Wesley Douthit and Eliza Staten, was born 18 November 1881, died 6 March 1955 in St. Louis City, Mo. He was buried on 11 March 1955 in Washington Park Cemetery, St. Louis Co., Mo. He married Belle Fallor, daughter of Neasie Fallor. Belle was born 18 June 1886 in Marina, Ark., died 17 February 1957 in St. Louis City, Mo. She was buried on 22 February 1957 in Washington Park Cemetery, St. Louis Co., Mo.

See James Wesley Douthit, death cert. no. 9537 (1955), Mo. Dept. of Health, Jefferson City; Belle Douthit, death cert. no. 10182 (1957), Mo. Dept. of Health, Jefferson City.

[26] Harvey Carson, son of Alex Carson and Ellen Amonette, was born 11 June 1883 in Mo., died 11 January 1916 in St. Louis City, Mo. He was buried on 12 January 1916 in Potosi, Washington Co., Mo.

See Harvey Carson, death cert. no. 3961 (1916), Mo. Dept. of Health, Jefferson City.

[27] Schofield Barracks in an army installation in Honolulu, Oahu, Hawaii.

[28] Belle Matkins was born between 1834 and November 1840 in Mo. or Ky., died on 31 December 1919 in Farmington, St. Francois Co., Mo. She was buried on 1 January 1920 in the Colored Masonic Cemetery, Farmington, St. Francois Co., Mo. She married (____). According to the 1900 census, Belle had given birth to twelve children, but by 1900 only five were living.

See Belle Matkins, death cert. no. 37187 (1919), Mo. Dept. of Health, Jefferson City; Belle Madkins [sic] household, 1900 U.S. census, St. Francois Co., Mo., pop. sch., Farmington, ED 98, SD 10, sh. 2A [printed], dw. 25, fl. 25; NA microfilm T623, roll 887; Bill [sic] Madkins household, 1910 U.S. census, St Francois Co., Mo., pop. sch., ED 96, SD 11, sh. 2B [printed], dw. 37, fl. 41; NA microfilm T624, roll 808.

[29] No death certificate could be found for any child with the name Lawrence (or Laurence) Matthias, Matthews, or variant spelling. However, a death certificate for Lawrence Villers, son of Gus Villers and Martha Clay, was located for the appropriate time period. Lawrence Villers was born 24 July 1904 in Farmington, St. Francois Co., Mo., died 2 April 1916 in St. Louis City, Mo. He was buried on 3 April 1916 in Farmington, St. Francois Co., Mo., prob-

ably in the Masonic Colored Cemetery.

See Lawrence Villers, death cert. no. 15907 (1916), Mo. Dept. of Health, Jefferson City.

[30] Sarah McMinn, daughter of Thos. Lester (b. New Madrid, Mo.) and Mary Kemp (b. Washington Co., Mo.), was born 7 October 1869 in Washington Co., Mo., died 15 February 1928 in Festus, Jefferson Co., Mo. She was buried on 17 February 1928 in Mt. Zion Cemetery, Festus, Jefferson Co., Mo. She married William McMinn, son of Jerry and Anna McMinn. William was born 17 July 1861 in Festus, Jefferson Co., Mo., died 17 October 1934 in St. Louis City, Mo. He was buried on 21 October 1934 in Festus, Jefferson Co., Mo., probably in Mt. Zion Cemetery.

See Sarah McMinn, death cert. no. 5410 (1928), Mo. Dept. of Health, Jefferson City; William McMinn, death cert. no. 37720 (1934), Mo. Dept. of Health, Jefferson City.

[31] In 1910, the fifteen year-old Jewel was living with her aunt, Hattie Cabbell [sic] in Chillicothe, Livingston Co., Mo. Jewel married on 31 July 1918 in Livingston Co., Mo., John W. Center. From 1920 until 1930, they lived in Chillicothe, Livingston Co., Mo. with their children: John W., Jr., b. ca. 1922 in Mo.; Hattie, b. ca. 1924 in Mo.; and Irene Berniece, b. ca. 1926 in Mo. However, by 1 April 1935, at least Jewell and her two daughters had moved to Kansas City, Jackson Co., Mo., and by 1940, Jewell and her two daughters had moved to Detroit, Wayne Co., Mich. where they were living with their cousin, Andrew Ward and his wife Alice.

See Livingston Co., Mo., Marriage Book X: 57; County Clerk's Office, Chillicothe; Hattie Cabbell [sic] household, 1910 U.S. census, Livingston Co., Mo., pop. sch., Chillicothe, ED 98, SD 2, sh. 4A [printed], dw. 76, fl. 80; NA microfilm T624, roll 796; J.W. Center household, 1920 U.S. census, Livingston Co., Mo., pop. sch., Chillicothe, ED 100, SD 2, sh. 2B, dw. 40, fl. 41; NA microfilm T625, roll 918; J.W. Center household, 1930 U.S. census, Livingston Co., Mo., pop. sch., Chillicothe, ED 59-5, SD 3, sh. 7B, dw. 196, fl. 199; NA microfilm T626, roll 1210; Andrew Ward household, 1940 U.S. census, Waynce Co., Mich., pop. sch., Detroit, ED 84-1278, SD 16, sh. 11B, hh. 206; NA microfilm T627, roll 1878.

[32] Martha M. (Clay) Villars, daughter of Lindsey Clay and Charlotte Staten, was born 14 July 1881 in Mo., died 4 April 1940 in Farmington, St. Francois Co., Mo. She was buried on 7 April 1940 in the Colored Masonic Cemetery, Farmington, St. Francois Co., Mo. She married Gustus Villars, son of Isaac Villars and Sarah Sides. Gustus was born 24 February 1880 in Mo., died 9

May 1922 in St. Louis City, Mo. He was buried on 12 May 1922 in Washington Park Cemetery, St. Louis Co., Mo.

See Martha M. Villars, death cert. no. 15950 (1940), Mo. Dept. of Health, Jefferson City; Gus Villars, death cert. no. 16936 (1922), Mo. Dept. of Health, Jefferson City.

[33] Emma J. (Evens) Harris, daughter of Alex and Martha Evens, was born 23 February 1869 in Farmington, St. Francois Co., Mo., died 7 June 1919 in Farmington, St. Francois Co., Mo. She was buried on 9 June 1919 in the Colored Masonic Cemetery, Farmington, St. Francois Co., Mo. She married Ed Harris.

See Mrs. Emma J. Harris, death cert. no. 20501 (1919), Mo. Dept. of Health, Jefferson City.

[34] Henry Burke aka Burks, son of Louis Burks and Mandy Burks, was born 22 April 1865 in Mo., died 25 November 1916 in St. Louis City, Mo. He was buried on 27 November 1916 in Farmington, St. Francois Co., Mo., probably in the Masonic Colored Cemetery.

See Henry Burks [sic], death cert. no. 39472 (1916), Mo. Dept. of Health, Jefferson City.

[35] Virginia M. "Virgie/Vergie" Pugh, daughter of Richard Jones and Henrietta Anthony, was born 4 December 1886 in Libertyville, St. Francois Co., Mo., died 28 June 1952 in St. Louis City, Mo. She was buried on 3 July 1952 in Washington Park Cemetery, St. Louis, Mo. She married Lewis or Louis D. Pugh, son of John Pugh and Harriett Braden. Lewis was born in 1873 in Mo., died 26 March 1914 in St. Louis City, Mo. He was buried on 28 March 1914 in Bethany, Harrison Co., Mo.

See Virginia M. Pugh, death cert. no. 26237 (1952), Mo. Dept. of Health, Jefferson City; Louis D. Pugh, death cert. no. 10960 (1914), Mo. Dept. of Health, Jefferson City.

[36] Laura Amonette, daughter of Henry Amonette and Emma Summers [sic] was born 23 May 1896 in Farmington, St. Francois Co., Mo., died 30 August 1942 in St. Louis City, Mo. She was buried on 6 September 1942 in Washington Park Cemetery, St. Louis Co., Mo. She married James Summerville, son of Cambridge Summerville. James was born 19 October 1862 in Tenn., died 15 October 1932 in St. Louis City, Mo. He was buried on 23 October 1932 in Washington Park Cemetery, St. Louis Co., Mo.

See Laura Summerville, death cert. no. 26231 (1942), Mo. Dept. of Health, Jefferson City; James Summerville, death cert. no. 34051 (1932),

Mo. Dept. of Health, Jefferson City.

[37] Rev. Frank P. Greenlee was born about 1868 in North Carolina. He married Mamie Jewell, daughter of Dan Jewell. Mamie was born 12 April 1878 in Woodville, Miss., died 21 February 1917 in Bonne Terre, St. Francois Co., Mo. She was buried in 1917 in Omaha, Nebraska. Sometime after Mamie's death, Frank married 2) Estella (Poston) Roberts, daughter of Samuel Poston. Estella was born about 24 March 1878 in Farmington, St. Francois Co., Mo., died 4 April 1920 in Poplar Bluff, Butler Co., Mo. She was buried on 7 April 1920 in Farmington, St. Francois Co., Mo., probably in the Masonic Colored Cemetery.

In 1920, Frank and Estella were living in Poplar Bluff, Butler Co., Mo.—along with Frank's step-son, Addison Roberts—where Frank was working as a pastor. Less than three months after their enumeration, Estella died on 4 April 1920.

See Frank P. Greenlee household, 1920 U.S. census, Butler Co., Mo., pop. sch., Poplar Bluff, ED 12, SD 12, sh. 25B, dw. 231, fl. 295; NA microfilm T625, roll 909; Mamie Greenlee, death cert. no. 7370 (1917), Mo. Dept. of Health, Jefferson City; Estella Greenlee, death cert. no. 15719 (1920), Mo. Dept. of Health, Jefferson City.

[38] Dr. Matthew O. Ricketts was a dentist. He was born in May 1852 in Louisville, Jefferson Co., Ky., died 15 January 1917 in St. Joseph, Buchanan Co., Mo. He was buried on 18 January 1917 in Ashland Cemetery, St. Joseph, Buchanan Co., Mo.

See Matthew O. Ricketts, death cert. no. 305 (1917), Mo. Dept. of Health, Jefferson City.

[39] David Staten, son of Ruben Staten and Elizabeth Coffman, was born 10 June 1851 in Ste. Genevieve Co., Mo., died 4 February 1917 in Saline Twp., Ste. Genevieve Co., Mo. He was buried on 6 February 1917 in the Stone Church Cemetery, Ste. Genevieve Co., Mo.

See David Staten, death cert. no. 7390 (1917), Mo. Dept. of Health, Jefferson City.

[40] Frank Scott, son of Wash Scott, was born about 1882 in Mo., died 24 February 1917 in St. Louis City, Mo. He was buried on 27 February 1917 in Horine Station, Jefferson Co., Mo. He was widowed at the time of his death.

See Frank Scott, death cert. no. 8473 (1917), Mo. Dept. of Health, Jefferson City.

[41] Oscar Reed, son of Artie Reed (b. Ill) and Velma Body (b. Mo.), was born

213

16 February 1917 in Mo., died 17 March 1917 in St. Louis City, Mo. He was buried on 19 March 1917 in Greenwood Cemetery, St. Louis, Mo.

See Oscar Reed, death cert. no. 12660 (1917), Mo. Dept. of Health, Jefferson City.

[42] Floyd Newell Kennedy, son of William Kennedy (b. Greenville, Mo.) and Louise Townson [sic] (b. [New] Tennessee, Mo.), was born 16 September 1900 in Coffman, Ste. Genevieve Co., Mo., died 7 April 1922 in Bowling Green, Pike Co., Mo. He was buried on 9 April 1922 in the [Colored] Masonic Cemetery, Farmington, St. Francois Co., Mo.

See Floyd Newell Kennedy, death cert. no. 13386 (1922), Mo. Dept. of Health, Jefferson City.

[43] Ferd "Fred" Madison, son of Peter Madison and Caroline Hutchins, was born 26 September 1870 in Bonne Terre, St. Francois Co., Mo., died 15 April 1917 in Farmington, St. Francois Co., Mo. He was buried on 17 April 1917 in Bonne Terre, St. Francois Co., Mo.

See Ferd [sic] Madison, death cert. no. 16036 (1917), Mo. Dept. of Health, Jefferson City.

[44] Harry L. Jacobs, son of Charles Jacobs and Mary Bollen, was born 8 October 1882 in Ste. Genevieve, Mo., died 17 April 1917 in Ste. Genevieve, Ste. Genevieve Co., Mo. He was buried on 19 April 1917 in Valle Spring Cemetery, Ste. Genevieve, Ste. Genevieve Co., Mo. He was single when he died from lobar pneumonia.

See Harry L. Jacobs, death cert. no. 16071 (1917), Mo. Dept. of Health, Jefferson City.

[45] Mary Theodocia "Docia" Bogy-Taylor was the daughter of Robert Taylor and Eliza E. (Bogy) Taylor Blackwell. Docia was born March 1870 or April 1870 in Bonne Terre, St. Francois Co., Mo., died 16 May 1917 in St. Louis City, Mo. She was buried on 18 May 1917 in Farmington, St. Francois Co., Mo., probably in the Masonic Colored Cemetery. She married 1) Peter Taylor, 2) on 17 November 1897 in St. Francois Co., Mo., Henry Drew, son of Joseph Drew and Margeret Fortener, 3) (____) Green. Henry was born 21 July 1872-1873 in Farmington, St. Francois Co., Mo., and died 7 December 1911 in Farmington, St. Francois Co., Mo. He was buried on 8 December 1911 in the County Cemetery, Farmington, St. Francois Co., Mo.

See Mary Green, death cert. no. 20491 (1917), Mo. Dept. of Health, Jefferson City; Ellen Bogy household, 1900 U.S. census, St. Francois Co., Mo., pop. sch., St. Francois twp., ED 98, SD 10, sh. 18B, dw. 343, fl. 351;

NA microfilm T623, roll 887; Ellen Hale household, 1870 U.S. census, St. Francois Co., Mo., pop. sch., Farmington post office, sh. 2-3, dw. 12, fl. 12; NA microfilm M593, roll 807; Frank George Drew, death cert. no. 42971 (1947), Mo. Dept. of Health, Jefferson City; Henry Drew, death cert. no. 42517 (1911), Mo. Dept. of Health, Jefferson City.

[46] Roxy Thompson, daughter of Chas. Dalford [sic] and Mary E. Poston, was born in 1892 in Mo., died 8 June 1917 in St. Louis City, Mo. She was buried on 10 June 1917 in Farmington, St. Francois Co., Mo., probably in the Masonic Colored Cemetery. Her daughter Stella was probably named after Roxy's elder sister, Stella.

Mary E. Poston was the daughter of Samuel Poston (b. Va.) and Sarah Kenedy [sic] (b. Mo.), she was born about 1871 in Mo., died 10 December 1921 in St. Louis City, Mo. She was buried on 13 December 1921 in Farmington, St. Francois Co., Mo., probably in the Masonic Colored Cemetery.

See Roxy Thompson, death cert. no. 23433 (1917), Mo. Dept. of Health, Jefferson City; Mary E. Poston, death cert. no. 33826 (1921), Mo. Dept. of Health, Jefferson City.

[47] Annie (-?-) Curtaindoll, daughter of Sarah, was born 4 October 1869 in Erin, Houston Co., Tenn., died 6 January 1945 in St. Louis City, Mo. She was buried on 11 January 1945 in Greenwood Cemetery, Hillsdale, St. Louis Co., Mo. She married Marshall W. Curtaindoll, son of Lawson Curtaindoll and Amanda Moose. Marshall was born 27 April 1874 in St. Charles, Mo., died 5 January 1948 in St. Louis City, Mo. He was buried on 9 January 1948 in Greenwood Cemetery, Hillsdale, St. Louis Co., Mo.

See Annie Curtaindoll, death cert. no. 179 (1945), Mo. Dept. of Health, Jefferson City; Marshall Curtaindoll, death cert. no. 2410 (1948), Mo. Dept. of Health, Jefferson City.

[48] Anna Emma "Annie" Sanders was born about 1871 in Madison Co., Mo., a daughter of William Sanders and Frances Valley/Valle. She married John W. Stiger. Anna died on 20 December 1952 in Fredericktown, Madison Co., Mo. and was buried on 20 December 1952 in Greenwood Cemetery, Madison Co., Mo. By 1920, Anna's husband had died and she was living as a widow in Fredericktown.

Frank J. Villars was born about 1883 in Mo. He married 1) on 23 March 1908 in Madison Co., Mo., Emma J. Abernathy, daughter of Charles Abernathy and Catherine McCombs, 2) before 1920, Nancy (____). Emma was born 17 February 1888 in Perry Co., Mo., died 9 January 1911 in Fredericktown, Madison Co., Mo. She was buried on 9 January 1911 in Fredericktown, Madison Co., Mo. Nancy was born about 1888 in Mo. By 1920, Frank and Nancy had moved to Jefferson Co., Mo.

Edward McFadden, son of Elbert McFadden, was born 13 August 1876 in Fredericktown, Madison Co., Mo., died 25 December 1937 in Fredericktown, Madison Co., Mo. He was buried on 28 December 1932 in Fredericktown, Madison Co., Mo. He married 1) on 14 November 1895 in Madison Co., Mo., Laura B. Sanders, daughter of William Sanders and Frances Valley/Valle, 2) before 1917, Georgia (____). Laura was born 16 July 1876 in Madison Co., Mo., died 1 June 1913 in Fredericktown, Madison Co., Mo. She was buried on 7 June 1913 in Fredericktown, Madison Co., Mo. Georgia was born about 1892 in Mo.

Anna Emma "Annie" Sanders and Laura B. Sanders were sisters, the daughter of William Sanders and Frances Valley/Valle. Frances Valley/Valle, daughter of Acan Valley and Frances Mack, was born 22 February 1846 in Madison Co., Mo., died 11 September 1910 in Fredericktown, Madison Co., Mo. She was buried on 12 September 1910 in Fredericktown, St. Francois Co., Mo.

See Anna Emma Stiger [sic], death cert. no. 42819 (1952), Mo. Dept. of Health, Jefferson City; Annie Stiger household, 1920 U.S. census, Madison Co., Mo., pop. sch., Fredericktown, ED 59, SD 11, sh. 15B, dw. 325, fl. 344; NA microfilm T625, roll 920; Villars-Abernathy Marr., Madison Co., Mo., Marriage Book X: 52; Co. Clerk's Office, Fredericktown; Edward McFadden, death cert. no. 45991 (1937), Mo. Dept. of Health, Jefferson City; Laura B. McFadden, death cert. no. 20235 (1913), Mo. Dept. of Health, Jefferson City; McFadden-Sanders Marr., Madison Co., Mo. Marriage Book X: 257; Co. Clerk's Office, Fredericktown; Emma Villars, death cert. no. 2380 (1911), Mo. Dept. of Health, Jefferson City; Frank Villars household, 1920 U.S. census, Jefferson Co., Mo., pop. sch., Kimmswick, ED 42, SD 11, sh. 14A, dw. 328, fl. 339; NA microfilm T625, roll 930; Edward McFadden household, 1920 U.S. census, Madison Co., Mo., pop. sch., Fredericktown, ED 59, SD 11, sh. 15B, dw. 328, fl. 347; NA microfilm T625, roll 920; Francis [sic] Sanders, death cert. no. 27874 (1910), Mo. Dept. of Health, Jefferson City.

[49] Lewis Cunningham, son of John Cunningham and Joanna Hill, was born 15 July 1875 in Mo., died single on 7 January 1918 in St. Louis City, Mo. He was buried on 10 January 1918 in Greenwood Cemetery, St. Louis, Mo. Lewis' death certificate provides a full name for his father, but only his mother's first name—Johanna. In his sister Lucy (Cunningham) Bridges death certificate, the mother's full name is Joanna Hill.

See Louis [sic] Cunningham, death cert. no. 3139 (1918), Mo. Dept. of Health, Jefferson City; Lucy Jane Bridges, death cert. no. 14330 (1933), Mo. Dept. of Health, Jefferson City.

[50] Louisa, or Louise, Lee was the daughter of Ben Jordan. She born in 1841 in Washington Co., Mo., died 28 May 1919 in Farmington, St. Francois Co., Mo. She was buried on 31 May 1919 in the County Colored Cemetery, probably the Masonic Colored Cemetery. She married Papin Lee.

See Louise Lee, death cert. no. 17941 (1919), Mo. Dept. of Health, Jefferson City.

[51] Arnie Wilburn, daughter of Henry Wilburn and Missouri Jackson, was born 16 April 1890 in Valle Mines, Mo., died 4 March 1918 in Jefferson Co., Mo. She was buried on 6 March 1918 in Mt. Zion Cemetery, Festus, Jefferson Co., Mo. She married John Jennings, son of James Jennings and Katherine Green. John was born 15 October 1876 in Belgrade, Washington Co., Mo., died 29 January 1919 in Crystal City, Jefferson Co., Mo. He was buried on 31 January 1919 in Mt. Zion Cemetery, Festus, Jefferson Co., Mo.

Both Arnie and her husband John had Pulmonary Tuberculosis, a disease which caused their early demise.

See Arnie Wilburn Jennings, death cert. no 9492-A (1918), Mo. Dept. of Health, Jefferson City; John Jennings, death cert. no. 1932 (1919), Mo. Dept. of Health, Jefferson City.

[52] Barney Pelty was a German-American, the son of Samuel Pelty and Helen Haas (both born in Germany). Barney was born 10 September 1880 in Farmington, St. Francois Co., Mo., died 24 May 1939 near Farmington, St. Francois Co., Mo. He was buried on 27 May 1939 in the Masonic Cemetery, Farmington, St. Francois Co., Mo. It is believed that he was buried in the European-American ("white") Masonic Cemetery as cemeteries were segregated at the time of his death. He married Eva Warsing.

See Barney Pelty, death cert. no. 19671 (1939), Mo. Dept. of Health, Jefferson City.

[53] Minnie Thornton, daughter of Richard Thornton and Maggie Pearner[?], was born 25 December 1897 in Mo., died 19 December 1933 in St. Louis City, Mo. She was buried on 23 December 1933 in Greenwood Cemetery, St. Louis, Mo. She married Charles Pryor, Jr., son of Charles Pryor, Sr. and Julia Godiere. Charles was born 6 February 1890 in Mo., died 27 December 1933 in St. Louis City, Mo. He was buried on 30 December 1933 in Greenwood Cemetery, St. Louis, Mo.

See Maggie Pryor, death cert. no. 41951 (1933), Mo. Dept. of Health, Jefferson City; Charles Pryor, Jr., death cert. no. 42183 (1933), Mo. Dept. of Health, Jefferson City.

[54] Myrtle Thornton, daughter of Richard or Godfrey Thornton and Maggie Perringer[?], was born 2 February 1890 in Mo., died 7 April 1926 in St. Louis City, Mo. She was buried on 10 April 1926 I Greenwood Cemetery, St. Louis, Mo. She married Frank Singleton.

See Myrtle Singleton, death cert. no. 14262 (1926), Mo. Dept. of Health, Jefferson City.

[55] Rebecca (Reed) Bridges, daughter of Robert Reed, was born 28 August 1874 in Mo., died 18 July 1951 in St. Louis City, Mo. She was buried on 22 July 1951 in Farmington (Masonic Colored Cemetery), St. Francois Co., Mo.

See Rebecca Bridges, death cert. no. 24343 (1951), Mo. Dept. of Health, Jefferson City.

[56] Rolla's death certificate is difficult to read due to the handwriting. However, the information that could be deciphered was that Rolla Johnson born on 5 January 1901 in Jefferson Co., Mo., the son of Lee Johnson (b. Wayne Co., Mo.) and Carrie [illegible]. He died on 8 March 1923 in Jefferson Co., Mo. from pulmonary tuberculosis, and was buried on 11 March 1923 in Mount [Zion] Cemetery, Festus, Jefferson Co., Mo.

See Rolla Johnson, death cert. no. 9502 (1923), Mo. Dept. of Health, Jefferson City.

[57] John Soloman Cobb was born on 10 September 1849 in Knox Co., Tenn., died 27 October 1919 in Cape Girardeau, Cape Girardeau Co., Mo. He was buried on 29 October 1919 in the Jackson Cemetery, Cape Girardeau Co., Mo. He married 1) on 29 November 1883 in Cape Girardeau Co., Mo., Elizabeth Eulenburg, 2) Mary A. Moore, daughter of H. Moore. Mary was born about 25 May 1845 in St. Louis, Mo., died 13 September 1919 in Cape Girardeau, Cape Girardeau Co., Mo. She was buried on 15 September 1919 in the Old Catholic Cemetery, Cape Girardeau Co., Mo.

See John Soloman [sic] Cobb, death cert. no. 29700 (1919), Mo. Dept. of Health, Jefferson City; Mary A. Cobb, death cert. no. 27151 (1919), Mo. Dept. of Health, Jefferson City.

[58] Vera Olega Brooks, daughter of Rev. John Lewis Brooks (born Meridian, Lauderdale Co., Miss.) and Fannie Nelson Taylor (born Mason, Tipton Co., Tenn.), was born 10 April 1899 in St. Louis, Mo., died 6 November 1919 in

St. Louis City, Mo. She was buried on 11 November 1919 in Father Dickson Cemetery, St. Louis, Mo. According to her death certificate, Vera died as a result of brain hemorrhaging. The coroner stated that her murder was due to a skull fracture caused by a blunt instrument. The murder appeared on the front page of the St. Louis Argus:

"MAN CONFESSED HE KILLED OWN SISTER-IN-LAW

Benjamin Saunders [sic] Murders His Wife's Sister, a Sumner High Girl, Because She Resents an In[su]lt.

Benjamin Sanders, 24 years old a chauffeur, must face trial for one of the most revolting crimes imaginable. Sanders admits murdering his sister-inlaw p[sic], Vera Olega Brooks, a Sumner High School girl, because she resented his improper advances toward her.

The crime was committed Thursday afternoon November 6. Sanders in company with Jerry Simms took an auto from the garage of H.E. Griesedieck, 3250 Hawthorn Boulevard, about 12:15, to Goode and Garfield where they met the Brooks girl and later picked up Gladys Emory and Adelaide Huff of 1718 Whittier and Florence Wyatt, 1802 Goode. They drove around for more than two hours through north St. Louis and Baden, after taking all the members of the party to their homes except Miss Brooks, he drove to the garage, arriving about 4 p.m. According to Sanders' confession, she sat in the garage while he washed the car. He says, "We talked about an hour and it led up to me accusing her of improper relations with another fellow, and I made advances to her, as she had known me a long time, she objected and told me she intended to tell her sister (Sander's wife) and her father and mother about it. He says he begged her not to tell, she insisted and he struck her on the head with a large iron furnace shacker [sic], knocking her down and rendering her unconscious. He claims to have tried to bring her to and finally struck her twice more, "to put her out of her misery, because she was suffering."

He then wrapped the body in a wheat sack and a sugar sack, placed it in the automobile and drove to the Compton avenue viaduct, where he threw out the body.

Her body was still warm when found at 5:50 by Ruben Carter and wife, 3430 Market St., her hat and text-books lay nearby.

Miss Brooks was 20 years old, the daughter of Rev. J.L. Brooks of Webster Groves and was boarding at 4231 W. Lucky. Sanders lived with his wife, Vera's sister, at 3101 Pine.

The funeral was held Monday and the remains interred in Father Dixon [sic] Cemetery."

The following year, Benjamin was enumerated as an inmate the Jefferson City State Penitentiary in Jefferson City, Cole Co., Mo. and remained incarcerated at least until the time the 1930 census was enumerated. Vera's father died in 1924 and her mother died in 1937; both were buried in Father Dickson Cemetery. Vera's siblings remained in St. Louis.

See Vera Brooks, death cert. no. 34399 (1919), Mo. Dept. of Health, Jefferson City; "Man Confesses He Killed Own Sister-In-Law," St. Louis Argus (St. Louis City, Mo.), 14 November 1919, pg. 1, col. 6; Ben Sanders entry, Jefferson City State Penitentiary, 1920 U.S. census, Cole Co., Mo., pop. sch., Jefferson City, ED 115, SD 183, sh. 18A, dw. 187, fl. 287; NA microfilm T625, roll 950; Benjamin Sanders entry, Jefferson City State Penitentiary, 1930 U.S. census, Cole Co., Mo., pop. sch., Jefferson City, ED 26-6, SD 12, sh. 36A, dw [not listed], fl. [not listed]; NA microfilm T626, roll 1184; John Lewis Brooks, death cert. no. 21457 (1924), Mo. Dept. of Health, Jefferson City; Fannie Nelson Brooks, death cert. no. 21294 (1937), Mo. Dept. of Health, Jefferson City.

[59] Fielding Douthit, son of Charles Douthit and Marih [sic] Franks, was born 2 November 1902 in Coffman, Ste. Genevieve Co., Mo., died 24 November 1919 in Saline Twp., Ste. Genevieve Co., Mo. He was buried on 26 November 1919 in Coffman, Ste. Genevieve Co., Mo. He was only 17 years old when he died.

See Fieldan [sic] Douihit [sic], death cert. no. 34089 (1919), Mo. Dept. of Health, Jefferson City.

[60] Sam Ross, son of Belle Matkins, was born about 1854 in Farmington, St. Francois Co., Mo., died 29 July 1924 in Jefferson Co., Mo. He was buried on 3 July 1924 in Mt. Zion Cemetery, Festus, Jefferson Co., Mo. He married Amanda "Mandy" (-?-).

Sam's death certificate gives an age at death of about 74. However, the informant for his death certificate was an unnamed step-daughter. His year of birth is likely that which was enumerated in the 1920 census, which given about 1854.

See Sam Ross, death cert. no. 20775 (1924), Mo. Dept. of Health, Jefferson City, Mo.; Sam Ross household, 1920 U.S. census, Jefferson Co., Mo., pop. sch., Festus, ED 35, SD 11, sh. 11A, dw. 225, fl. 239; NA microfilm T625, roll 930.

[61] Reverend Richard Davis, son of Wm. Green and Nina Davis (both b. Kentucky) was born about 1853 in Mo., died 10 January 1920 in Kansas City, Jackson Co., Mo. He was buried on 14 January 1920 in Highland Cemetery. He married Nellie.

See Rev. Richard Davis, death cert. no. 1082 (1920), Mo. Dept. of Health, Jefferson City.

[62] Benjamin Ransom was born 27 January 1835 in South Carolina, died 29 January 1920 in Festus, Jefferson Co., Mo. He was buried on 31 January 1920 in Bonne Terre, St. Francois Co., Mo. At the time of his death, he was divorced.

See Benjamin Ransom, death cert. no. 1798 (1920), Mo. Dept. of Health, Jefferson City.

[63] Mary A. Wade, daughter of Andrew J. Wade and Lulu Hull, was born 16 November 1894 in Jackson, Cape Girardeau Co., Mo., died 5 February 1920 in Webster Groves, St. Louis Co., Mo. She was buried on 7 February 1920 in Jackson, Cape Girardeau Co., Mo. She married Henry Renfro/Renfroe.

See Mary A. Renfro, death cert. no. 9025 (1920), Mo. Dept. of Health, Jefferson City.

[64] Dr. O.A. Smith was Owen A. Smith. Listed as "white" on his death certificate, Dr. Smith was a European American doctor, the son of Alfred A. Smith and Isabelle Miller. Dr. Smith was born on 31 March 1868 in Jerseyville, Jersey Co., Ill., died on 2 December 1934 in Farmington, St. Francois Co., Mo. He was buried on 3 December 1934 in Parkview Cemetery. He Married Nellie A. Taylor, daughter of James Taylor and Isabell Ritchie. Nellie was born 5 December 1866 in Scotland, died 15 November 1955 in Cantwell, St. Francois Co., Mo. She was buried on 17 November 1955 in Parkview Cemetery, Farmington, St. Francois Co., Mo.

See Owen A. Smith, death cert. no. 44203 (1934), Mo. Dept. of Health, Jefferson City; Nellie A. Smith, death cert. no. 37943 (1955), Mo. Dept. of Health, Jefferson City.

[65] Cosetta Wilburn, daughter of Henry Wilburn and Minnie Burkes [sic], was born 12 July 1911 in Mo., died 13 February 1920 in St. Louis City, Mo. She was buried on 17 February 1920 in "…Washington U…." Her death at the age of eight was due to pulmonary tuberculosis.

See Cosetta Wilburn, death cert. no. 10314 (1920), Mo. Dept. of Health, Jefferson City.

[66] Laura (Amonette) House, daughter of Henry Amonette and Sarah Green, was born 19 December 1872 in Mo., died 25 April 1956 in St. Louis City, Mo. She was buried on 1 May 1956 in Greenwood Cemetery, Hillsdale, St. Louis Co., Mo.

Laura's death certificate only provides her parents' names as Henry Amonette and Sarah ???. However, her brother's death certificate lists their mother's maiden name as Green.

See Laura House, death cert. no. 18049 (1956), Mo. Dept. of Health, Jefferson City; Henry Scott Amonette, death cert. no. 26707 (1939), Mo. Dept. of Health, Jefferson City.

[67] Hiram Green died 7 April 1920 in St. Louis City, Mo. He was buried on 10 April 1920 in Greenwood Cemetery, Hillsdale, St. Louis Co., Mo. According to his death certificate, he was born about 1872. However, the 1910 census enumerates him as being born about 1865 in Mo.

See Hiram Green, death cert. no. (1920), Mo. Dept. of Health, Jefferson City; Hiram Green household, 1910 US census, St. Louis City, Mo., pop. sch., Ward 4, ED 55, SD 10, sh. 12A, dw. 118, fl. 260; NA microfilm T624, roll 812.

[68] Elvira McGee, daughter of Mason Hill, was born 24 April 1861 in Mo., died 10 April 1920 in St. Louis City, Mo. She was buried on 13 April 1920 in Father Dickson Cemetery, St. Louis, Mo. At the time of her death, she was widowed. She married on 23 May 1884 in St. Francois Co., Mo., Joseph A. McGee.

In 1870, the ten year-old Elvira Hill was living in the household of Ruben Staten—all of whom were incorrectly enumerated as "white"—in Ste. Genevieve Co., Mo. By 1880, the nineteen year-old Elvira was living in St. Francois Co., Mo., in the household of her uncle, James W. Douthit. Sometime after her marriage to Joseph A. McGee in 1884, the couple moved to East Carondelet, St. Clair Co., Ill. where their daughter Arizona was born on 1 August 1892.

See Elvira McGee, death cert. no. 17829 (1920), Mo. Dept. of Health, Jefferson City; St. Francois Co., Mo. Marriages A:53, Recorder's Office, Farmington; Ruben Staton [sic] household, 1870 U.S. census, Ste. Genevieve Co., Mo., pop. sch., Avon post office, sh. 24, dw. 163, fl. 180; NA microfilm M593, roll 807; James W. Douthett [sic] household, 1880 U.S. census, St. Francois Co., Mo., pop. sch., Farmington, ED 118, SD 2, sh. 28D, dw.. 235, fl. 238; NA microfilm T9, roll 714; Arizona Jackson, death cert. no. 31725 (1950), Mo. Dept. of Health, Jefferson City.

[69] Addison Roberts Jr., son of Addison Roberts, Sr., and Estelle Poston, was born 5 May 1909 in Indianapolis, Ind., died 14 January 1959 in St. Louis City, Mo. He was buried on 19 January 1959 in Greenwood Cemetery, Hillsdale, St. Louis Co., Mo. He married Bernadine. The informant for his death

certificate was Dollean Alexander.

     See Addison Roberts, death cert. no. 3426 (1959), Mo. Dept. of Health, Jefferson City.

[70] Freeman Franks, son of Sonnie Franks and Ella Tow[n]send (both b. Coffman, Mo.), was born 15 June 1893 in Farmington, St. Francois Co., Mo., died 26 June 1932 in St. Louis City, Mo. He was buried on 5 July 1932 in Father Dickson Cemetery, St. Louis, Mo. According to his death certificate, Freeman died from a, "…Gunshot Wound of Buttocks, caused by bullet fired from a gun in the hands of one John Ballard, (Col), at 16th and Morgan, 1/30/32 [sic], at about 3 A.M. JUSTIFIABLE HOMICIDE…"

     See Freeman Franks, death cert. no. 24129 (1932), Mo. Dept. of Health, Jefferson City.

[71] Minnie was born in 1877 in Summitt [si], Mo., the daughter of John Hudsey and Delia Rodges [sic]. She died on 10 October 1920 in St. Louis City, Mo., and was buried on 13 October 1920 in Bonne Terre, St. Francois Co., Mo. The informant was Henry G. Robinson.

     See Minnie Robinson, death cert. no. 32723 (1920), Mo. Dept. of Health, Jefferson City.